Progressive Business Plan for a Child Day Care

Copyright © 2017 by Progressive Business Consulting, Inc.
Pembroke Pines, FL 33027

NON-DISCLOSURE AGREEMENT

_____ (Company)., and _____ (Person Name), agrees:

_____ (Company) Corp. may from time to time disclose to _____ (Person Name) certain confidential information or trade secrets generally regarding Business plan and financials of _____ (Company) corp.

_____ (Person Name) agrees that it shall not disclose the information so conveyed, unless in conformity with this agreement. _____ (Person Name) shall limit disclosure to the officers and employees of _____ (Person Name) with a reasonable "need to know" the information, and shall protect the same from disclosure with reasonable diligence.

As to all information which _____ (Company) Corp. claims is confidential, _____ (Company) Corp. shall reduce the same to writing prior to disclosure and shall conspicuously mark the same as "confidential," "not to be disclosed" or with other clear indication of its status. If the information which _____ (Company) Corp. is disclosing is not in written form, for example, a machine or device, _____ (Company) Corp. shall be required prior to or at the same time that the disclosure is made to provide written notice of the secrecy claimed by _____ (Company) Corp.. _____ (Person Name) agrees upon reasonable notice to return the confidential tangible material provided by it by _____ (Company) Corp. upon reasonable request.

The obligation of non-disclosure shall terminate when if any of the following occurs:
(a) The confidential information becomes known to the public without the fault of _____ (Person Name), or;
(b) The information is disclosed publicly by _____ (Company) Corp., or ;
(c) a period of 12 months passes from the disclosure, or;
(d) the information loses its status as confidential through no fault of _____ (Person Name).

In any event, the obligation of non-disclosure shall not apply to information which was known to _____ (Person Name) prior to the execution of this agreement.

Dated: _____

_____
_____ (Company) Corp.
_____(Person Name)

Business and Marketing Plan Instructions

1. If you purchased this Business Plan Book via Amazon's Print-on-Demand System, please send proof-of-purchase to Probusconsult2@Yahoo.com and we will email you the file.

2. Complete the Executive Summary section, as your final step, after you have completed the entire plan.

3. Feel free to edit the plan and make it more relevant to your strategic goals, objectives and business vision.

4. We have provided all of the formulas needed to prepare the financial plan. Just plug in the numbers that are based on your particular situation. Excel spreadsheets for the financials are available on the microsoft.com website and www.simplebizplanning.com/forms.htm
http://office.microsoft.com/en-us/templates/

5. Throughout the plan, we have provided prompts or suggestions as to what values to enter into blank spaces, but use your best judgment and then delete the suggested values (?).

6. The plan also includes some separate worksheets for additional assistance in expanding some of the sections, if desired.

7. Additionally, some sections offer multiple choices and the word 'select' appears as a prompt to edit the contents of the plan.

8. Your feedback, referrals and business are always very much appreciated.

Thank you

Nat Chiaffarano, MBA
Progressive Business Consulting, Inc.
Pembroke Pines, FL 33027
ProBusConsult2@yahoo.com

"Progressive Business Plan for a Child Day Care"

Copyright Notice
Copyright © 2017   Nat Chiaffarano, MBA
Progressive Business Consulting, Inc
All Rights Reserved.   ISBN: 9781549741630

This program is protected under Federal and International copyright laws. No portion of these materials may be reproduced, stored in a retrieval system or transmitted in any manner whatsoever, without the written consent of the publisher.

Limits of Liability / Disclaimer of Warranty
The author and the publisher of "Progressive Business Plan for a Child Day Care", and all accompanying materials have used their best efforts in preparing this program. The author and publisher make no representations and warranties with respect to the accuracy, applicability, fitness or completeness of the content of this program. The information contained in this program is subject to change without notice and should not be construed as a commitment by the author or publisher.

The authors and publisher shall in no event be held liable for any loss or damages, including but not limited to special, incidental, consequential, or other damages. The program makes no promises as to results or consequences of applying the material herein: your business results may vary in direct relation to your detailed planning, timing, availability of capital and human resources, and implementation skills.

This publication is not intended for use as a source of legal, accounting, or professional advice. As always, the advice of a competent legal, accounting, tax, financial or other professional should be sought. If you have any specific questions about your unique business situation, consider contacting a qualified business consultant. The fact that an organization or website is referred to as a 'resource' or potential source of information, does not mean that the publisher or authors endorse the resource. Websites listed may also have been changed since publication of the book.

Child Day Care Business Plan
_____ (date)

Business Name: _____
Plan Time Period: 2017 - 2019

Founding Directors:
Name: _____
Name: _____

Contact Information:
Owner: _____
Address: _____
City/State/Zip: _____
Phone: _____
Cell: _____
Fax: _____
Website: _____
Email: _____

Submitted to: _____
Date: _____
Contact Info: _____

This document contains confidential information. It is disclosed to you for informational purposes only. Its contents shall remain the property of _____ (business name) and shall be returned to _____ when requested. This is a business plan and does not imply an offering of securities.

Child Day Care Business Plan: Table of Contents

Section	Description	Page
1.0	**Executive Summary**	___
1.1.0	Tactical Objectives	___
1.1.1	Strategic Objectives	___
1.2	Mission Statement	___
1.2.1	Core Values Statement	___
1.3	Vision Statement	___
1.4	Keys to Success	___
2.0	**Company Summary**	___
2.1	Company Ownership	___
2.2	Company Licensing and Liability Protection	___
2.3	Start-up To-do Checklist	___
2.4.0	Company Location	___
2.4.1	Company Facilities	___
2.5.0	Start-up Summary	___
2.5.1	Inventory	___
2.5.2	Supply Sourcing	___
2.6	Start-up Requirements	___
2.7	SBA Loan Key Requirements	___
2.7.1	Other Financing Options	___
3.0	**Products and Services**	___
3.1	Service Descriptions	___
3.1.1	Product Descriptions	___
3.2	Alternate Revenue Streams	___
3.3	Production of Products and Services	___
3.4	Competitive Comparison	___
3.5	Sale Literature	___
3.6	Fulfillment	___
3.7	Technology	___
3.8	Future Products and Services	___
4.0	**Market Analysis Summary**	___
4.1.0	Secondary Market Research	___
4.1.1	Primary Market Research	___
4.2	Market Segmentation	___
4.3	Target Market Segment Strategy	___
4.3.1	Market Needs	___
4.4	Buying Patterns	___
4.5	Market Growth	___

Section	Description	Page
4.6	Service Business Analysis	____
4.7	Barrier to Entry	____
4.8	Competitive Analysis	____
4.9	Market Revenue Projections	____
5.0	**Industry Analysis**	____
5.1	Industry Leaders	____
5.2	Industry Statistics	____
5.3	Industry Trends	____
5.4	Industry Key Terms	____
6.0	**Strategy and Implementation Summary**	____
6.1.0	Promotion Strategy	____
6.1.1	Grand Opening	____
6.1.2	Value Proposition	____
6.1.3	Positioning Statement	____
6.1.4	Distribution Strategy	____
6.2	Competitive Advantage	____
6.2.1	Branding Strategy	____
6.3	Business SWOT Analysis	____
6.4.0	Marketing Strategy	____
6.4.1	Strategic Alliances	____
6.4.2	Monitoring Marketing Results	____
6.4.3	Word-of-Mouth Marketing	____
6.5	Sales Strategy	____
6.5.1	Customer Retention Strategy	____
6.5.2	Sales Forecast	____
6.5.3	Sales Program	____
6.6	Merchandising Strategy	____
6.7	Pricing Strategy	____
6.8	Differentiation Strategies	____
6.9	Milestone Tracking	____
7.0	**Website Plan Summary**	____
7.1	Website Marketing Strategy	____
7.2	Development Requirements	____
7.3	Sample Frequently Asked Questions	____
8.0	**Operations**	____
8.1	Security Measures	____
9.0	**Management Summary**	____
9.1	Owner Personal History	____

Section	Description	Page
9.2	Management Team Gaps	____
9.2.1	Management Matrix	____
9.2.2	Outsourcing Matrix	____
9.3	Employee Requirements	____
9.4	Job Descriptions	____
9.4.1	Job Description Format	____
9.5	Personnel Plan	____
9.6	Staffing Plan	____
10.0	**Business Risk Factors**	____
10.1	Business Risk Reduction Strategies	____
10.2	Reduce Customer Perceived Risk Strategies	____
11.0	**Financial Plan**	____
11.1	Important Assumptions	____
11.2	Break-even Analysis	____
11.3	Projected Profit and Loss	____
11.4	Projected Cash Flow	____
11.5	Projected Balance Sheet	____
11.6	Business Ratios	____
12.0	**Business Plan Summary**	____
13.0	**Potential Exit Strategies**	____
	Appendix	____
	Helpful Resources	____
	Marketing Worksheets	____
	Sample Business Forms	____
	Child Daycare Laws	____

1.0 Executive Summary

Industry Overview

This industry provides day-care services for infants and children. These establishments generally care for preschool children, but may care for older children when school is not in session, such as during the summer or after school hours. Establishments may also offer some educational programs.

The daycare industry is thriving, and will continue to do so as the financial demands make working parents the required standard. Approximately one-half of the children in the United States today are cared for by someone other than an immediate family member during some portion of each day. In two-thirds of two-parent homes, both parents work, providing a large and ever growing consumer base for the day-care industry. In addition, 12 million children, more than 20% of the children in the United States, live with single parents who need child care in order to work.

The industry consists of establishments that provide paid care for infants, toddlers, preschool children, or older children in before- and after-school programs. Two main types of child care make up the child day care services industry: center-based care and family child care. Formal child day care centers include preschools, child care centers, and Head Start centers. Family child care providers care for children in their home for a fee and are the majority of self-employed workers in this industry, which does not include occasional babysitters or persons who provide unpaid care in their homes for the children of relatives or friends.

The for-profit sector of this industry includes centers that operate independently or as part of a local or national chain. Nonprofit child day care organizations may provide services in religious institutions, YMCAs and other social and recreation centers, colleges, public schools, social service agencies, and worksites ranging from factories to office complexes. The number of for-profit establishments has grown rapidly in response to demand for child care services. Within the nonprofit sector, there has been strong growth in Head Start, the federally funded child care program designed to provide disadvantaged children with social, educational, and health services.

Business Overview

_____ (company name) _____ (was/is in the process of being) formed to provide first class, safe and secure child care services in the _____ area to children from ____ (#) months to ___ (#) years of age. Our goal is to provide a safe, supervised, long-term, daily care for a child while the child's parents are working or unable to assume child care responsibilities. We will also offer after school programs, such as tutoring and activities such as arts and crafts, and _____ (gymnastics?), and a drop-off child care service.

With the increasing number of households either headed by a single parent or where both parents work (dual income family), professional and trustworthy childcare is more important than ever. In the interest of children's health and safety, many states are applying more strict licensing requirements to childcare facilities and childcare workers, but we expect to have no problem exceeding these requirements.

In order to succeed, _____ (company name) will have to do the following:
1. Make superior customer service our number one priority.
2. Stay abreast of trends in the child care industry.
3. Precisely assess and then exceed the expectations of all clients.
4. Form long-term, trust-based relationships with parents to secure profitable repeat business and referrals.
5. Create a safe, educational and fun experience for the children.

Customer Service
We will take every opportunity to help the customer, regardless of what the revenue might be. We will outshine our competition by doing something "extra" and offering added-value, such as a Young Parent Program. We will treat clients with respect and help them like we would help a friend. We will take a long-term perspective and focus on the client's possible lifetime value to our business.

Plan Objective
The purpose of this document is to provide a strategic business plan for our company. The plan has been adjusted to reflect the particular strengths and weaknesses of _____ (company name). Actual financial performance will be tracked closely and the business plan will be adjusted when necessary to ensure that full profit potential is realized.

Business Structure
The business _____ (will be/was) incorporated on _____ (date) in the state of _____, as a _____ (Corporation/LLC), and intends to register for Sub-chapter 'S' status for federal tax purposes. This will effectively shield the owner(s) from personal liability and double taxation.

Business Goals
Our business goal is to continue to develop the _____ (company name) brand name. To do so, we plan to execute on the following:
1. Offer quality child care at a competitive price.
2. Focus on quality controls and ongoing operational excellence.
3. Recruit and train the very best, background checked employees.
4. Create a marketing campaign with a consistent look and message content.

Mission Statement
Our Mission is to address the following customer pain points or unmet needs and wants, which will define the opportunity for our business:
_____
In order to satisfy these unmet needs and wants, we will propose the following unique solutions, which will create better value for our customers:

Location
_____ (company name) will be located in the _____ (complex name) on _____ (street address) in _____ (city), ____ (state). The _____ (purchased/leased) space is easily accessible and provides ample parking for ____ (#) customers and staff. The location is attractive due to the area demographics, which reflect our target customer profile. The facilities will include office space for the principals and bookkeeper, a toy and game storage area, locker area, indoor and outdoor play areas, a sick room, snack/kitchen area, and book and music centers.

Competitive Edge
_____ (company name) will compete well in our market by offering competitive prices, high-quality customer-centric child care services, innovative after-school programs, transport services, nutritional meals and healthy snack foods, lower staff/child ratios, creative extracurricular programs, stricter teacher qualifications and formal background screening practices, and leading edge educational programs. For budget constrained parents, we plan to offer a daycare program option that does not offer an educational component, but rather focuses on arts and crafts, and organized playtime. We will provide quality customer service to all wards and parents that patronize our center and offer competitive prices and discounts based on family size, loyalty and referrals. We will build a state-of-the-art facility for the kids in our day care center. We will also have quality control experts who will ensure that our employees deliver the quality that is abiding by the health and safety rules and regulations, as demanded by the appropriate authorities. Furthermore, we will maintain an excellent reputation for trustworthiness and integrity with parents and the community we serve.

Target Market
We will target the community developments of _____ and _____, which are within a ___ mile radius of our facility. Our target customers are dual-income, and single parent, middle class families who value the importance of early learning programs and quality day care for their children. We are going to concentrate mainly on working families who have got kids that need to be in daycare centers.

Marketing Plan
With the help of an aggressive marketing plan, _____ (company name) expects to experience steady growth. _____ (company name) plans to attract its customers through the use of local newspaper advertisements, circulating flyers, a systematic series of direct mailings, news releases in local newspapers, a website, online directories, networking with local organizations, a sales rep to approach commercial accounts and Yellow Page ads. We will also become an active member of the local Early Child Development organization.
Resource: http://childcareaware.org/providers/planning-for-success/marketing-your-program/

Content Marketing Strategies will include:

1. Blogging topics such as "Benefits of Child Daycare vs Staying at Home" and "How to Deal with Separation Anxiety on Both Sides."
2. FAQ items to provide general information and answers to commonly asked questions for parents.
3. Infographics outlining the advantages of early child development from a daycare.
4. Trend Reports and statistics of the value of child care development through areas of education, socialization, stimulation, and general child development.
5. Checklists and sample timelines of when they should be considering their options.
6. Subscriptions to our Parent e-Newsletter.
7. Download our New Parent Guide
8. Survey Results Reports
9. Comparison white papers to assess the evaluation criteria for the parents options.
10. E-Books outlining the top reasons to enroll a child in a daycare.
11. Webinar to provide information on the advantages of enrolling a child in a daycare over alternative forms of child care.
12. Case Studies of real families who were on the fence when considering their options.
13. Curriculum overview or outline.
14. Testimonials from the actual parents of enrollees.

Resource:
ttps://blog.hubspot.com/marketing/inbound-marketing-for-daycares

The Management Team

_____ (company name) will be lead by _____ (owner name) and _____ (co-owner name). ____ (owner name) has a _____ degree from ___ (institution name) and a ____ background within the industry, having spent ____ (#) years with ____ (former employer name or type of business). During this tenure, ___ (he/she) helped grow the business from $_____ in yearly revenue to over $___. ____ (co-owner name) has a ___ background, and while employed by __ was able to increase operating profit by __ percent. These acquired skills, work experiences and educational backgrounds will play a big role in the success of our child day care center. Additionally, our president, _____ (name), has an extensive knowledge of the _____ area and has identified a niche market retail opportunity to make this venture highly successful, combining his ___ (#) years of work experience in a variety of businesses. _____ (owner name) will manage all aspects of the business and service development to ensure effective customer responsiveness while monitoring day-to-day operations. Qualified and trained sales associates personally trained by _____ (owner name) in customer service skills will provide additional support services. Support staff will be added as seasonal or extended hours mandate.

Recap of Past Successful Accomplishments

____ (company name) is uniquely qualified to succeed due to the following past successes:
1. **Entrepreneurial Track Record**: The owners and management team have helped to launch numerous successful ventures, including a _____.

2. **Key Milestones Achieved**: The founders have invested $___ to-date to staff the company, build the core technology, acquire starting inventory, test market the _____ (product/service), realize sales of $_____ and launch the website.

Start-up Funding
_____ (owner name) will financially back the new business venture with an initial investment of $_____, and will be the principal owner. Additional funding in the amount of $_____ will be sought from _____, a local commercial bank, with a SBA loan guarantee. This money will be needed to start the company. This loan will provide startup capital, financing for a selected site lease, remodeling renovations, inventory supply purchases, pay for permits and licensing, instructor training and certification, purchase equipment and cover expenses during the first year of operation.

Financial Projections
We plan to open for business on _____ (date), and start with an initial enrollment of ___ students. _____ (company name) is forecasted to gross in excess of $_____ in sales in its first year of operation, ending _____ (month/ year). Profit margins are forecasted to be at about ____ percent. Second year operations will produce a net profit of $_____. This will be generated from an investment of $_____ in initial capital. It is expected that payback of our total invested capital will be realized in less than _____ (#) months of operation. It is further forecasted that cash flow becomes positive from operations in year _____ (one/two?). We project that our net profits will increase from $_____ to over $ _____ over the next three years.

Financial Profile Summary

Key Indicator	2017	2018	2019
Total Revenue			
Expenses			
Gross Margin			
Operating Income			
Net Income			
EBITDA			

EBITDA = Revenue - Expenses (excluding tax, interest, depreciation and amortization)
  EBITDA is essentially net income with interest, taxes, depreciation, and amortization added back to it, and can be used to analyze and compare profitability between companies and industries because it eliminates the effects of financing and accounting decisions.
Gross Margin (%) = (Revenue - Cost of Goods Sold) / Revenue
Net Income = Total revenue - Cost of sales - Other expenses - Tax

Exit Strategy
If the business is very successful, ____ (owner name) may seek to sell the business to a third party for a significant earnings multiple. Most likely, the Company will hire a qualified business broker to sell the business on behalf of _____ (company name). Based

on historical numbers, the business could generate a sales premium of up to __(#) times earnings.

Summary

Through a combination of a proven business model and a strong management team to guide the organization, _____ (company name) will be a long lasting, profitable business. We believe our ability to create future product and service opportunities and growth will only be limited by our imagination and our ability to attract talented people who understand the concept of branding.

1.1 Key Strategic Objectives

The following strategic objectives will specify quantifiable results and involve activities that can be easily tracked. They will also be realistic, tied to specific marketing strategies and serve as a good benchmark to evaluate our marketing plan success. (Select Choices)

1. To create a company whose primary goal is to exceed customer expectations.
2. To develop a cash flow that is capable of paying all salaries, as well as grow the business, by the end of the _____ (first?) year.
3. To be an active networking participant and productive member of the community by _____ (date).
4. Create over _____ (50?) % of business revenues from repeat customers by _____ (date).
5. Achieve an overall customer satisfaction rate of ____ (100?) % by _____ (date).
6. Get a business website designed, built and operational by _____ (date), which will include an online shopping cart.
7. Achieve total sales revenues of $_____ in _____ (year).
8. Open a second location by the end of Fiscal _____ (year) and begin franchise efforts by the end of Fiscal _____ (year).
9. Realize gross margins higher than _____ (85?) percent by _____ (date).
10. Achieve net income more than ___ (10?) percent of net sales by the ____ (#) year.
11. Increase overall sales by _____ (20?) percent from prior year through superior service and word-of-mouth referrals.
12. Reduce the cost of new customer acquisition by ___ % to $ _____ by _____ (date).
13. Turn in profits from the _____ (#) month of operations.
14. Expand operations to include all of the _____ (city) area, including _____, _____ and _____.
15. Provide employees with continuing training, benefits and incentives to reduce the employee turnover rate to _____ %.
16. To pursue a growth rate of ____ (20?) % per year for the first ____ (#) years.
17. The enrollment in our facility of at least ___ (#) different families in the first _____ (#) months.
18. Reduce the cost of new customer acquisition by ___ % to $ ___ by _____ (date).
19. Provide employees with continuing training, benefits and incentives to reduce the

employee turnover rate to _____%.
20. Enable the owner to draw a salary of $ _____ by the end of year ____ (one?).
21. To reach cash break-even by the end of year ____ (one?).
22. Increase market share to ___ percent over the next ___ (#) months.
23. Become one of the top ___ (#) players in the emerging _____ category in __ (#) months.
24. Increase Operating Profit by ___ percent versus the previous year.
25. To have over ____ (#) toddlers/babies within the first 12 months of operations.
26. To generate a minimum revenue of _____ US dollars within the first 12 months of operations.
27. To achieve a sustainable growth at the rate of _____% annual sales growth

1.1.1 Strategic Objectives

We will seek to work toward the accomplishment of the following strategic objectives, which relate back to our Mission and Vision Statements:
1. Improve the overall quality of our child care services.
2. Make the family experience better, faster and more customer friendly.
3. Strengthen personal relationships with customers.
4. Enhance affordability and accessibility.
5. Foster a spirit of innovation.

1.2.0 Mission Statement   (select)

Our Mission Statement is a written statement that spells out our organization's overall goal, provides a sense of direction and acts as a guide to decision making for all levels of management. In the mission statement, our goal will be to identify the customer pain we intend to satisfy, and what our company will do to satisfy it. In developing the following mission statement we will encourage input from employees, volunteers, and other stakeholders, and publicize it broadly in our website and other marketing materials.

It is the Mission of _____ (company name) to develop a community of professional care givers with the credentials to not only enhance children's early social and motor skills, but to also teach them basic learning skills.

Our mission is to be a leader in the growth and development of children and to create a curriculum tailored specifically for children that is taught in a fun, safe and nurturing, care giving environment. Our mission is to make sure that all kids that passes through our day care center have the best of foundations for their next educational hurdles.

Our mission is to realize 100% student satisfaction, and generate long-term profits through referrals and repeat business. Our goal is to set ourselves apart from the competition by making customer satisfaction our number one priority and to provide

customer service that is responsive, informed and respectful.
Our goal is to inspire young children to confidently explore, create, and become involved in the learning process through their five senses. Our mission is to provide affordable, first-class care giving and education by providing a broad range of integrated programs and services, and innovative learning approaches.
Our mission is to improve child care accessibility for all community residents and promote cultural diversity.

1.2.1 Mantra

We will create a mantra for our organization that is three or four words long. Its purpose will be to help employees truly understand why the organization exists. Our mantra will serve as a framework through which to make decisions about product and business direction. It will boil the key drivers of our company down to a sentence that defines our most important areas of focus and resemble a statement of purpose or significance.
Our Mantra is _____

1.2.2 Core Values Statement

The following Core Values will help to define our organization, guide our behavior, underpin operational activity and shape the strategies we will pursue in the face of various challenges and opportunities:
    Being respectful and ethical to our customers and employees.
    Building enduring relationships with clients.
    Seeking innovation in our industry.
    Practicing accountability to our colleagues and stakeholders.
    Pursuing continuous improvement as individuals and as a business entity.
    Performing tasks on time to satisfy the needs of our internal and external clients.
    Taking active part in the organization to meet the objectives and the establishment of continuous and lasting relationships.
    Offering professional treatment to our clients, employees, shareholders, and the community.
    Continuing pursuit of new technologies for the development of the projects that add value for our clients, employees, shareholders, and the community.
    Personal and professional improvement through education.
    Teamwork to achieve our goals.
    Honesty and integrity in all areas of our professional relationships.
    Loyalty to the team and dedication to achieving our mission.

1.3 Vision Statement   (select)

The following Vision Statement will communicate both the purpose and values of our organization. For employees, it will give direction about how they are expected to behave and inspires them to give their best. Shared with customers, it will shape customers' understanding of why they should work with our organization.

_____ (company name) will strive to become one of the most respected and favored day care centers in the area. It is our desire to become a landmark business in _____ (city), ____ (state), and become known not only for the quality of our products and services, but also for our community and charity involvement.

_____ (company name) is dedicated to operating with a constant enthusiasm for learning about the child care business, being receptive to implementing new ideas, and maintaining a willingness to adapt to changing market needs and wants. To be an active and vocal member of the community, and to provide continual reinvestment through participation in community activities and financial contributions.

In five years,_____ (company name) will be an area leader in the child care industry, and plans will be developed and implemented to pursue national business through the franchising of our business model concept.

1.4 Keys to Success

In broad terms, the success factors relate to providing what our clients want, and doing what is necessary to be better than our competitors. The following critical success factors are areas in which our organization must excel in order to operate successfully and achieve our objectives:

1. Service our client needs with personalized attention and expert knowledge.
2. A good location that enables the servicing of our residential community.
3. Launch a website to showcase our services and customer testimonials, provide helpful information and facilitate online registrations.
4. Local community involvement and business partnerships.
5. Conduct a targeted and cost-effective marketing campaign that seeks to differentiate our care giving and educational services from traditional daycare offerings.
6. Institute a program of profit sharing among all employees to reduce employee turnover and improve productivity.
7. Control costs and manage budgets at all times in accordance with company goals.
8. Institute management processes and controls to insure the consistent replication of operations.
9. Recruit screened employees with a passion for delivering exceptional day care.
10. Institute an employee training to insure the best child care techniques are consistently practiced.
11. Network aggressively within the community, as word of mouth will be our most powerful advertising asset.
12. Maintaining a highly regarded reputation for excellence in care giving, education and community involvement.

13. Adhering to our strategic business plan for growth and expansion, and reinvesting in the business and its employees.
14. Provide a low staff-to-child ratio to facilitate personalized child attention and a quality experience.
15. Provide a safe and secure environment.
16. Staying abreast of new day care service concepts.
17. Building our brand awareness, which will drive customers to increase their usage of our services and make referrals.
18. Maintaining a reputable and untarnished reputation in the community.
19. Business planning with the flexibility to make changes based on gaining new insightful perspectives as we proceed.
20. Building trust by circulating and adhering to our Code of Ethics and Service Guarantees.
21. The offering of a flexible schedule of available child care hours.
22. Competitive pricing in conjunction with a differentiated service business model.
23. Must report all signs of child abuse and allegations of sexual activity between children.
24. Develop a checklist to make the cleaning and sanitizing of the daycare regularly a top priority to prevent the spread of germs.
25. A basic knowledge about child development.
26. Must be extremely reliable and give parents as much warning as possible about schedule changes or availability.
27. Must thoroughly research state's rules and regulations concerning licensed family day care business, usually listed under 'Department of Human Services'.
28. Must prepare for state's safety inspection of the day care facility.
29. Must adequately invest in the added furniture, toys and supplies needed to accommodate a large number of children throughout the day.
30. Join a family child care association that provides a parent referral service for members, practical advice and instructional classes, and profession updates on the state and national levels.
31. The environment must be safe, clean, uncluttered, bright, colorful and inviting.
32. Work with a lawyer to make a contract between the provider and the child's parents.
33. Take CPR and first aid classes to insure that you are able to handle any emergencies, and keep a first aid kit filled and updated.
34. Arrange for safe sleeping areas for the kids, free of mobiles, bumpers and overly fluffy bedding.
35. Research nutritional needs and ways to arrange colored food to make meals and snacks more attractive to children.
36. Plan an educational curriculum that will challenge the children.
37. Day care providers need to stay informed of federal program and proposals because of the direct consequences on new and existing day care businesses.
38. Because of recent court cases, day-care providers must have a substantial knowledge of the laws for operating a center or providing care in the home.
39. An important step in precluding lawsuits filed by parents is to require them to sign a consent form which outlines the policies of the center and the procedures

to be followed in special situations and emergencies. Also, the responsibilities and expectations of the day-care provider and the parents should be clearly understood.
40. Proper insurance coverage is essential to cover the costs of lawsuits, liabilities, and unexpected expenses.
41. Be certain that you have researched and fully understand your local government requirements before opening your child care center.
42. Start by offering in-home babysitter services to build up experience as well as create clients that will likely be interested in our day care center.
43. Ensure that you always have a first-aid-kit ready and easily accessible.
44. Purchase safe and adequate bedding for each child.
45. Make sure that you can meet local regulations on safe sleeping arrangements.
46. Make meal plans that include healthy snacks and meals planned in advance.
47. Ensure that all games, puzzles, toys and play equipment are appropriate for the age of the children you will have under your care.
48. Immediately discard broken or otherwise dangerous toys and equipment.
49. Provide some educational time because parents will be very happy to know that their children are learning new things.
50. Get inspected by your local Social and Rehabilitation Service, Department of Human Services, Department of Children & Families or Child Safety Department.
51. Create your accounting system, advertising ideas and scheduling process.
52. Keep good records on every child under your care.
53. Realize the networking benefits of becoming a Certified Women's Business Enterprise (WBE).
54. Identify the skills you need, but don't personally have, and then hire people with those skills to enable you to grow your business.
55. Hire people with an attitude that reflects how excited they are about the promise of early childhood education, and then train for skills.
56. Become familiar with the number of government programs that help low-income families pay for child care so the adults can stay in the work force.
57. Recognize and reward employee excellence to motivate the whole team.
Source:
www.flipmycenter.com/6-ways-to-run-a-more-successful-child-care-center/
58. Create the documentation and develop a system for coaching new preschool teachers.
Source:
www.naeyc.org/blogs/sfriedmannaeycorg/2013/07/advice-new-preschool-teacher
www.brighthubeducation.com/teaching-preschool/125439-collection-of-resources-and-lessons-for-teaching-preschool/
59. Carefully screen all workers for a love of children and make certain they aren't easily frustrated.
Source:
http://www.businessknowhow.com/businessideas/daycare.htm
60. Understand what sets your daycare apart from your competitors: the décor, the curriculum, the teaching philosophy, extracurricular activities like sports teams or cooking classes, teacher experience or educations, expanded

	open hours and days, and expound upon it as a competitive advantage.
61.	Stay abreast of parents' desire for their children to have an educational experience in daycare. Source: www.carelulu.com/resources/childcare-providers/successful-child-care-business/
62.	Do the research to become an expert in potty training and biting prevention. Source: http://www.simplydaycare.com/daycare-tips.html
63.	Install sensor activated faucets to reduce germ spreading and water bills. Resource: www.FaucetDirect.com
64.	Use real estate sites like Loopnet.com and Zillow.com to provide helpful demographic analyses of the neighborhood and the need for a child day care center.

2.0 Company Summary

_____ (company name) is a start-up _____ (Corporation/Limited Liability Company) consisting of _____ (#) principle officers with combined industry experience of _____ (#) years. The owner of the company will be investing a significant amount of _____ (his/her) own capital into the company and will also be seeking a loan to cover start-up costs and future growth.

____ (company name) will be located in a ___ (purchased/rented) _____ (suite/complex) in the _____ on _____ (address) in _____ (city), _____ (state). The facilities _____ (will be/were designed) to meet strict design standards, under the supervision of the _____ County Child Care licensing board.

We will do the upfront research to determine which of the following services are most needed in our community and prioritize the launching of those services:
1. Full-time care during traditional weekday hours
2. After-school care
3. Nontraditional hours (very early mornings, evenings, overnight care, weekdays and/or weekends)
4. Drop-in or on-demand care, either during traditional or nontraditional hours
5. Part-time care
6. Parents' night out (weekend evening care)
7. Age-based care
8. Transportation

The company plans to use its existing contacts and customer base to generate short-term sales. Its long-term profitability will rely on focusing on referrals, networking within community organizations and a comprehensive marketing program that includes public relations activities and a structured referral program.

Our daycare center will employ the following fundamental concepts for the services offered:
1. Premier Care Giving Services
2. Learning, Mentoring and Tutoring Services
3. Community Advancement and Involvement
4. Advanced Developmental Programs
5. An Activity Based and Structured Curriculum.

Sales are expected to reach $_____ within the first year and to grow at a conservative rate of _____ (20?) percent during the next two to five years.

Facilities Renovations
The necessary renovations are itemized as follows: Estimate
    Partition of space into functional areas and offices.   _____
    Build storage areas for toys, games and books.   _____
    Painting and other general cosmetic repairs   _____

Install play equipment. _____
Other _____ _____
Total: _____

Operations

_____ (company name) will open for business on _____ (date) and will maintain the following business hours:

Monday through Thursday:	_____	(7 to 6 ?)
Friday:	_____	(7 to 8 ?)
Saturday:	_____	(8 to 5 ?)
Sunday:	_____	(Closed ?)

The company will invest in customer relationship management software (CRM) to track sales and collect customer information, including names, email addresses, key reminder dates and preferences. This information will be used with email, e-newsletter and direct mail campaigns to build personalized fulfillment programs, establish customer loyalty and drive revenue growth.

2.0.1 Traction (optional)

We will include this section because investors expect to see some traction, both before and after a funding event and investors tend to judge past results as a good indicator of future projections. It will also show that we can manage our operations and develop a business model capable of funding inventory purchases. Traction will be the best form of market research and present evidence of customer acceptance.

Period _____
Product/Service Focus _____
Our Sales to Date: _____
Our Number of Users to Date: _____
Number of Repeat Users _____
Number of Pending Orders: _____
Value of Pending Orders: _____
Reorder Cycle Period: _____
Key Reference Sites _____
Mailing List Subscriptions _____
Competitions/Awards Won _____
Notable Product Reviews _____
Actual Percent Gross Profit Margin _____
Industry Average: GPM _____
Actual B/(W) Industry Average _____

Note: Percent Gross Profit Margin equals the sales receipts less the cost of goods sold divided by sales receipts multiplied by 100.

2.1 Company Ownership

_____ (company name) is a _____ (Sole-proprietorship/ Corporation/Limited Liability Corporation (LLC)) and is registered to the principal owner, _____ (owner name). The company was formed in _____ (month) of ____ (year). It will be registered as a Subchapter S to avoid double taxation, with ownership allocated as follows: _____ (owner name) ____ % and _____ (owner name) ____ %.

The owner is a _____ (year) graduate of _____ (institution name), in _____ (city, ____ (state), with a _____ degree. He/she has ____ years of executive experience in the _____ (?) industry as a _____, performing the following roles: _____.
His/her major accomplishments include: _____
_____.

Ownership Breakdown:

Shareholder Name	Responsibilities	Number and Class of Shares	Percent Ownership

The remainder of the issued and outstanding common shares are retained by the Company for __ (future distribution / allocation under the Company's employee stock option plan).

Shareholder Loans
The Company currently has outstanding shareholder loans in the aggregate sum of $_____. The following table sets out the details of the shareholder loans.

Shareholder Name	Loan Amount	Loan Date	Balance Outstanding

Directors
The Company's Board of Directors, which is made up of highly qualified business and industry professionals, will be a valuable asset to the Company and be instrumental to its development. The following persons will make up the Board of Directors of the Company:

Name of Person	Educational Background	Past Industry Experience	Other Companies Served

2.2 Company Licensing & Liability Protection

The business will consider the need to acquire the following types of insurances. This will require extensive comparison shopping, through several insurance brokers, listed with our state's insurance department:
1. Workman's Compensation,
2. Business Policy: Property & General Liability Insurance
3. Health insurance.
4. Commercial Auto Insurance
5. Professional Liability (Errors and Omissions Insurance)
6. State Unemployment Insurance
7. Life Insurance
8. Disability Insurance
9. Business Interruption Insurance (Business Income Insurance)
10. Crime Insurance

General liability protects against claims of injury or property damage involving clients. Workman's compensation covers employees in case of harm attributed to the workplace. The property and liability insurance protects the building from theft, fire, natural disasters, and being sued by a third party. Employee health insurance will be provided for the full time employees. Professional Liability Insurance is important when a business is involved with contracts. Life and Disability Insurance may be required if a bank loan is secured.

Liability Insurance includes protection in the face of day-to day accidents, unforeseen results of normal business activities, and allegations of abuse or molestation, food poisoning, or exposure to infectious disease.
Abuse and Molestation Insurance coverage will defend us from such allegations and, when necessary, pay the amount we are legally liable to pay up to the limit we purchase.
Student Accident Insurance - This type of policy will pay for medical bills incurred by the injured children up to a set dollar amount (typically $5,000 or $10,000).
Property Insurance - Property Insurance should take care of the repairs less whatever deductible you have chosen.
Loss of Income Insurance will replace our income during the time the business is shutdown. Generally this coverage is written for a fixed amount of monthly income for a fixed number of months.

To help save on insurance cost and claims, management will do the following:
1. Stress employee safety in our employee handbook.
2. Screen employees with interview questionnaires and will institute pre-employment drug tests and comprehensive background checks.
3. Videotape our equipment and inventory for insurance purposes.
4. Create an operations manual that shares safe techniques.
5. Limit the responsibilities that we choose to accept in our contracts.
6. Consider the financial impact of assuming the exposure ourselves.
7. Establish loss prevention programs to reduce the hazards that cause losses.

8. Consider taking higher deductibles on anything but that which involves liability insurance because of third-party involvement.
9. Stop offering services that require expensive insurance coverage or require signed releases from clients using those services.
10. Improve employee training and initiate training sessions for safety.
11. Require Certificate of Insurance from all subcontractors.
12. Make staff responsible for a portion of any damages they cause.
13 We will investigate the setting-up of a partial self-insurance plan.
14. Convince underwriters that our past low claims are the result of our ongoing safety programs and there is reason to expect our claims will be lower than industry averages in the future.
15. At each renewal, we will develop a service agreement with our broker and get their commitment to our goals, such as a specific reduction in the number of incidents.
16. We will assemble a risk control team, with people from both sides of our business, and broker representatives will serve on the committee as well.
17. When an employee is involved in an accident, we will insist on getting to the root cause of the incident and do everything possible to prevent similar incidents from re-occurring.
18. At renewal, we will consult with our brokers to develop a cost-saving strategy and decide whether to bid out our coverage for competitive quotes or stick with our current carrier.
19. We will set-up a captive insurance program, as a risk management technique, where our business will form its own insurance company subsidiary to finance its retained losses in a formal structure.
20. Review named assets (autos and equipment), drivers and/or key employees identified on policies to make sure these assets and people are still with our company.
21. As a portion of our business changes, that is, closes, operations change, or outsourcing occurs, we will eliminate unnecessary coverage.
22. We will make sure our workforce is correctly classified by our workers' compensation insurer and liability insurer because our premiums are based on the type of workers used.
23. We will become active in Trade Organizations or Professional Associations, because as a benefit of membership, our business may receive substantial insurance discounts.
24. We will adopt health specific changes to our work place, such as adopting a no smoking policy at our company and allow yoga or weight loss classes to be held in our break room.
25. We will consider a partial reimbursement of health club membership as a benefit.
26. We will find out what employee training will reduce rates and get our employees involved in these programs.

The required business insurance package will be provided by _____ (insurance carrier name). The business will open with a ____ (#) million dollar liability insurance policy, with an annual premium cost of $ _____..

All required licenses to own and operate a daycare business will be obtained through the local city and county government offices. Each state has its own guidelines for the caregiver or staff qualifications, proper physical environment, proper health and safety practices, good nutrition, maximum number of children and maximum number in each age group in a family child-care facility. States also have guidelines regarding the number of caregivers required per number of children in each age group for commercial facilities.

Note: In addition to complying with state-specific licensing requirements, owners of daycare centers are responsible for demonstrating competence in the field of child care and development. Many daycare center owners choose to obtain either the Child Development Associate credential from the Council for Professional Recognition (www.cdacouncil.org/cda_obt.htm) or the National Administrator Credential from the National Child Care Association (www.nccanet.org/). Owners who hire employees are also encouraged to have their employees become certified by a program similar to the Certified Childcare Professional credential. While the credentialing process is distinct from licensing, both mandate minimum guidelines in terms of education, background and experience

Accreditation
Once we are established as a family child care provider, we will look into accreditation through the National Association for Family Child Care (NAFCC). Accreditation is awarded to family child care providers who meet eligibility requirements and quality standards. NAFCC is the only nationally recognized accreditation system specifically for family child care providers and is the highest indicator available to demonstrate that a family child care program is a quality environment.
Resource: www.nafcc.net.

Note: Most States do not regulate family child care providers who care for just a few children, typically between ages 2 and 5. Providers who care for more children are required to be licensed and, in a few States, have some minimal training. Once a provider joins the industry, most States require the worker to complete a number of hours of training per year. In nearly all States, licensing regulations require criminal record checks for all child day care staff. Many local governments regulate family child care providers who are not covered by State regulations. Home safety inspections and criminal background checks are usually required of an applicant.

Note: Wait to be contacted by the Department of Family and Protective Services if you have applied to become a licensed or registered daycare home. The department will inspect your home to make sure that you comply with the minimum standards. The standards changes depending on the kind of daycare you wish to operate and are subject to change with the laws of your state.

The daycare business will need to acquire the following special licenses and permits to qualify for insurance coverage:
1.   A sales tax license is required through the State Department of Revenue.

2. A County and/or City Occupational License.
3. Daycare Business License from State Licensing Agency (Office of Child Services) County Department of Children and Family Services
4. Permits from the Fire Department and State Health Department.
5. Building Code Inspections by the County Building Department.
6. Sign Permit

Note: In most states, you are legally required to obtain a business license, and a dba certificate. A business license is usually a flat tax assessment and a percentage of your gross income. A dba stands for Doing Business As, and it is the registration of your trade name if you have one. You will be required to register your trade name within 30 days of starting your business. Instead of registering a dba, you can simply form an LLC or Corporation and it will have the same effect, namely register your business name.

Resources:
Workers Compensation Regulations
    http://www.dol.gov/owcp/dfec/regs/compliance/wc.htm#IL
New Hire Registration and Reporting
    www.homeworksolutions.com/new-hire-reporting-information/
State Tax Obligations
    www.sba.gov/content/learn-about-your-state-and-local-tax-obligations

Note: Check with your local County Clerk and state offices or Chamber of Commerce to make sure you follow all legal protocols for setting up and running your business.
Note: To find out about your local business licensing office, visit SBA.gov. This government website compiles information on business licenses and permits at the state level.

Resource:
www.sba.gov/blogs/starting-child-care-business-government-tools-and-resources-can-help-0

Resources:
Block Insurance   www.blockinsurance.com
Child Care Insurance   www.childcareinsuranceprofessionals.com
Insurance Information Institute   www.iii.org/individuals/business/
National License Directory   www.sba.gov/licenses-and-permits
National Resource Center for Health & Safety in Child Care and Early Education:
    http://nrckids.org/STATES/states.htm
    http://nrckids.org/index.cfm/resources/state-licensing-and-regulation-information/
Licensing Resource: www.daycarematch.com/resources.asp
National Child Care Association   www.nccanet.org
U.S. Dept. of Health and Human Svcs   www.childcare.gov/
Independent Insurance Agents & Brokers of America   www.iiaa.org
National Association of Surety Bond Producers   www.nasbp.org
Find Law   http://smallbusiness.findlaw.com/starting-business/starting-business-

Business Licenses	licenses-permits/starting-business-licenses-permits-guide.html
	www.iabusnet.org/business-licenses
Legal Zoom	www.legalzoom.com

2.3 Start-up To-Do Checklist

1. Describe your business concept and model, with special emphasis on planned multiple revenue streams and services to be offered.
2. Create Business Plan and Opening Menu of Products and Services.
3. Determine our start up costs of Child Day Care Center, and operating capital and capital budget needs.
4. Seek and evaluate alternative financing options, including SBA guaranteed loan, equipment leasing, social networking loan (www.prosper.com) and/or a family loan (www.virginmoney.com).
5. Do a name search: Check with County Clerk Office or Department of Revenue and Secretary of State to see if the proposed name of business is available.
6. Decide on a legal structure for business.
   Common legal structure options include Sole Proprietorship, Partnership, Corporation or Limited Liability Corporation (LLC).
7. Make sure you contact your State Department of Revenue, Secretary of State, and the Internal Revenue Service to secure EIN Number and file appropriate paperwork. Also consider filing for Sub-Chapter S status with the Federal government to avoid the double taxation of business profits.
8. Protect name and logo with trademarks, if plan is to go national.
9. Find a suitable location with proper zoning.
10. Research necessary permits and requirements your local government imposes on your type of business. (Refer to: www.business.org)
11. Call for initial inspections to determine what must be done to satisfy Fire Marshall, and Building Inspector requirements.
12. Adjust our budget based on build-out requirements.
13. Negotiate lease or property purchase contract.
14. Obtain a building permit.
15. Obtain Federal Employee Identification Number (FEIN).
16. Obtain State Sales Tax ID/Exempt Certificate.
17. Open a Business Checking Account.
18. Obtain Merchant Credit Card Account.
19. Obtain City and County Business Licenses.
20. Create a prioritized list for equipment, furniture and décor items.
21. Comparison shop and arrange for appropriate insurance coverage with product liability insurance, public liability insurance, commercial property insurance and worker's compensation insurance.
22. Locate and purchase all necessary equipment and furniture prior to final inspections.
23. Get contractor quotes for required alterations.

24. Manage the alterations process.
25. Obtain information and price quotes from possible supply distributors.
26. Set a tentative opening date.
27. Install 'Coming Soon' sign in front of building and begin word-of-mouth advertising campaign.
28. Document the preparation, project and payment process flows.
29. Create your accounting, purchasing, payroll, marketing, loss prevention, employee screening and other management systems.
30. Start the employee interview process based on established job descriptions and interview criteria.
31. Contact and interview the following service providers: uniform service, security service, trash service, utilities, telephone, credit card processing, bookkeeping, cleaning services, etc.
32. Schedule final inspections for premises.
33. Correct inspection problems and schedule another inspection.
34. Set a Grand Opening date after a month of regular operations to get the bugs out of the processes.
35. Make arrangements for website design.
36. Train staff.
37. Schedule a couple of practice lessons for friends and interested prospects.
38. Be accessible for direct customer feedback.
39. Distribute comment cards and surveys to solicit more constructive feedback.
40. Remain ready and willing to change your business concept and offerings to suit the needs of your actual customer base.

2.3.1   EMPLOYER RESPONSIBILITIES CHECKLIST

1. Apply for your SS-4 Federal Employer Identification Number (EIN) from the Internal Revenue Service. An EIN can be obtained via telephone, mail or online.
2. Register with the State's Department of Labor (DOL) as a new employer. State Employer Registration for Unemployment Insurance, Withholding, and Wage Reporting should be completed and sent to the address that appears on the form. This registration is required of all employers for the purpose of determining whether the applicants are subject to state unemployment insurance taxes.
3. Obtain Workers Compensation and Disability Insurance from an insurer. The insurance company will provide the required certificates that should be displayed.
4. Order Federal Tax Deposit Coupons – Form 8109 – if you didn't order these when you received your EIN. To order, call the IRS at 1-800-829-1040; you will need to give your EIN. You may want to order some blanks sent for immediate use until the pre-printed ones are complete. Also ask for the current Federal Withholding Tax Tables (Circular A) – this will explain how to withhold and remit payroll taxes, and file reports.
5. Order State Withholding Tax Payment Coupons. Also ask for the current Withholding Tax Tables.

6. Have new employees complete an I-9 Employment Eligibility Verification form. You should have all employees complete this form prior to beginning work. Do not send it to Immigration and Naturalization Service – just keep it with other employee records in your files.
7. Have employees complete a W-4 Employees Withholding Allowance Certificate.

2.4.0 Company Location

A great location for our child daycare will be one that is easy to access, safe and secure. It will have a secure parking area. Safe and secure will be important because most parents always put it on the first list when they are looking for daycare. Parents are always looking for places that offer minimum risk of worries and tension.

_____ (company name) will be located in the _____ (complex name) in _____ (city), ___ (state). It is situated on a _____ (turnpike/street/avenue) just minutes from _____ (benchmark location), in the neighborhood of _____. It borders a large parking lot which is shared by all the businesses therein.

The location has the following advantages:
It is easy to locate and accessible to a number of major roadways.
Good visibility
Plentiful parking.
Proximity to _____ and _____ growth areas.
Proximity to businesses in same affinity class with same ideal client profiles.
Reasonable rent.
Proximity to the growing residential community of _____.
Proximity to the _____ neighborhood school.
In the _____ shopping center where parents with children are likely to frequent or pass by.
Shares a facility with the _____ community organization.
Proximity to the _____ light industrial park with a sizeable workforce.
Area has low crime rate.
Safe drop-off zone.

Resource:
www.hoppingin.com/starting-a-daycare-center-part-1-location-and-square-footage/

2.4.1 Company Facilities

_____ (company name) signed a _____ (#) year lease for _____ (#) square foot of space. The cost is very reasonable at $____/sq. foot. We also have the option of expanding into an additional _____ sq. ft. of space and subletting the space. A leasehold improvement allowance of $___ /sq. ft. would be given. Consolidated area maintenance fees would be $___/month initially. _____ (company name) has obtained a _____ (three) month option on this space effective _____ (date), the submission date of this business plan, and has deposited refundable first and last lease payments, plus a $ _____ security deposit with the leasing agent.

Note:
It will be very important to understand the difference between a net or gross lease. Gross means the monthly lease rate includes everything. A net lease means that in addition to price per square-foot, the tenant will have to pay their share of property taxes, water bills, utilities, landlord's insurance, and common area repairs or maintenance.

The facilities will include office space for the principals, storage area for toys and games, book center, music center, classrooms, cafeteria/kitchen, infant care room, reception area, sick room, parent communications room, hallways, bathrooms and indoor and outdoor play areas. Note: Should allocate at least 20% of the leased area to non-classroom space.

The facilities will feature the following:
1. Computer lab equipped with state-of-the-art hardware and software.
2. Indoor gym area with climbing, sliding and other play equipment.
3. The outdoor play area will be furnished with age appropriate playground equipment.
4. Outdoor basketball courts and sandbox.
5. Puppet Theater (optional)
6. Special events/ reading room.
7. Secure fencing around the entire perimeter.
8. Access to natural light.
9. _____

2.4.2 Facilities Design

In designing our center, we will make certain of the following critical design issues:
1. Two points of exit from the center
2. Up-to-code kitchen with three-compartment sink and grease trap
3. Fire alarm system hooked up to a central box
4. Buzz-in security system

Our day care center will have one room that is large and open. This will be the main room for the children. It will be where the children play, eat and even rest. The room will be large enough to have in it areas not divided by walls. We will use the back of the room for cots and naps, the center part of the room for tables and meals and the front part for play and storage. We will use the walls for storage shelves and bin units.

Note:
We will need to research the square-foot-per-child requirement in our town, city, and state, which may be 35 sq/ft per child.

There will be two bathrooms to the floor plan, along with a kitchen and an office for staff. One of the bathrooms will be placed off of the playroom, so the children have access to it. Another bathroom near the office will be for staff use only. The kitchen will have a stove, microwave, refrigerator, sink and countertop. The children's meals will be prepared in the kitchen. An office will provide private and organized space for the staff away from the main room . We will design storage spaces in the office for the staff. Our facility will have at least two outside entrances. The main door will be on the front of the building and be the main entrance. A back door will provide a second fire exit. Each room will have windows for fire exits and to let in light. Ramps and rails will be added into the design to make the day care center handicap accessible if the center will have special-needs children attending. All stairs will have railings, and grip rails will be added for safety in the children's bathroom. We will add the locations of fire extinguishers and smoke detectors to the design. The eating area will be close to a kitchen or other warming or cooking facility. The diaper area will be away from the eating area and close to a bathroom, or at least a sink. The diapering area will have counters or tables to change diapers, with storage of all equipment right at hand. Equipment storage will include areas for diapers, cleaning supplies for disinfecting the changing surface after diapering, and sanitary storage or disposal for soiled diapers. The indoor play area will be cheerful, well lighted, and invite exploration. There will be an outdoor play area as well that is equally inviting to explore. The environment will be designed with children in mind and furniture will be child sized. Materials will be accessible and displays will be safe and at the child's eye level. We will double check our design against standards and regulations of our state. We will make sure that the building's electrical system will meet code requirements since it will need to pass several code inspections.

The facility has a state-of-the-art security and surveillance system with video monitors of each classroom that parents can remotely access. The facility will provide older children with a minimum of 10 minutes a day of personal computer time, and each teacher will have a classroom computer so that they can communicate with parents by email. Other amenities at the daycare include a commercial kitchen and playgrounds for three separate age groups.

Because the perfect wall color in our daycare will increase the children's mood, we will wisely decide the color scheme. The wall color of nap room will be differentiated from the playing room. The nap room will be soothing and calm children while the daycare play room will be more colorful and cheerful. We will also allocate certain room area where the wall color will be neutral. The neutral color can be the place to hang children art projects. For the learning area, yellow will be a great choice since it can create a sense of warmth, and increase the children's energy level and creativity.

We will not put the same color to the entire wall because it will create the feeling of boredom. To raise children energy levels, orange, red and purple will be used. Another color that will be perfect for daycare is blue. It will be a great choice to create a mural wall. Blue is also great for the nap room, since it can be associated with the ocean or sky design. Natural green is also a great color to soothe children. We will also add a tree or forest painting to create a more interesting environment. We will stay away from dark green shades since it cannot stimulate children interest during daycare time. We will paint the walls of the display area with white color, because it will be the perfect background for the children's hand paintings and drawings. The best method to create the perfect daycare wall color will be to match it with the ceiling. In the nap room, we will choose a light blue for the wall and a lighter blue shade for the ceiling. We will match the furniture with the daycare wall color.

Design Layout for Infants
The infant classroom will have a place for cribs or sleeping places. The napping area will be separated from the play area, providing a quiet atmosphere for snoozing children. The sleeping area will be as far away from the kitchen, ringing telephone, and classroom door as possible. The sleeping area will be softly lit. Our infants will have a safe room, free from debris and choking hazards, to explore the environment. Special attention will be paid to the flooring materials because infants spend most of their day on the floor, creeping, crawling and rolling. We will separate the infant classroom into separate learning centers. A soft climbing area, an area for pulling to a stand, and ample room for crawling without many obstacles are some of the other areas we will include in our design.

Toddlers
The toddler classrooms will have a preschool feel to them, with shelving and tables used to create learning centers. Most toddlers will nap in the afternoon on cots, instead of cribs, freeing up more space for play and learning. A large group gathering area will be designed using a large rug or carpet squares, to provide ample space for a classroom of toddlers. The toddler classroom will contain a sensory table that will be available at all times, a quiet reading area, and an area for creating art. All sensory and art spaces will be in an area that can be cleaned easily, and near a sink. Quiet reading areas will contain soft pillows or chairs for sitting comfortably and exploring books. We will provide spaces on the floor for larger toys such as wooden train sets, large Lego sets, and building blocks. A kitchen will be included in the floor plan. An area for manipulative toys will also contain a low table with several chairs.

Preschool
Preschool classrooms will provide large enough to provide space for more children. The materials contained in a preschool setting will be more challenging than the toddler classroom, but the basic floor plan of a daycare classroom can be the same.
Art and sensory areas will be larger than in the toddler classroom, and will contain more materials to explore. The preschool classroom will have a dedicated science area with different kinds of rocks, plants, seeds, magnifying lenses, and magnets. We will use the science area to display some nonfiction books in a bookcase. The quiet reading areas will contain pillows and soft seating for reading. A listening center with CD players with headphones will be located nearby for listening to music or recorded stories. our preschool classroom will also contain an area for computers.
Source: www.brighthubeducation.com/toddler-activities-learning/91602-floor-plans-to-use-in-daycare/

2.5.0 Start-up Summary

The start-up costs for the Child Day Care Center will be financed through a combination of an owner investment of $ _____ and a short-term bank loan of $ _____. The total start-up costs for this company are approximately $ _____ and can be broken down in the following major categories:

1. Computer hardware & software $ _____
2. Equipment $ _____
3. Office Furniture, Work Tables and Fixtures $ _____
4. Inventory $ _____
5. Working Capital $ _____
   For day-to-day operations, including payroll, etc.
6. Renovations/Buildout $ _____
   Includes architect, lighting update, flooring, etc.
7. Marketing/Advertising Expenses $ _____
   Includes sales brochures, direct mail, opening expenses.
8. Rent and Utility Deposits $ _____
9. Pick-up Van $ _____
10. Contingency Funds $ _____
11. Other (Includes training, legal expenses, software, etc.) $ _____
Total: $ _____

The company will require $ _____ in initial cash reserves and additional $ _____ in assets. The start-up costs are to be financed by the equity contributions of the owner in the amount of $ _____, as well as by a ____ (#) year commercial loan in the amount of $ _____. The funds will be repaid through earnings.
These start-up expenses and funding requirements are summarized in the tables below.

2.5.1 Inventory

Inventory:	Supplier	Qty	Unit Cost	Total
Arts & Crafts Supplies				
Toys, Games and Puzzles				
Books, Movies, Music				
Classroom Supplies				
Bathroom Supplies				
Teaching Supplies				
Meal Plan Supplies				
Snacks/Beverages				
Plastic Plates/Utensils				

Wipes   _____
Diapers   _____
Disinfectants   _____
Disposal Bags   _____
Cleaning Supplies   _____
Labels   _____
Business Forms   _____
Marketing Materials   _____
Office Supplies   _____
Computer Supplies   _____
Contracts   _____
Board Markers   _____
First Aid Kit/Supplies   _____
Misc. Supplies   _____
Totals: _____

Resources:
Kaplan Teaching Supplies   www.kaplanco.com/

2.5.2 Supply Sourcing

We will search for and contact several wholesale suppliers for our _____. We will first contact the National Association of Wholesaler-Distributors, and ask our contact person if they can supply a list of daycare supply wholesalers. We will also visit the Tradepub.com website, and order some free trade publications on retailing. We will read through the classified ads for potential _____ wholesalers. We will consider the wholesalers that offer the best mix of lowest unit cost of _____ products, the fastest re-order turnaround service, and the best open credit terms. We will meet up with suppliers and inquire if we can avail discounted prices if we buy in bulk.

Initially, _____ (company name) will purchase all of its equipment from _____ and supplies from _____, the _____ (second/third?) largest supplier in _____ (state), because of the discount given for bulk purchases. However, we will also maintain back-up relationships with two smaller suppliers, namely _____ and _____. These two suppliers have competitive prices on certain products.

Resources:
http://www.childcarecatalog.com/
http://www.stay-a-stay-at-home-mom.com/forms-contracts-for-home-daycare.html
http://daycareinventory.com/
www.goodsearch.com/coupons/honor-roll-childcare-supply

Lakeshore Learning Materials: offers one of the broadest selections–books, toys, paints, tricycles, climbing equipment and more.

PlayCore: offer outdoor equipment, including playgrounds and sand boxes.

2.5.4　Equipment Leasing

Equipment Leasing will be the smarter solution allowing our business to upgrade our equipment needs at the end of the term rather than being overly invested in outdated equipment through traditional bank financing and equipment purchase. We also intend to explore the following benefits of leasing some of the required equipment:

1. Frees Up Capital for other uses.
2. Tax Benefits
3. Improves Balance Sheet
4. Easy to add-on or trade-up
5. Improves Cash Flow
6. Preserves Credit Lines
7. Protects against obsolescence
8. Application Process Simpler

Our leasing strategy will also be shaped by the following factors:
1. Estimated useful life of the equipment.
2. How long our business plans to use the equipment.
3. What our business intends to do with the equipment at the end of the lease.
4. The tax situation of our business.
5. The cash flow of our business.
6. Our company's specific needs for future growth.

List Any Leases:

Leasing Company	Equipment Description	Monthly Payment	Lease Period	Final Disposition

Resources:
LeaseQ　　　　　　　　　　　　www.leaseq.com
An online market place that connects businesses, equipment dealers, and leasing companies to make selling and financing equipment fast and easy. The LeaseQ Platform is a free, cloud based SaaS solution with a suite of on-demand software and data solutions for the equipment leasing industry. Utilizes the Internet to provide business process optimization (BPO) and information services that streamline the purchase and financing of business equipment across a broad array of vertical industry segments.

Innovative Lease Services　　　　http://www.ilslease.com/equipment-leasing/
This company was founded in 1986 and is headquartered in Carlsbad, California. It is accredited by the Better Business Bureau, a long standing member of the National Equipment Finance Association and the National Association of Equipment Leasing Brokers and is the official equipment financing partner of Biocom.

2.5.4 Funding Source Matrix

Funds Source	Amount	Interest Rate	Repayment Terms	Use

2.5.5 Distribution or Licensing Agreements (if any)

Note: These are some of the key factors that investors will use to determine if we have a competitive advantage that is not easily copied.

Licensor	License Rights	License Term	Fee or Royalty

2.5.6 Trademarks, Patents and Copyrights (if any)

Our trademark will be virtually our branding for life. Our choice of a name for our business is very important. Not only will we brand our business and services forever, but what may be worthless today will become our most valuable asset in the years to come. A trademark search by our Lawyer will be a must, because to be told down the road that we must give up our name because we did not bother to conduct a trademark search would be a devastating blow to our business. It is also essential that the name that we choose suit the expanding product or service offerings that will be coming down the pike.
Note: These are some of the key factors that investors will use to determine if we have a competitive advantage that is not easily copied.

Resources:
Patents/Trademarks   www.uspto.gov
Copyright   www.copyright.gov

2.5.7 Innovation Strategy (optional)

____ (company name) will create an innovation strategy that is aligned with not only our firm's core mission and values, but also with our future technology, supplier, and marketing strategies. The objective of our innovation strategy will be to create a sustainable competitive advantage . Our education and training systems will be designed to equip our staff with the foundations to learn and develop the broad range of skills needed for innovation in all of its forms, and with the flexibility to upgrade skills and adapt to changing market conditions. To foster an innovative workplace, we will ensure that employment policies facilitate efficient organizational change and encourage the expression of creativity, engage in mutually beneficial strategic alliances and allocate adequate funds for research and development. Our radical innovation strategies include _____ to achieve first mover status. Our incremental innovation strategies will include modifying the following _____ (products/services/processes) to give our customers added value for their money.

2.5.8   Summary of Sources and Use of Funds

Sources:
Owner's Equity Investment $ _____
Requested Bank Loans $ _____
Total: $ _____

Uses:
Capital Equipment $ _____
Beginning Inventory $ _____
Start-up Costs $ _____
Working Capital $ _____
Total: $ _____

2.5.9   Funding To Date   (optional)

To date, _____'s (company name) founders have invested $_____ in _____ (company name), with which we have accomplished the following:
1.   _____ (Designed/Built) the company's website
2.   Developed content, in the form of ___ (#) articles, for the website.
3.   Hired and trained our core staff of __(#) full-time people and ___ (#) part-time people.
4.   Generated brand awareness by driving ___ (#) visitors to our website in a ___(#) month period.
5.   Successfully _____ (Developed/Test Marketed) ___ (#) new _____ (products/services), which compete on the basis of _____.
6.   _____ (Purchased/Developed) and installed the software needed to _____ (manage _____ operations?)
7.   Purchased $ _____ worth of _____ (supplies)
8.   Purchased $ _____ worth of _____ equipment.

2.6 Start-up Requirements

Start-up Expenses: Estimates
    Legal   400
    Accountant   300
    Accounting Software Package   300
    Licenses & Permits   300
    Market Research Survey   300
    Office Supplies   300
    Sales Brochures   300
    Direct Mailing   500
    Other Marketing Materials   2000
    Logo Design   500
    Advertising (2 months)   2000
    Consultants   1000
    Insurance   1200
    Rent (2 months security)   3000
    Rent Deposit   1500
    Utility Deposit   600
    DSL Installation/Activation   100
    Telephone System Installation   200
    Telephone Deposit   200
    Expensed Equipment   1000
    Website Design/Hosting   2000
    Computer/Printer
    Used Office Equipment/Furniture   2000
    Toy, game and book storage   300
    Organization Memberships   300
    Facility Renovations/Buildout   5000
    Playground Prep Expenses   1000
    Activity Supplies   500
    Cleaning Supplies   200
    Food Preparation Supplies   500
    Food Costs
    Training Materials
    Signs
    Other
Total Start-up Expenses   _____ (A)

Start-up Assets:
    Cash Balance Required   (T)   5000
    Start-up Equipment   See schedule
    Start-up Inventory   See schedule
    Other Current Assets
    Long-term Assets
Total Assets   _____ (B)

Total Requirements _____ (A+B)

Start-up Funding
Start-up Expenses to Fund _____ (A)
Start-ups Assets to Fund _____ (B)
Total Funding Required: _____ (A+B)

Assets
Non-cash Assets from Start-up _____
Cash Requirements from Start-up _____ (T)
Additional Cash Raised _____ (S)
Cash Balance on Starting Date _____ (T+S=U)
Total Assets: _____ (B)

Liabilities and Capital
Short-term Liabilities:
Current Borrowing _____
Unpaid Expenses _____
Accounts Payable _____
Interest-free Short-term Loans _____
Other Short-term Loans _____
Total Short-term Liabilities _____ (Z)

Long-term Liabilities:
Commercial Bank Loan _____
Other Long-term Liabilities _____
Total Long-term Liabilities _____ (Y)
Total Liabilities _____ (Z+Y = C)

Capital
Planned Investment
Owner _____
Family _____
Other _____
Additional Investment Requirement _____
Total Planned Investment _____ (F)
Loss at Start-up (Start-up Expenses) (-) _____ (A)
Total Capital (=) _____ (F+A=D)
Total Capital and Liabilities _____ (C+D)

Total Funding _____ (C+F)

Expense Forecast Notes:
Once a center is up and running, payroll to meet mandated staff-to-child ratios will be the largest line item, devouring roughly 70% of sales. State laws vary, but in general you

need about one staff member per 12 preschool-age children; one per six children ages 2 to 4; and one per every four infants. (Health insurance and other fringe benefits are uncommon.) Then come the rent and property taxes, eating another 15% of sales; meals and supplies, 4%; insurance, 3%; and maintenance, 2%. Knowledgeable operators might clock 5% pretax operating margins, assuming decent occupancy rates.

Source:
www.forbes.com/2007/04/04/child-care-startup-ent-fin-cx_mf_0405
fundchildcareexpenses.html

2.6.1 Capital Equipment List

We will stock foodservice equipment and a wide variety of educational and play-related equipment, that is age appropriate, to keep children occupied.

Equipment Type	Model	Quantity	Unit Cost	Total Est.
Computer System				1000
Printer				
Fax Machine				200
Digital Camera				500
Copy Machine				600
Phone System				
Answering Machine				200
TV and DVD Player				
Security System				
Vehicle				9000
Exterior Playground Equipment				5000
Indoor Soft Play Equipment				
Non-toxic Play & Educational Toys				4000
First Aid Kits				
Fire Extinguishers				
Smoke Detectors				
Carbon Monoxide Detectors				
Rest and Tumbling Mats				
Nap Time Bedding				
Classroom Furniture				
Activity Tables				
Classroom Boards				
Kitchen Equipment				
Laundry Equipment				
Surge Protector				
Accounting Software				
Microsoft Office Software				
Day Care Management Software				

Electronic Scale	_____
Tape Dispensers	_____
Calculator	_____
Refrigerator	_____
Plastic Stacking Chairs	_____
Microwave	_____
Paper Shredder	_____
Internet Broadband Connection	_____
Other	_____

Total Capital Equipment _____

Note: Equipment costs are dependent on whether purchased new or used or leased. All items that are assets to be used for more than one year will be considered a long-term asset and will be depreciated using the straight-line method.

List of Daycare Playground Equipment

Swings	Plastic slide
Rocking toy	Toy car
Electric train	Ball pool
Bicycles	Spring horse
Toy house	Toy game
Merry go round	Seesaw
Building blocks	

2.7.0   SBA Loan Key Requirements

In order to be considered for an SBA loan, we must meet the basic requirements: 1. Must have been turned down for a loan by a bank or other lender to qualify for most SBA Business Loan Programs. 2. Required to submit a guaranty, both personal and business, to qualify for the loans. 3. Must operate for profit; be engaged in, or propose to do business in, the United States or its possessions; 4. Have reasonable owner equity to invest; 5. Use alternative financial resources first including personal assets.

All businesses must meet eligibility criteria to be considered for financing under the SBA's 7(a) Loan Program, including: size; type of business; operating in the U.S. or its possessions; use of available of funds from other sources; use of proceeds; and repayment. The repayment term of an SBA loan is between five and 25 years, depending on the lift of the assets being financed and the cash needs of the business.

Working capital loans (accounts receivable and inventory) should be repaid in five to 10 years. The SBA also has short-term loan guarantee programs with shorter repayment terms.

A Business Owner Cannot Use an SBA Loan:

To purchase real estate where the participant has issued a forward commitment to the developer or where the real estate will be held primarily for investment purposes. To finance floor plan needs. To make payments to owners or to pay delinquent withholding taxes. To pay existing debt, unless it can be shown that the refinancing will benefit the small business and that the need to refinance is not indicative of poor management.

SBA Loan Programs:
Low Doc: www.sba.gov/financing/lendinvest/lowdoc.html
SBA Express   www.sba,gov/financing/lendinvest/sbaexpress.html
Basic 7(a) Loan Guarantee Program
> For businesses unable to obtain loans through standard loan programs. Funds can be used for general business purposes, including working capital, leasehold improvements and debt refinancing.
> www.sba.gov/financing/sbaloan/7a.html

Certified Development Company 504 Loan Program
> Used for fixed asset financing such as purchase of real estate or machinery.
> www. Sba.gov/gopher/Local-Information/Certified-Development-Companies/

MicroLoan 7(m) Loan Program
> Provides short-term loans up to $35,000.00 for working capital or purchase of fixtures.
> www.sba.gov/financing/sbaloan/microloans.html

2.7.1   Other Financing Options

Non-profit daycare facilities are typically more likely to receive grant funding than commercial child care centers. States or municipalities with a Small Business Administration or Department of Development do offer low interest loans and start-up funds for new ventures that will create jobs and enhance the quality life in a community

Government grants may require additional matching funds or an in-kind volunteer commitment. Daycare facilities that serve children in an impoverished rural or urban area or offer services for children with disabilities are typically eligible for grant funds. Award amounts vary by grant terms, annual amount of funds available and number of children to be served.

Private foundations that focus on the care and education of the young child also offer seed money and financial support to child care facilities. Requests for funding are typically accepted once annually. To increase chances for success in a quest for funds, prepare a multi-year business plan, detailed report of daycare center programs and community demographics.
Resource: http://www.childcare.net/grantsusa.shtml

1.   National Children's Facilities Network   http://www.ncfn.org/

2. Community Investment Collaborative for Kids
   http://www2.nccic.org/ccpartnerships/profiles/cick.htm
3. Grants
   A. Contact your state licensing office.
   B. Child Care Resource and Referral Agency
   C. Children's and Family Service Office
   D. Foundation Grants to Individuals: www.fdncenter.org
   E. US Grants   www.grants.gov
   F. Foundation Center   www.foundationcemter.org
   G. The Grantsmanship Center   www.tgci.com
   H. The offering of a Young Parents Program (YPP) may qualify us to be a recipient of a Greenleaf Foundation grant, to support its specialized counseling services to teen mothers on topics including child safety, prenatal care and general issues related to teenage pregnancy. F
   I. Check with local Chamber of Commerce
   J. The Catalog of Federal Domestic Assistance is a major provider of business grant money. https://www.cfda.gov/
   K. The Federal Register is a good source to keep current with the continually changing federal grants offered.
   L. FedBizOpps is a resource, as all federal agencies must use FedBizOpps to notify the public about contract opportunities worth over $25,000.
   M. Fundsnet Services   www.fundsnetservices.com/
   N. Childcare.net   www.childcare.net/grantsusa.shtml

4. Friends and Family Lending   www.virginmoney.com
5. National Business Incubator Association   http://www.nbia.org/
6. Women's Business Associations   http://www.nawbo.org/
7. Childcare.net   http://www.childcare.net/grantsusa.shtml
8. Peer-to-Peer Programs   www.lendingclub.com
9. Extended Credit Terms from Suppliers   30/60/90 days.
10. Community Bank with existing deposit relationship.
11. Prepayments from Customers
12. Seller Financing: When purchasing an existing child day care center.
13. Business Funding Directory   www.businessfinance.com
14. FinanceNet   www.financenet.gov
15. SBA Financing   www.sbaonline.sba.gov
16. Micro-Loans   www.accionusa.org/
17. Private Investor
18. Use retirement funds to open a business without taxes or penalty. First, establish a C-corporation for the new business. Next, the C-corporation establishes a new retirement plan. Then, the owner's current retirement funds are rolled over into the C-corporation's new plan. And last, the new retirement plan invests in stock of the C-corporation. Warning: Check with your accountant or financial planner. Resource: http://www.benetrends.com/
19. Business Plan Competition Prizes
    www.nytimes.com/interactive/2009/11/11/business/smallbusiness/Competitions-

table.html?ref=smallbusiness
20. Unsecured Business Cash Advance based on future credit card transactions.
21. Kick Starter   www.kickstarter.com
22. Tech Stars   www.techstars.org
23. Capital Source   www.capitalsource.com
   www.msl.com/index.cfm?event=page.sba504
   Participates in the SBA's 504 loan program. This program is for the purchase of fixed assets such as commercial real estate and machinery and equipment of a capital nature, which are defined as assets that have a minimum useful life of ten years. Proceeds cannot be used for working capital.
24. Commercial Loan Applications   www.c-loans.com/onlineapp/
25. Sharing assets and resources with other non-competing businesses.
26. Angel Investors   www.angelcapitaleducation.org
27. The Receivables Exchange   http://receivablesxchange.com/
28. Bootstrap Methods: Personal Savings/Credit Card/Second Mortgages
29. Community-based Crowd-funding   www.profounder.com
                                             www.peerbackers.com
   A funding option designed to link small businesses and entrepreneurs with pools of prospective investors. Crowdfunding lenders are often repaid with goods or services.
30. On Deck Capital   www.ondeckcapital.com/
   Created the Short Term Business Loan (up to $100,000.00) for small businesses to get quick access to capital that fits their cash flow, with convenient daily payments.
31. Royalty Lending   www.launch-capital.com/
   With royalty lending, financing is granted in return for future revenue or company performance, and payback can prove exceedingly expensive if a company flourishes.
32. Stock :Loans   Southern Lending Solutions, Atlanta. GA.
                            Custom Commercial Finance, Bartlesville, OK
   A stock loan is based on the quality of stocks, Treasuries and other kinds of investments in a businessperson's personal portfolio. Possession of the company's stock is transferred to the lender's custodial bank during the loan period.
33. Lender Compatibility Searcher   www.BoeFly.com
34. Strategic Investors
   Strategic investing is more for a large company that identifies promising technologies, and for whatever reason, that company may not want to build up the research and development department in-house to produce that product, so they buy a percentage of the company with the existing technology.
35. Bartering
36. Small Business Investment Companies   www.sba.gov/INV
37. Cash-Value Life Insurance
38. Employee Stock Option Plans   www.nceo.org
39. Venture Capitalists   www.nvca.org
40. Initial Public Offering (IPO)
41. Meet investors through online sites, including LinkedIn (group discussions),

Facebook (BranchOut sorts Facebook connections by profession), and CapLinked (enables search for investment-related professionals by industry and role).

42. SBA Community Advantage Approved Lenders
www.sba.gov/content/community-advantage-approved-lenders
43. Small Business Lending Specialists
https://www.wellsfargo.com/biz/loans_lines/compare_lines
http://www.bankofamerica.com/small_business/business_financing/
https://online.citibank.com/US/JRS/pands/detail.do?ID=CitiBizOverview
https://www.chase.com/ccp/index.jsp?pg_name=ccpmapp/smallbusiness/home/page/bb_business_bBanking_programs
44. Startup America Partnership   www.s.co/about
Based on a simple premise: young companies that grow create jobs. Once startups apply and become a Startup America Firm, they can access and manage many types of resources through a personalized dashboard.
45. United States Economic Development Administration   www.eda.gov/
46. Small Business Loans   http://www.iabusnet.org/small-business-loans
47. Resources   http://childcareaware.org/child-care-providers
48. Tax Increment Financing (TIF)
A public financing method that is used for subsidizing redevelopment, infrastructure, and other community-improvement projects. TIF is a method to use future gains in taxes to subsidize current improvements, which are projected to create the conditions for said gains. The completion of a public project often results in an increase in the value of surrounding real estate, which generates additional tax revenue. Tax Increment Financing dedicates tax increments within a certain defined district to finance the debt that is issued to pay for the project. TIF is often designed to channel funding toward improvements in distressed, underdeveloped, or underutilized parts of a jurisdiction where development might otherwise not occur. TIF creates funding for public or private projects by borrowing against the future increase in these property-tax revenues.
49. Gust   https://gust.com/entrepreneurs
Provides the global platform for the sourcing and management of early-stage investments. Gust enables skilled entrepreneurs to collaborate with the smartest investors by virtually supporting all aspects of the investment relationship, from initial pitch to successful exit.
49. Goldman Sachs 10,000 Small Businesses   http://sites.hccs.edu/10ksb/
50. Earnest Loans   www.meetearnest.com
51. Biz2Credit   www.biz2credit.com
52. Funding Circle   www.fundingcircle.com
A peer-to-peer lending service which allows savers to lend money directly to small and medium sized businesses
53. Lending Club   www.lendingclub.com
54. Equity-based Crowdfunding   www.Indiegogo.com
www.StartEngine.com
www.SeedInvest.com
55. National Funding   www.nationalfunding.com
Their customers can to get working capital, merchant cash advances, credit card

processing, and, equipment leasing.
56. Quick Bridge Funding　　www.quickbridgefunding.com
Offers a flexible and timely financing program to help assist small and medium sized businesses achieve their goals.
57. Kabbage　　www.kabbage.com
The industry leader in providing working capital online.
58. SBA Financing Info　　https://business.usa.gov/access-financing
www.sba.gov/blogs/7-tips-starting-successful-and-legal-child-care-business

Resource:　　www.sba.gov/category/navigation-structure/starting-managing-business/starting-business/local-resources

http://usgovinfo.about.com/od/moneymatters/a/Finding-Business-Loans-Grants-Incentives-And-Financing.htm

The U.S. Department of Education 21st Community Learning Centers Program supports the creation of learning centers for students in low-performance and/or high-poverty school areas. You can call 800-872-5327, email 21stCCLC@ed.gov, or visit the Web at http://www.ed.gov/21stcclc for more information.

The Afterschool Investments Project Web site at http://nccic.acf.hhs.gov/afterschool/index.html provides information about resources for after-school programs. The New State Developments section at http://nccic.acf.hhs.gov/afterschool/newstatedev.html has information about grants available for after-school programs. Visit the Web at http://nccic.acf.hhs.gov/afterschool/financing_ap.html for more information.

The Afterschool.gov Web site offers information to the public about Federal resources to support after-school programs. The Running a Program section has information about getting money for programs, starting partnerships, evaluating programs, finding volunteers, and starting programs. Visit the Web at htttp://www.afterschool.gov/xhtml/group/g_8.html for more information.

First Children's Finance　　**www.firstchildrensfinance.org**
Provides financing, training and business-development assistance to child care businesses. Also provide consulting and planning assistance to government agencies, intermediaries and regional child care organizations. A nonprofit Community Development Financial Institution (CDFI), they currently lend in Iowa, Kansas, Michigan, Minnesota, Missouri, North Dakota, South Dakota, Texas, Washington and Wisconsin.

Economic development tools, such as redevelopment (tax increment) funds and Community Development Block Grants (CDBG), can be used to revitalize neighborhoods and encourage new child care businesses, which create jobs and revenue.

Examples:

The City of South San Francisco built a 100-child center in an office park to help retain and grow its significant biotech industry. The Redevelopment Agency used $2.7 million of bond funds to construct the 8,500-square-foot facility and then leased it to a nonprofit operator. Other public and private funds were leveraged to support start-ups.

Several New York municipalities use State Enterprise Zone tax credits to develop child care facilities within their jurisdictions.

Federal **Community Development Block Grant (CDBG)** Program funds commonly subsidize child care operations or facility construction and renovation for low-income populations (Anderson 2006). Starting new child care businesses is an eligible economic development activity. San Jose and San Mateo County in California, among others, fund family child care home business development projects that provide training, technical assistance, and start-up resources. Other cities support consortia of family child care providers to help them access economies of scale in purchasing and management. The nonprofit Acre Family Child Care Network in Lowell, Massachusetts, oversees 39 homes that serve an average of 234 children daily (Stoney 2004).

Other economic development strategies used to strengthen the child care sector include business management training, collective purchasing arrangements for providers, and community outreach regarding tax credits and subsidies for families (Warner et al. 2004). Source: https://www.planning.org/research/family/briefingpapers/childcare.htm

Child and Adult Care Food Program

CACFP provides aid to child and adult care institutions and family or group day care homes for the provision of nutritious foods that contribute to the wellness, healthy growth, and development of young children, and the health and wellness of older adults and chronically impaired disabled persons.
Source:
http://www.fns.usda.gov/cacfp/child-and-adult-care-food-program

3.0 Product and Services

In this section, we will not only list all of our planned products and services, but also describe how our proposed products and services will be differentiated from those of our competitors and solve a real problem or fill an unmet need in the marketplace...

We plan to offer child care services for the following age groups:
1. Infant – a child from 3 months to 12 months in age.
2. Toddler – a child from 13 to 36 months in age.
3. Pre-school – a child between the ages of three and five.
4. School Age - Care for a child in first grade, or the time he/she enters school, through fifteen years of age. Programs for school-age children occur after the school day ends.

Our developmental programs are designed to reinforce basic social, listening, independence and motor skills.

Our hours of operation will be from___ (6:30) AM to ____ (7:30) PM, Monday through Friday.

We will offer the following extracurricular activities as part of a comprehensive program:
1. Arts and Crafts   2. Dance
3. Gymnastics   4. Homework Mentoring
5. Tutoring   6. Basic Computer Skills

Special programs include the following:
1. Children birthday party hosting services   2. Basketball tournaments
3. Summer Programs   4. Young Parents Program

Our Snack Menu:
1. Fresh Fruits   2. Mixed Fruit Cups.
3. Fruit Juices   4. Flavored Milks
5. Oatmeal Cookies   6. Graham Crackers
7. Yogurt Pops   8. Applesauce
9. Jello   10. Non-fat Granola

Resource: Child Care Food Program   www.ccfproundtable.org/index.asp

Products:
Educational Books and DVDs.
Logo-imprinted T-shirts
Learning Games

3.1 Service Description

In creating our service descriptions, we will provide answers to the following types of questions:
1. What does the service do or help the customer to accomplish?
2. Why will people decide to buy it?
3. What makes it unique or a superior value?
4. How expensive or difficult is it to make or copy by a competitor?
5. How much will the service be sold for?

_____ (company name) will offer the following basic services:

1. **Full-time Child Day Care Center**
   Full time children come 4 or more days/night per week.
   Children benefit from social development, nurturing, nutrition, behavioral discipline, age-appropriate play activities and educational activities.
2. **Part-time Child Day Care Center**
   Part-time children come 3 days/night or less per week.
3. **After School Care (Extended Day Program)**
   A child care program for school-aged children. This program provides supervision, academic enrichment, and recreation for children after school hours. We will make it easier for parents to choose a quality after-school care program that can have a tremendous impact on their child's academics, self-esteem and overall happiness. We will transport school-aged children from school back to the center, provide a healthy snack, and then start kids on their homework, so that it is mostly done by the time parents arrive.
4. **After School Tutoring**
   Our program provides a dedicated space for homework. Our committed teachers communicate with parents about homework completed at the center and items that need completion at home.
5. **Fitness Programs**
   Daily fitness activities are critically important for children's developing bodies. In our program, children will participate in fun activities and adopt healthy habits that can last a lifetime.
6. **Drop-In Care (Parents Night Out)**
   A child care program that parents may use as back up or unscheduled child care. The drop-in care facilities focus on fun activities for kids and often include mealtimes and special theme events to provide parents with a worry-free evening or time away from kids.
7. **Drop-Off Child Care.   (On-Demand Care)**
   These facilities provide care for children for short periods of time while parents run errands or go to appointments.
8. **Weekend Evening Care**
9. **24-Hour Child Care**
   Most 24-hour child care is provided through large companies as a convenience for their employees.
10. **Overnight Care**

Childcare for children staying with the care provider after 1:00 AM.
11. **Evening Care**
Childcare for children staying with the provider after 6:00 PM and leaving before 1AM the following day.
12. **Sick or Ill Child Care (Special Needs)**
Child care services provided to a child who has a mild sickness, chronic illness and/or special medical condition. The child receives physical and occupational therapy and the chance to interact with other children.
13. **Transportation Services**
A transportation service exclusively created to transport children to and from school, day care, after school activities, recreational programs, etc.
14. **Summer Programs**
Feature a variety of special programs and activities in a safe and secure camp-like atmosphere.

All of our programs will be designed for specific age groups and contain the following developmental activity components:

1. Physical
2. Intellectual
3. Social
4. Emotional
5. Language

3.1.1 Our Service Benefits

Research indicates that children who attend quality daycare programs benefit in the following ways:
1. Children who attended a high-quality day care program were four times more likely to have earned college degrees as adults.
2. They were also more likely to have held a job and avoided needing public assistance than the control group.
3. A recent study published in The Journal of American Medical Association suggests that children who are at high risk of emotional problems may see those problems diminish if they attend a quality day care program.
4. Being in a child care center provides these children with more opportunities for social interactions and lessens the time they spend with their mother, or other caregiver, who may suffer from emotional issues.
5. Long-running U.S. National Institutes of Health study has shown that children who attended a high quality program score higher on achievement and cognitive tests as high school students.
6. Children who attend a day care may benefit mothers, as well, because a study suggests that mothers may actually be more involved in their children's school lives once they reach kindergarten.
7. Children in daycare will develop social skills at a young age and be exposed to school readiness skills.

Resource: www.firstchildrensfinance.org/businessresourcecenter/centers-2/marketing/marketing-tools/

3.2 Alternative Revenue Streams

1. Classified Ads in our Newsletter
2. Vending Machine Sales
3. Children Birthday Parties
4. Children's Transport (Cab) Service
   Resource: National Child Transport Association
5. Errand Running/ Concierge Business
6. Exercise and Yoga Classes
7. Drama and Singing Classes
8. Artist Workshops
9. Educational Products

3.3 Production of Products and Services

We will use the following methods to locate the best suppliers for our business:
- Attend trade shows to spot upcoming trends, realize networking opportunities and compare prices.

- Subscribe to appropriate trade magazines, journals, newsletters and blogs.
Childcare Management Magazine www.childcareintro.com/childcare_management
Momscape www.momscape.com/
Baby Center www.babycenter.com/303_home-daycare_1512906.bc
Child Care Central
www.childcarecentral.com/Provider-Articles/52/starting-home-daycare-tips.html

- Join our trade association to make valuable contacts, get listed in any online directories, and secure training and marketing materials.
Child Care Aware America

Child Development Policy Institute www.cdpi.org
A nonprofit, non-partisan agency concerned with child care and development issues. CDPI has one of the few paid lobbyists for the child care field.

Zero to Three www.zerotothree.org
A national, nonprofit, multidisciplinary organization that advances their mission to support the healthy development and well-being of infants, toddlers and their families by informing, educating and supporting adults who influence the lives of infants and toddlers.

National Association for Family Child Care www.nafcc.org/
Administers state child care licensing rules and accreditation standards which set a minimum standard of quality for child care programs.

The National Association for the Education of Young Children.
The NAEYC administers the largest and most widely recognized national, voluntary, professionally sponsored accreditation system for all types of early childhood schools and child care centers.

Child Care Association Directory
www.americatakingaction.com/childcare/dcassociations.html

ChildCare Education Institute®   http://www.cceionline.edu/
Provides high-quality, distance education certificates and child care training programs in an array of child care settings, including preschool centers, daycare, family child care, prekindergarten classrooms, nanny care, and more online training. Over 100 English and Spanish child care training courses are available online to meet licensing, recognition program, and Head Start training requirements. CCEI also has online certification programs that provide the coursework requirement for national credentials including the Online CDA, Director and Early Childhood Credential. CCEI is nationally accredited by the Accrediting Commission of the Distance Education and Training Council (DETC), has been accredited as an Authorized Provider by the International Association for Continuing Education and Training (IACET), and is authorized under the Nonpublic Postsecondary Educational Institutions

Child Care Business Owner Institute   http://childcarebusinessowner.com

National Resource Center for Health and Safety in Child Care and Early Education
http://nrckids.org/index.cfm/resources/state-licensing-and-regulation-information/

Child Care Resource & Referral Agencies (R&Rs)
R&Rs can be resources to assess the local child care market, identify operators, design experts, and funding, and assist in developing policies to support child care development.

American Business Women's Association

3.4 Competitive Comparison

According to _____ County Records, the city of _____, _____ (state) has only ____ (#) licensed child care facilities. We expect to filling the growing local market need for this vital service.

According to US Census 2000 data, the city of _____ has _____ (#) single family homes. There are only ___ (#) other child care facilities in the neighborhood. _____ (company name) will differentiate itself from its local competitors by offering an alternative to these traditional day care approaches at a competitive price based on the expanded value of our services.

Our market strategy is based on providing an activity based learning environment. We will offer the services of professional caregivers with the credentials to enhance a child's early social, motor and learning skills.

By forming strategic referral alliances with local pediatrics offices and fitness centers, we plan to become the market leader in child care services, and developmental and educational offerings for children.

_____ (company name) does not have to pay for under-utilized staff. Our flexible employee scheduling procedures and use of part-timers ensure that the store is never overstaffed during slow times. We will also adopt a pay-for-performance compensation plan, and use referral incentives to generate new business.

We will reinvest major dollars every year in professional and educational materials. We will participate in online webinars to bring clients the finest selection of day care products and services, and industry trend information. Our prices will be competitive with other day care centers that offer far less in the way of benefits, innovative services, and program selection.

3.5 Sales Literature

_____ (company name) has developed sales literature that illustrates a professional organization with vision. _____ (company name) plans to constantly refine its marketing mix through a number of different literature packets. These include the following:
- direct mail with introduction letter and product price sheet.
- product information brochures
- press releases
- new product/service information literature
- email marketing campaigns
- website content
- corporate brochures

A copy of our informational brochure is attached in the appendix of this document. This brochure will be available to provide referral sources, leave at seminars, and use for direct mail purposes.

3.6 Fulfillment

The key fulfillment and delivery of services will be provided by our director/owner, licensed instructors and staff workers. The real core value is the industry expertise of the founder, and staff education, experience, training and certifications.

3.7 Technology

___(company name) will employ and maintain the latest technology to enhance its office management, inventory management, payment processing, customer profiling and record keeping systems

We will acquire software that enable our center to better manage the following:
1. **Child Info Management**
    These programs will provide quick access profiles to all of our center's children. Information that can be obtained from the software includes:
    A. Medical histories.
    B. Child and parents/guardian photos.
    C. Parent/guardians information, such as address, phone number and email.
    D. Logs of the child's achievements or incidents throughout the day.
    E. Emergency contacts.
    F. Graphs detailing attendance records.

2. **Time-Punch System**
    These programs keep track of students' attendance. They also enable administrators to quickly message parents/guardians and staff. The software:
    A. Allows parents/guardians to sign their children in and out, thereby reducing attendance errors.
    B. Permits siblings to punch in at the same time, instead of separately.
    C. Enables automated messages to appear when staff or parents/guardians sign in, thereby reducing miscommunication.
    D. Allow parents/guardians to message staff directly.
    E. Sends automated reminders to guardians and staff that have not signed in on time.

3. **Scheduling Software**
    This software will help to save time and money. The software will:
    A. Keep track of signed-in children.
    B. Provide online access to parents to manage their children's attendance schedules.
    C. Create daily appointment reports.
    D. Schedule customizable automatic e-mail appointment reminders.
    E. Track sales.
    F. Set recurring staff appointment-scheduling.
    G. Create and manage classes and events.

Resources:
Procare Child Care Software   www.procaresoftware.com/
                www.procareblog.com/2011/09/19/text-messaging-daycare/
The management tool of choice for more than 25,000 child-centered businesses. Procare's flexible modular format simplifies management of child and family information in a variety of business settings including: child care centers, daycare providers, preschool and after school programs, school districts, enrichment programs, gymnastics clubs, child activity centers and similar facilities.

Childcare Sage Management Software   www.childcaresagemarketing.com/

Appointment-Plus   www.appointment-plus.com/industries/day-care

Software Directory   http://childcarecrm.com/partners

Daycare Mobile Apps
www.gocanvas.com/content/blog/post/canvas-launches-daycare-apps

Mobile Apps: Daycare Forms
gocanvas.com/mobile-forms-apps/search?terms=daycare&commit.x=0&commit.y=0#.
Ex: www.gocanvas.com/mobile-forms-apps/3615-Daycare-Activity-Authorization-Form

Child Care Reports   www.himama.com/childcare/how_it_works
Designed specifically to make it faster and more personal than paper based child care reports.

Daycare Wait List Software   http://www.daycarewaitlist.com/

AWE Digital Learning Software   www.awelearning.com/en/markets/childcare/

Mobile POS Systems
Vend   www.vendhq.com/
A retail POS software, inventory management, ecommerce & customer loyalty for iPad, Mac and PC. Easily manage & grow your business in the cloud.

Shopkeep   www.shopkeep.com
Charges a monthly fee of $49 per register. It customizes service for retail, quick service, restaurants and bars with features including inventory monitoring, staff management and customer marketing. Administrators can monitor business stats through an online back-end, which also syncs with an iOS app for iPhone. Shopkeep's system can also be integrated with MailChimp to manage emails to a customer listserv and Quickbooks accounting software for an additional fee.

LevelUp   www.thelevelup.com/
 LevelUp charges a 1.95% rate for every transaction, as well as $50 per scanner, which plugs into most POS systems or the $100 LevelUp Tablet. The scanner reads a QR code displayed on a customer's smartphone or uses near field communication technology to allow the customer to pay with the likes of ApplePay or Google Wallet. LevelUp reminds customers when they have not visited the businesses after a set period of time and provides a rewards program. Customers also have the option of leaving feedback for the owner through the LevelUp app.

Revel   http://revelsystems.com/
An award-winning iPad Point of Sale solution for single and multi-location businesses.

Mobile Phone Credit Card Reader   https://squareup.com/pos
Square, Inc. is a financial services, merchant services aggregator and mobile payments company based in San Francisco, California. The company markets several software and hardware products and services, including Square Register and Square Order. Square Register allows individuals and merchants in the United States, Canada, and Japan to accept offline debit and credit cards on their iOS or Android smartphone or tablet computer. The app supports manually entering the card details or swiping the card through the Square Reader, a small plastic device which plugs into the audio jack of a supported smartphone or tablet and reads the magnetic stripe. On the iPad version of the Square Register app, the interface resembles a traditional cash register.

Google Wallet   https://www.google.com/wallet/
A mobile payment system developed by Google that allows its users to store debit cards, credit cards, loyalty cards, and gift cards among other things, as well as redeeming sales promotions on their mobile phone. Google Wallet can be used near field communication (NFC) to make secure payments fast and convenient by simply tapping the phone on any PayPass-enabled terminal at checkout.

Apple Pay   http://www.apple.com/apple-pay/
A mobile payment and digital wallet service by Apple Inc. that lets users make payments using the iPhone 6, iPhone 6 Plus, Apple Watch-compatible devices (iPhone 5and later models), iPad Air 2, and iPad Mini 3. Apple Pay does not require Apple-specific contactless payment terminals and will work with Visa's PayWave, MasterCard's PayPass, and American Express's ExpressPay terminals. The service has begun initially only for use in the US, with international roll-out planned for the future.
Resource:
www.wired.com/2017/01/shadow-apple-pay-google-wallet-expands-online-reach/

WePay   https://www.wepay.com/
An online payment service provider in the United States. WePay's payment API focuses exclusively on platform businesses such as crowdfunding sites, marketplaces andsmall business software. Through this API, WePay allows these platforms to access its payments capabilities and process credit cards for the platform's users.

Chirpify
Connects a user's PayPal account with their Twitter account in order to enable payments through tweeting.

Article: www.prnewswire.com/news-releases/tips-to-leverage-mobile-payments-in-your-marketing-strategy-300155855.html

3.8   Future Products and Services

_____ (company name) will continually expand our offering of services based on daycare industry trends and changing client needs. We will not only solicit feedback via surveys and comments cards from clients on what they need in the future, but will also work to develop strong relationships with all of our clients and vendors.

We also plan to open ____ (#) additional locations in the _____ area starting in _____ (year). Franchise start-ups will be offered in _____ (city) after _____ (#) years of successful operation. We plan to expand our line of educational products as a source of holiday gift items.

We plan to add a latchkey program for the children of working parents, which will offer before-school and after-school care for children, ages 6 to 12, from 7 to 8 a.m., and 3 to 6 p.m. weekdays. We will also provide transportation to and from local schools in the area.

We plan to offer tutoring services, art classes and work to prevent childhood obesity in conjunction with 'The Nutrition and Physical Activity Self-Assessment for Child Care (NAP SACC) Program', which is a research-tested intervention designed to enhance policies, practices, and environments in child care by improving the:

- nutritional quality of food served,
- amount and quality of physical activity
- staff-child interactions
- facility nutrition and physical activity policies and practices and related environmental characteristics

The NAP SACC intervention primarily addresses the inter-personal and organizational levels of the socio-ecologic model.

Resource: https://riskfactor.cancer.gov/mfe/instruments/benjamin-nap-sacc-nutrition-and-physical- activity-self-assessment-for-child-care-instrument/

Sell Complementary Products and Services
We plan to become a reseller for green or other kid-friendly products and print a take-home catalog so parents can "keep their kids as safe at home as they are at daycare.

We also plan to offer after-hours babysitting appointments for parents in exchange for a commission. We will offer this additional service right from the front desk.

In addition to our regular programs, we will also hold special events during the summer and winter that are fun for all ages. A summer barbecue and holiday parties will give families a chance to connect and network through our daycare center. Our goal will be to become a community resource.

Niche Daycare Services
In order to improve our competitiveness, we plan to offer the following types of unique

childcare services:

1. 24 hour Child Care
   Most daycare centers open at 6 am and close at 6 pm. Daycare that offers its services 24 hours a day, seven days a week, is a growing trend and a necessity for some families that work long or overnight shifts.

2. Vacation Daycare
   Families on vacation will be able to make a reservation with our daycare business, which will provide high-level child-care services on a 24-hour basis.

3. Green Daycare
   As a green child care center, we will take special measures to ensure that the environment provides the best in health for children, offering locally-grown or organic food, the use of non-toxic cleaning solutions, and celebrating multiculturalism. We will ban the use of harmful chemicals and pesticides. Children will also be taught to respect the earth and its precious natural resources.

4. Sick Daycare
   We will satisfy the need for a childcare center that serves as an infirmary for mildly ill children on an emergency basis. Each day more than 350,000 children under the age of 14 years with both parents working are too sick to attend school or child care.
   Resource: National Association for Sick Child Care

5. Drop In-Childcare
   Drop-in daycare will basically involve providing back-up childcare when something unexpected comes up for a parent. While not around the clock care, drop-in childcare is usually open 7 days a week and offers later hours of service.

Wraparound Service Programs
Because parents want a wider menu of child care choices, we will provide a variety of care options based on their current needs.
1. We will provide at home nanny services for infants.
2. We will provide a trained in-home provider for a toddler
3. We will provide daycare center facilities for preschoolers.
4. We will provide occasional care service options, such as babysitters, drop-in care, and child care co-ops.
5. We will provide after school enrichment programs for latch key children.

Customized Corporate Day Care Programs
We plan to build and manage onsite or near site day-care centers for companies, because more corporations are evaluating offering day-care facilities as a key benefit to retain talent. The corporation will pay us a monthly management fee for managing the facility, and the corporation will decide the fee to be paid by their employees, which is usually

subsidized. We will facilitate the fee collection from the parents which will be credited to the corporation.

Other Possible Revenue Sources

1. **Place holding fee.** If you pre-register your child in advance, you may be charged a non- refundable "holding fee" to reserve your child's space.
2. **Initial registration fee** (typically one-time per child). This is typically a nonrefundable administrative fee. AVERAGE: $10-$200.
3. **Re-registration fee.** If you withdraw and then re-enroll your child. AVERAGE: $25-$50.
4. **Early drop-off and late pick-up fee.** This fee applies if you need to drop your child off early or you are late picking your child up. AVERAGE: by-minute fee of $1-$10.
5. **Meal/snack fee.** If meals and snacks are *not* included with tuition, you may have the option to pack food for your child or pay a fee to have this provided. AVERAGE: Varies by type; average <$1 per snack and $2-$4 per meal.
6. **Late payment/NSF fee.** This fee applies if you are late with your scheduled payments or your payment does not go through. AVERAGE: $20-$50
7. **Activity/supplies fee(s).** Some daycares charge a flat extra fee, others charge by the activity. AVERAGE: $10-$30
8. **Camera/video fees.** This newer fee offers parents the option to tune in to a live camera video feed during the day to watch their children at the daycare.
9. **Failure to sign your child in/out or safe arrival call fee.** If the daycare cannot verify your child's whereabouts due to your failure to notify. AVERAGE: $5-$10 per incident or call.
10. **Extra clothes/diapers/wipes fee.** If your child needs more than what is supplied with the flat rate or more than what you send. AVERAGE: $1-$5 per item.
11. **Special needs.** These fees can range from potty training to special meals.

Source: http://thekrazycouponlady.com/tips/family/7-strategies-for-keeping-daycare-costs-and-fees-low/

4.0 Market Analysis Summary

Our Market Analysis will serve to accomplish the following goals:
1. Define the characteristics of the target market.
2. Serve as a basis for developing a sales and promotional strategy.
3. Influence the website design.

_____ (company name) offers daycare services that are vitally important to today's required dual income family.

From 1970 to 1993, the proportion of dual-earner couples increased from 39 percent to 61 percent of all married couples. In 2002, only 7 percent of all U.S. households consisted of married couples with children in which only the husband worked. Dual-income families with children made up more than two times as many households. Even families with two incomes and no children outnumbered the traditional family by almost two to one.

There are over ___ (#) facilities in the _____ area that provide child care services similar to _____ (our company name), and all of them has a growing, large client base, and a successful business. In fact, according to recent national business statistics, about 85% of licensed child care facilities succeed and make a profit in their first year of operation. Consequently, there is no doubt that there is ample room in the market for a high-quality, child care facility that places an emphasis on child development and education.

4.1 Secondary Market Research

We will research demographic information for the following reasons:
1. To determine which segments of the population, such as Hispanics and the elderly, have been growing and may now be underserved.
2. To determine if there is a sufficient population base in the designated service area to realize the company's business objectives.
3. To consider what products and services to add in the future, given the changing demographic profile and needs of our service area.

We will pay special attention to the following general demographic trends:
1. Population growth has reached a plateau and market share will most likely be increased through innovation and excellent customer service.
2. Because incomes are not growing and unemployment is high, process efficiencies and sourcing advantages must be developed to keep prices competitive.
3. The rise of non-traditional households, such as single working mothers, means developing more innovative and personalized programs.
4. As the population shifts toward more young to middle aged adults, ages 30 to 44, and the elderly, aged 65 and older, there will be a greater need for child-rearing and geriatric mobile support services.

5. Because of the aging population, increasing pollution levels and high unemployment, new 'green' ways of dealing with the resulting challenges will need to be developed.

We will collect the demographic statistics for the following zip code(s):
_____

We will use the following sources: www.census.gov, www.zipskinny.com, www.city-data.com, www.demographicsnow.com, www.esri.com/data/esri_data/tapestry and www.claritas.com/claritas/demographics.jsp. This information will be used to decide upon which targeted programs to offer and to make business growth projections.
Resource: www.sbdcnet.org/index.php/demographics.html

Snapshots of consumer data by zip code are also available online:
http://factfinder.census.gov/home/saff/main.html?_lang=en
http://www.esri.com/data/esri_data/tapestry.html
http://www.claritas.com/MyBestSegments/Default.jsp?ID=20

1. **Total Population** _____
2. **Number of Households** _____
3. **Population by Race:** White ____% Black ____%
   Asian Pacific Islander ____% Other ____%
4. **Population by Gender** Male ____% Female ____%
5. **Income Figures:** Median Household Income $_____
   Household Income Under $50K ____%
   Household Income $50K-$100K ____%
   Household Income Over $100K ____%
6. **Housing Figures** Average Home Value - $_____
   Average Rent $_____
7. **Homeownership:** Homeowners ____% _____
   Renters ____% _____
8. **Education Achievement** High School Diploma ____% _____
   College Degree ____% _____
   Graduate Degree ____% _____
9. **Stability/Newcomers** Longer than 5 years ____% _____
10. **Marital Status** ____% Married ____% Divorced ____% Single
    ____% Never Married ____% Widowed ____% Separated
11. **Occupations** ____%Service ____% Sales ____% Management
    ____% Construction ____% Production
    ____% Unemployed ____% Below Poverty Level
12. **Age Distribution** ____%Under 5 years ____%5-9 yrs ____%10-12 yrs
    ____% 13-17 yrs ____%18-years
    ____% 20-29 ____% 30-39 ____% 40-49 ____% 50-59
    ____% 60-69 ____% 70-79 ____% 80+ years
13. **Prior Growth Rate** _____% from _____ (year)
14. **Projected Population Growth Rate** _____%

15.   Employment Trend   _____

Secondary Market Research Conclusions
This area will be demographically favorable for our business for the following reasons:

_____

_____

Resources:
www.sbdcnet.org/index.php/demographics.html
www.allbusiness.com/marketing/segmentation-targeting/848-1.html
http://factfinder2.census.gov/faces/nav/jsf/pages/index.xhtml

4.1.1   Primary Market Research

We plan to develop a survey for primary research purposes and mail it to a list of local home and parenting magazine subscribers, purchased from the publishers by zip code. We will also post a copy of the survey on our website and encourage visitors to take the survey. We will use the following survey questions to develop an Ideal Customer Profile of our potential client base, so that we can better target our marketing communications. To improve the response rate, we will include an attention-grabbing _____ (discount coupon/ dollar?) as a thank you for taking the time to return the questionnaire.

1. What is your zip-code?
2. Are you single, divorced, separated, widowed or married?
3. Are you male or female?
4. What is your age?
5. What is your approximate household income?
6. What is your educational level?
7. What is your profession?
8. Are you a dual income household?
9. Do you have children? If Yes, what are their ages?
10. What are your favorite magazines?
11. What is your favorite local newspaper?
12. What is your favorite radio station?
13. What are your favorite television programs?
14. What organizations are you a member of?
15. Does our community have adequate child care facilities?   Yes / No
16. Are any of your children currently enrolled in daycare?   Yes / No
17. What are the ages of your children currently in daycare?
18. Are you satisfied with your child care arrangements?
19. Who currently provides your current daycare arrangements?
            ___ Family member   ___ In-home caregiver
            ___ Outside home caregiver   ___ Child care center
            ___ Nursery School   ___ Other _____
20. What are their strengths as child care providers?

21. What are their weaknesses or shortcomings?
22. What would it take for us to earn your daycare business?
23. What is the best way for us to market our daycare services?
24. What is your general need for child care?
    Circle Months: J F M A M J J A S O N D
    Circle Days: S M T W T F S
    Indicate Hours: _____
25. How much do you currently pay for child care?
26. Would you be willing to pay a higher fee for better child care services?
27. Are your child care fees subsidized by the government?
28. If your child is in school, how do you handle days off from school?
    ___ Take time off   ___ Spouse takes time off
    ___ Friend/relative provides care in my home.
    ___ Friend/relative provides care in their home.
    ___ Other _____
29. Would you prefer to have your child in a facility near where you work?
30. Do you live in _____ community?
31. Do you work or study in _____ community?
32. Do you plan to return to work in the near future?
33. Do you think you will be in need of daycare in the near future?
34. What are the ages of your children who will require care?
35. What type of child care arrangements would you prefer?
    ___ Daycare center   ___ Regulated private home daycare
    ___ Play school   ___ Nursery School
    ___ Occasional use caregiver   ___ Regulated private hone daycare
    ___ Parent/child drop-in program ___ Other
36. Describe your experience with other daycare centers.
37. Please rank (1 to 18) the importance of the following factors when choosing a daycare center:
    ___ Right education focus   ___ Environment
    ___ Hours of service   ___ Safety
    ___ Convenient location   ___ Staff-to-child ratio
    ___ Group size   ___ Staff education and experience
    ___ Square feet of facility per child. ___ Staff turnover
    ___ Accreditation.   ___ Customer Service
    ___ Program Selection   ___ Scheduling Convenience
    ___ Value Proposition   ___ Price
    ___ Referral   ___ Other _____
38. What information would you like to see in a daycare company newsletter?
39. Which online social groups have you joined? Choose the ones you access.
    ___ Facebook   ___ MySpace
    ___ Twitter   ___ LinkedIn
    ___ Ryze   ___ Ning
40. What types of new daycare programs would most interest you?
41. What are your suggestions for realizing a better daycare experience?
42. Are you satisfied with your ward's progress so far?

43. Do you think the atmosphere we have created for your child is suitable?
44. Are you comfortable with our customer service?
45. If you are not satisfied with our customer service relations, what areas would you want us to work on?
46. Do you think our fee is moderate?
47. How much will be too much to pay as a fee for your ward at our center?
48. Are there added services you want us to start?
49. Would you freely recommend a client?
50. If no, what are the reasons?
51. Are you on our mailing list? Yes/No If No, can we add you?   Yes / No

Please note any comments or concerns about child day care services.
We very much appreciate your participation in this survey. If you provide your name, address and email address, we will sign you up for our e-newsletter, inform you of our survey results, advise you of any new daycare facilities opening in your community, and enter you into our monthly drawing for a free _____.
Name   Address   Email   Phone

4.1.2 Voice of the Customer

To develop a better understanding of the needs and wants of our Child Day Care Center customers, we will institute the following ongoing listening practices:

1. Focus Groups
   Small groups of customers (6 to 8) will be invited to meet with a facilitator to answer open-ended questions about priority of needs and wants, and our company, its products or other given issues. These focus groups will provide useful insight into the decisions and the decision making process of target consumers.
2. Individual Interviews
   We will conduct face-to-face personal interviews to understand customer thought processes, selection criteria and day care preferences.
3. Customer Panels
   A small number of customers will be invited to answer open-ended questions on a regular basis.
4. Customer Tours
   We will invite customers to visit our facilities to discuss how our processes can better serve them.
5. Visit Customers
   We will observe customers as they actually use our products to uncover the pains and problems they are experiencing during usage.
6. Trade Show Meetings
   Our trade show booth will be used to hear the concerns of our customers.
7. Toll-free Numbers
   We will attach our phone number to all products and sales literature to encourage

the customer to call with problems or positive feedback.
8. Customer Surveys
We will use surveys to obtain opinions on closed-ended questions, testimonials, constructive feedback, and improvement suggestions.
9. Mystery Shoppers
We will use mystery shoppers to report on how our employees treat our customers.
10. Salesperson Debriefing
We will ask our salespeople to report on their customer experiences to obtain insights into what the customer faces, what they want and why they failed to make a sale.
11. Customer Contact Logs
We will ask our sales personnel to record interesting customer revelations.
12. Customer Serviceperson's Hotline
We will use this dedicated phone line for people to report problems.
13. Discussions with competitors.
14. Installation of suggestion boxes to encourage constructive feedback. The suggestion card will have several statements customers are asked to rate in terms of a given scale. There are also several open ended questions that allow the customer to freely offer constructive criticism or praise. We will work hard to implement reasonable suggestions in order to improve our service offerings as well as show our commitment to the customer that their suggestions are valued.

4.2 Market Segmentation

Market segmentation is a technique that recognizes that the potential universe of users may be divided into definable sub-groups with different characteristics. Segmentation enables organizations to target messages to the needs and concerns of these subgroups. We will segment the market based on the needs and wants of select customer groups. We will develop a composite customer profile and a value proposition for each of these segments. The purpose for segmenting the market is to allow our marketing/sales program to focus on the subset of prospects that are "most likely" to purchase our child day care services. If done properly this will help to insure the highest return for our marketing/sales expenditures.

____ (company name) will focus on meeting the local community need for full-time or part-time child care services within a ____ mile radius of _____ (neighborhood).
1. **Full-time Working Couples (Dual Income Families)**
This client base will establish a consistent revenue base and ensure the financial stability of the business. Our community networking activities will be very important in this regard. Additionally, it will be very important to keep parents satisfied with our child safety and development efforts to keep their children enrolled in our daycare center.
2. **Single-Parent Households**

Some of this base is subsidized by public funds, and shows no sign of decreasing in size.
3. **Upper-Income Working Professionals.**
   This base has the surplus income to pursue a top-quality pre-school education for their children. These personally ambitious people are typically willing to pay a premium to have their children attend the best and most sophisticated child care facilities and experience the ultimate in personalized developmental guidance.
4. **After School Care**
   This client base will provide a higher profit margin because the instructor-to-student ratios are higher, and the students require more specialized educational and tutoring services. These clients are looking for stay-of-trouble enrichment programs and homework assistance for latch key kids.
5. **Part-time Workers and Drop-Ins**
   This group originates from the local fitness centers and business part-time workers, and will comprise about ____ (20?) percent of our total revenues. However, this group will be important to our word-of-mouth marketing strategy and the development of alternative revenue sources.

Composite Ideal Customer Profile:

By assembling this composite customer profile we will know what customer needs and wants our company needs to focus on and how best to reach our target market. We will use the information gathered from our customer research surveys to assemble the following composite customer profile:

Ideal Customer Profile

Who are they?
  age
  gender
  occupation
  location: zip codes
  income level
  marital status
  ethnic group
  education level
  family life cycle
  number of household members
  household income
  homeowner or renter
  association memberships
  leisure activities
  hobbies/interests
  core beliefs
Where are they located (zip codes)?
Most popular product/service purchased?
Lifestyle Preferences?   Trendsetter/Trend follower/Other _____
How often do they buy?
What are most important purchase factors? Price/Brand Name/Quality/Financing/Sales

What is their key buying motivator?
How do they buy it?
Where do they buy it from (locations)?
What problem do they want to solve?
What are the key frustrations/pains that these customers have when buying?
What search methods do they use?
What is preferred problem solution?

Convenience/Packaging/Other _____

Cash/Credit/Terms/Other _____

Table: Market Analysis

Number of Potential Attendees

Potential Customers	Growth	2017	2018	2019
Under 5 years	10%			
5 to 9 years	10%			
10 to 12 years	10%			
Over 12 years	10%			
Other	10%			
Totals:	10%			

Alternative Approach:

Number of Potential Customers

Potential Customers	Growth	2017	2018	2019
Full-time Working Families	10%			
Single Working Parent	10%			
Upper-Income Professionals	10%			
After School Students	10%			
Part-time Workers	10%			
Drop-In Shopper	10%			
Totals:	10%			

4.3 Target Market Segment Strategy

Our target marketing strategy will involve identifying a group of customers to which to direct our child day care services. Our strategy will be the result of intently listening to and understanding customer needs, representing customers' needs to those responsible for product production and service delivery, and giving them what they want. In developing our targeted customer messages we will strive to understand things like: where they work, worship, party and play, where they shop and go to school, how they spend their leisure time, what organizations they belong to, and where they volunteer their time. We will use research, surveys and observation to uncover this wealth of information to get our product details and brand name in front of our customers when they are most receptive to receiving our messaging.

Target Market Worksheet   (optional)

Note: Use this worksheet to explore potential target markets for your products and services.

Product Benefits: Actual factor (cost effectiveness, design, performance, etc.) or perceived factor (image, popularity, reputation, etc.) that satisfies what a customer needs or wants. An advantage or value that the product will offer its buyer.

Products Features: One of the distinguishing characteristics of a product or service that helps boost its appeal to potential buyers. A characteristic of a product that describes its appearance, its components, and its capabilities. Typical features include size and color.

Product or Service	Product/ Service Benefits	Product/ Service Features	Potential Target Markets

The target market for _____ (company name) is full-time working couples. Referral marketing, direct-mail campaigns and community activities will be the primary types of marketing strategies employed. Enhancing our reputation for trust with families and in the community will be crucial in establishing our brand image and obtaining the planned market share growth that we have forecasted.

Target City's Administration for Children Services
We will target this City Agency because it allocates funds and oversees child care programs for low-income families. It chooses new child care contractors. The agency works with day care providers to facilitate the signature and submission of their contracts.

Target Local Schools and Churches
Many churches and schools keep a list of local businesses that would be beneficial to their families and parishioners.

Target Schools
We will target schools that offer on-site programs because they want to avoid kids going home to an empty house until parents get off work. We will offer to manage these programs as an independent outside contractor.

Target Local Medical Professionals
We will talk to our local pediatricians and make sure our local hospital knows about our daycare services and programs. We will offer a good day rate for parents who might need a safe place they can drop one child off during the day while they attend to someone who is sick or has to stay in the hospital.

Target Real Estate Agents
We will provide them with flyers or business cards and ask them to hand them out to new families moving to the area.

Target Concierge Services
These companies are often asked to make child daycare recommendations.

Target Single Parent Women
The divorce rate remains extremely high by historical standards. Meanwhile, the proportion of births occurring out of wedlock continues to increase at a steady pace. If this trend persists, the proportion of children in one-parent families with working parents will rise even further.

Target Dual Income Families
Because of work obligations, this segment does not have the time during the day to care for or nurture the development of their child. To this group, we will promote our one-stop child care services via a direct mail campaign and our networking activities. We will also work with the local newspaper to prepare a press release that describes the child development benefits of our services to families.

Target Retired People and Seniors
Grandparents are increasingly being asked to take care of their grand children. We will prepare a seminar that discusses viable alternative solutions to this trend and the family benefits to be realized by using our daycare facility.

Target Corporations
More companies are partnering with child care centers to offer discounted rates or even special hours for employees, as a means of increasing employee retention and productivity. We will visit Employers in our area and introduce our company to human resources and or management. in any business. We will tell them about our daycare and be sure to leave some business cards behind. We will ask if we can place flyers on a bulletin board in the cafeteria. We will ask them if they'll consider referring employees who might have use for our daycare services and offer their employees a special discounted rate in exchange for exclusive access to their employees.

Ex: http://yourstory.com/2017/02/the-little-company/
The Little Company builds and manages onsite or near site day-care centers for companies.

Target Resorts and Other Travel Destinations
We will approach these types of businesses and offer to manage their on-site daycare services using an outsourced contractor agreement or provide information about our drop-in service for their guests.

Target Local Ethnic Groups
Ongoing demographic trends suggest that, in the coming decades, early childhood programs will be serving a population of children which is increasingly diverse in

economic resources, racial and ethnic background, and family structure.

Our plan is to reach out to consumers of various ethnic backgrounds, especially Hispanics, who comprise nearly 13 percent of the country's total population. In addition to embarking on an aggressive media campaign of advertising with ethnic newspapers and radio stations, we will set up programs to actively recruit bilingual employees and make our store more accessible via signage printed in various languages based on the store's community. We will accurately translate our marketing materials into other languages. We will enlist the support of our bilingual employees to assist in reaching the ethnic people in our surrounding area through a referral program. We will join the nearest _____ (predominate ethnic group) Chamber of Commerce and partner with _____ (Hispanic/Chinese/Other?) Advocacy Agencies. We will also develop clinics and programs that reflect cultural influences and brand preferences.

Helpful Resources:
1. U.S. census Bureau Statistics   www.census.gov
2. U.S. Dept. of Labor/Bureau of Labor Statistics   www.bls.gov/data/home.htm

4.3.1 Market Needs

According to a 2011 report by the U.S. Census Bureau, approximately 12,499,000 children younger than five are under regular childcare arrangements. Of those 12.49 million, 4.7 million spent their days in some kind of organized daycare facility. However, there are several million more preschool aged children who are not under any stable daycare routine. But studies have shown that high quality, professional childcare offers toddlers growth opportunities that are not available in the homes of most free daycare providers.

Child development experts believe that the lack of a consistent routine can be detrimental to the social and intellectual development of children. Furthermore, developmental psychologists have found a positive correlation between consistent, paid childcare, and the levels of self esteem and confidence exhibited by children under that care.

With decreasing real wages, the typical family now requires dual or supplemental incomes to survive. This continuing trend has created a growing need for quality child care services, of which, we expect to capture a share of this market. But, during this recession, many parents have lost their jobs, making child care unnecessary, while others have taken pay cuts, making it unaffordable.

There is also a need to provide care 24/7 for shift workers, including hospital staff and police.

4.4 Buying Patterns

A Buying Pattern is the typical manner in which consumers purchase goods or services or firms place their purchase orders in terms of amount, frequency, timing, etc. In determining buying patterns, we will need to understand the following:
- Why consumers make the purchases that they make?
- What factors influence consumer purchases?
- The changing factors in our society.

The economic recovery will greatly benefit the day care industry. As parents and guardians, particularly females, rejoin the workforce, demand for day care services will grow. Additionally, the expected increase in disposable incomes will allow families to spend more on child care, including high-value services like early education programs. One key area of growth for the industry is employer-sponsored child care services, which will become increasingly important as companies ramp up their efforts to attract and retain staff.

Price, service, staff-to-child ratio, certification and reputation are critical success factors in the child care services industry. _____ (company name) will compete well in our market by offering competitive prices, high quality child care services, a lower staff-to-child ratio and educational programs given by certified instructors. We will also strive to maintain an excellent reputation with parents and the community.

___ (company name) will gear its offerings, marketing, and pricing policies to establish a loyal client base. Our affordable pricing, attractive facility, educational programs, and basic quality services will be welcomed in _____ (city) and contribute to our success.

4.5 Market Growth

We will assess the following general factors that affect market growth:

Current Assessment

1. Interest Rates
2. Government Regulations
3. Perceived Environment Impact
4. Consumer Confidence Level
5. Population Growth Rate
6. Unemployment Rate
7. Political Stability
8. Currency Exchange Rate
9. Innovation Rate
10. Home Sales
11. Overall Economic Health

The dispersion of day-care centers largely reflects variations in the geographic distribution of children. Geographic distribution is also influenced by the cost and supply of child care; labor, income and housing affordability patterns and child-care subsidy policies. In addition, varying state and local regulations and licensing requirements affect employment in this industry. Government agencies generally review, among other things, the ratio of staff-to-enrolled children. Overall, however, the spread of establishments in the United States closely follows the national share of population.

Our business will be positioned to take advantage of several extremely positive industry trends:
1. The under-five population is projected to grow 55% from 2000-2050.
2. The effects of the baby boom echo (those born between 1977-2002) will be increasingly felt. Long-range projections indicate a rising number of annual births from 4.2 million in 2010 to 4.8 million in 2028.
3. Rising numbers of double-income families and single-parent families continue to cause waiting lists in child care centers in the U.S.

The _____ area is expected to grow _____% annually. The _____ zip code area is expected to grow ____% annually. These estimates are based on the most recent US Census Data and the _____ County Chamber of Commerce figures.

The general industry analysis shows that _____ (city) is expected to experience substantial population, housing and commercial business growth. This suggests that as more families continue to move into the _____ area, there will be an increasing demand for quality daycare services, and this makes it a prime location for a daycare center business.

4.6 Service Business Analysis

In 2017, the Day Care industry is expected to generate $46.6 billion in revenue. Day-care services are often a necessary expense for working families, a factor that mitigates revenue volatility for the industry. Over the past five years, in spite of the economic recession, revenue has kept growing, supported by rising birthrates prior to the recession and the fact that child care represents a relatively nondiscretionary expense for households, according to IBISWorld. From 2008 to 2017, industry revenue is expected to rise at an average annual rate of 1.4%. Nevertheless, revenue growth slowed because rising unemployment during the recession enabled newly jobless parents to provide child care themselves. This factor, however, was mitigated by an ongoing focus on child development, with a greater number of parents investing in day cares and preschools that include high-value services, such as personalized education. In 2017, industry revenue is projected to rise 1.6% as parents begin to reenter the workforce and disposable income rises, which will result in greater use of day-care services.

The industry largely comprises non-employing operators; in fact, non-employers make up over 90.0% of the companies in the industry. Over the past five years, the number of companies offering day-care services has grown, supported by continuing demand for child-care services and low barriers to entry. From 2008 to 2017, the number of enterprises is estimated to increase at an average annual rate of 2.7%, to 871,700 operators.

Beyond 2017, the industry will continue to prosper. Decreasing unemployment will lead to more parents reentering the workforce, raising demand for child-care services. Additionally, large players will likely benefit from parents' increased focus on child development and education programs, a key growth area for the industry. Large players will therefore offer more personalized development services for children. Early education will be a strong marketing tool to attract new customers.

The child care industry is split between large, commercially-run child care centers, like KinderCare and smaller, locally-owned centers. There are companies at all levels, from the basic baby sitter services, to national franchised chains. There are service providers that offer standard business hours to companies that offer evening and night hours. There are scheduled services and no reservation drop-off services. Price, quality and reputation drives parental choices.

We will compete with the small care centers, which is where the main competition exists, on the basis of innovative and flexible programs, and a well-trained professional staff, motivated by a pay-for-performance component to their compensation package.

The child care services industry includes the following business models:
1. **Franchised Child care Centers**
   These are typically larger facilities that offer care to a wide range of ages. The child care is adequate, but somewhat impersonal by virtue of its large size.
2. **Licensed locally and independently owned Child Care Facilities**
   Small business facilities that offer child daycare services. Some handle a wide range of ages, while others specialize with a specific age group or learning program.
3. **Family Child Care Homes**
   Individuals that offer child daycare services in their homes. The quality pf these ranges considerably.
4. **Specific Interest Based Programs**
   Businesses that offer specialized instruction such as gymnastics, martial arts and dance.
5. **Church Child Care Facilities**
   Religious organizations that offer child daycare services in their communities.

The Program/Curriculum:
The program or curriculum we offer will be varied according to child age. For children aged three and under, programs will emphasize play activities that enhance development as opposed to formal educational curricula. Four and five year olds will benefit from school readiness activities that combine elements of formal education with play and free expression. All programs will include both small and large group activities, and a balance

between rest and activity.

4.7 Barriers to Entry

_____ (company name) will benefit from the following combination of barriers to entry, which cumulatively present a moderate degree of entry difficulty or obstacles in the path of other child care businesses wanting to enter our market.

1. Industry Experience.
2. Community Networking
3. Referral Program Set-up
4. People Skills
5. Marketing Skills
6. Facility Design
7. Operations Management
8. Cash Flow Management
9. Website Design
10. Certification

4.7.1 Porter's Five Forces Analysis

We will use Porter's five forces analysis as a framework for the industry analysis and business strategy development. It will be used to derive the five forces which determine the competitive intensity and therefore attractiveness of our market. Attractiveness in this context refers to the overall industry profitability.

Competitors The degree of rivalry is high in this segment, but less when compared to the overall category. There are ____ (#) major competitors in the _____ area and they include: _____

Threat of Substitutes
Substitutes are moderate for this industry. These include other child day care centers, corporate day care centers, preschool centers, babysitters, family or homemaker child care, pre-kindergarten classrooms, and nanny care.

Bargaining Power of Buyers
Buyer power is moderate in the business. Buyers are sensitive to quality, security, safety and pricing as the segment attempts to capitalize on the pricing and quality advantage.

Bargaining Power of Suppliers
Supplier power is low in the industry. Inventory must be obtained from a number of distributors. A high level of operational efficiency for managing supplies can be achieved.

Threat of New Entrants
Relatively high in this segment. The business model can be easily copied.

Conclusions: _____ (company name) is in a competitive field and has to move fast to retain its competitive advantage. The key success factors are to develop operational efficiencies, innovative programs, cost-effective marketing and customer service excellence.

4.8 Competitive Analysis

Competitor analysis in marketing and strategic management is an assessment of the strengths and weaknesses of current and potential competitors. This analysis will provide both an offensive and defensive strategic context through which to identify our business opportunities and threats. We will carry out continual competitive analysis to ensure our market is not being eroded by developments in other firms. This analysis will be matched with the target segment needs to ensure that our products and services continue to provide better value than the competitors. The competitive analysis will show very clearly why our products and services are preferred in some market segments to other offerings and to be able to offer reasonable proof of that assertion.

Competitor	What We Can Do and They Can't	What They Can Do and We Can't

We will conduct good market intelligence for the following reasons:
1. To forecast competitors' strategies.
2. To predict competitor likely reactions to our own strategies.
3. To consider how competitors' behavior can be influenced in our own favor.

Overall competition in the area is _____ (weak/moderate/strong).

Competitive analysis conducted by the company owners has shown that there are ____ (# or no other?) companies currently offering the same combination of child care services in the _____ (city) area. However, the existing competitors offer only a limited range of child care programs. In fact, of these _____ (#) competitors only _____ (#) offered a range of child care services and packaged options comparable with what _____ (company name) plans to offer to its clients.

Main Competitors

		Strengths	Weaknesses
1.	Catholic Church Day Care	Established	Religious Focus Unlicensed facility
2.	Martial Arts America	Established	No tutoring
3.	Family Child Care Homes	Personal Service	Small Capacity
4.	Dance Schools	Activities	Female Oriented.
5.	KinderCare	Established	Impersonal Chain

Resource: www.manta.com/mb_54_B315F_9VT/child_day_care_services/redford_mi

Self-assessment

Competitive Rating Assessment: 1 = Weak ....5 = Strong

	Our Company	Prime Competitor	Compare
Our Location			
Our Facilities			
Our Services and Amenities			
Our Management Skills			
Our Training Programs			
Our Research & Development			
Our Company Culture			
Our Business Model			
Overall Rating			

Rationale: _____

The following establishments are considered direct competitors in _____ (city):

Competitor	Address	Market Share	Primary Focus	Secondary Prod/Svcs	Strengths	Weaknesses

Indirect Competitors include the following:
_____
_____

Alternative Competitive Matrix

Competitor Name: Us _____   _____   _____

Location
Distance
Website
Comparison Items:
Sales Revenue
Programs
Registration Fee
Profitability
Market Share
Brand Name
Services Included
Funding Source
Target Market
Operating Hours
Pricing Strategy
Yrs in Business
Reputation
Marketing Strategy
Sales Brochure/Catalog
Website

Sales Revenues   _____
No. of Staff   _____
Competitive Advantage _____
Comments   _____

Competitor Profile Matrix

Critical Success Factors	Our Score	Competitor 1 Rating Score	Competitor 2 Rating Score	Competitor 3 Rating Score
Advertising				
Service Quality				
Price Competition				
Management				
Financial Position				
Customer Loyalty				
Brand Identity				
Market Share				
Total				

We will use the following sources of information to conduct our competition analysis:

1. Competitor company websites.
2. Mystery shopper visits.
3. Annual Reports (www.annual reports.com)
4. Thomas Net (www.thomasnet.com)
5. Trade Journals
6. Trade Associations
7. Sales representative interviews
8. Research & Development may come across new patents.
9. Market research can give feedback on the customer's perspective
10. Monitoring services will track a company or industry you select for news. Resources: www.portfolionews.com www.Office.com
11. Hoover's www.hoovers.com
12. www.zapdata.com (Dun and Bradstreet) You can buy one-off lists here.
13. www.infousa.com (The largest, and they resell to many other vendors)
14. www.onesource.com (By subscription, they pull information from many sources)
15. www.capitaliq.com (Standard and Poors).
16. Obtain industry specific information from First Research (www.firstresearch.com) or IBISWorld, although both are by subscription only, although you may be able to buy just one report.
17. Get industry financial ratios and industry norms from RMA (www.rmahq.com) or by using ProfitCents.com software.
18. Company newsletters
19. Industry Consultants
20. Suppliers
21. Customer interviews regarding competitors.

22. Analyze competitors' ads for their target audience, market position, product features, benefits, prices, etc.
23. Attend speeches or presentations made by representatives of your competitors.
24. View competitor's trade show display from a potential customer's point of view.
25. Search computer databases (available at many public libraries).
26. Review competitor Yellow Book Ads.
27. www.bls.gov/cex/ (site provides information on consumer expenditures nationally, regionally, and by selected metropolitan areas).
28. www.sizeup.com
29. Business Statistics and Financial Ratios   www.bizstats.com

Resource:
www.sba.gov/business-guide/plan/market-research-competitive-analysis
sba.gov/business-guide/plan/market-research-competitive-analysis#researchresources

4.9 Market Revenue Projection

For each of our chosen target markets, we will estimate our market share in number of customers, and based on consumer behavior, how often do they buy per year? What is the average dollar amount of each purchase? We will then multiply these three numbers to project sales volume for each target market.

Target Market	Number of Customers	No. of Purchases per Year	Average Dollar Amount per Purchase	Total Sales Volume
	A x	B	x C	= D

_____
_____
_____

Using the target market number identified in this section, and the local demographics, we have made the following assessments regarding market opportunity and revenue potential in our area:

Potential Revenue Opportunity =

	_____	Local Daycare Population
(x)	_____	Expected ___ % Market Share
(=)	_____	Number of likely local clients
(x)	$ _____	Average annual fee dollar amount
(=)	$ _____	Annual Revenue Opportunity.

Or

Age Group   No. of Clients   (x) Monthly Fee   (=)   Monthly Income

Infants   _____   _____   _____
Toddlers   _____   _____   _____
Pre-School   _____   _____   _____
School Age   _____   _____   _____
Total: _____
Annualized: (x)   12
Annual Revenue Potential: _____

Recap

Month   Jan Feb Mar Apr May Jun Jul Aug Sep Oct Nov Dec   Total
Products
_____

Services
_____

Gross Sales: _____
(-) Returns   _____
Net Sales   _____

Revenue Assumptions:
1. The sources of information for our revenue projection are:
   _____
2. If the total market demand for our product/service = 100%, our projected sales volume represents ____% of this total market.
3. The following factors might lower our revenue projections:
   _____

5.0 Industry Analysis

NAICS Code 624410, **Child Day Care Svcs**
SIC 7299: Miscellaneous Personal Services, Not Elsewhere classified.
Head Start centers operating in conjunction with elementary schools are classified in **SIC 8211: Elementary and Secondary Schools.**

The US child-care industry includes about 40,000 commercial companies with combined annual revenue of $22 billion, and 25,000 nonprofit organizations, with combined annual revenue of $10 billion. Large firms include Knowledge Learning, Bright Horizons Family Solutions, and ABC Learning Centers. The industry is highly fragmented. The top 50 companies hold less than 20 percent of the market. The average facility of one of the larger companies has $700,000 in annual revenue and employs 120.

Job and income growth drive demand for child-care centers. The profitability of individual companies depends on good marketing and efficient operations. Large companies have economies of scale in advertising and administration. Smaller companies can compete effectively in local markets by owning convenient locations. The industry is highly labor-intensive, as annual revenue per worker is only about $30,000.

Child-care centers provide supervision and educational programs for pre-school and school-age children. The type of care varies according to a child's age, which may range from 6 weeks to 16 years. Most commercial companies operate child-care centers that are open to the public, but some operate corporate-sponsored centers for employees' children. Most commercial facilities concentrate on a small age range, since each age group requires a different program.

A typical facility of a national operator occupies 12,000 square feet, with kitchen and bathrooms, and accommodates 150 children. Hours may be from 6:00 am to 6:00 pm. Educational programs, usually feature age-specific learning curriculum.

The industry derives the majority of its revenue from standard child-care services, which accounts for 56.9% of the industry's revenue, according to the latest data from the US Census. These include child-care centers, family day care, nanny or babysitting services. Child-care centers are licensed facilities that offer relatively large numbers of enrollments. Child-care centers are typically slightly more expensive than nanny or babysitting services. According to the latest data from Child Care Aware of America, the average annual cost of full-time center-based child care for a four-year-old ranged from about $4,515 in Tennessee to nearly $12,320 in Massachusetts in 2013.

Source: http://www.ibisworld.com/industry/default.aspx?indid=1618

Resource: www.sbdcnet.org/small-business-research-reports/daycare-business-2012

5.1 Key Industry Statistics

1. Overall, families with a preschool child who pay for child care devote about 10% of their incomes to child care, but this figure ranges from only 6% for families with annual incomes of $50,000 or more to 23% for families with annual incomes under $15,000.
2. In 2005, 61 percent of children from birth through age six, and not in kindergarten, spent time in non-parental child care. Twenty-two percent were cared for by a relative, 14 percent by a non-relative but in a home, and 36 percent in center-based programs. Center-based programs may include day care centers, pre-kindergartens, nursery schools, Head Start programs, and other early childhood education programs
3. Among children ages 0 to 6 (and not yet in kindergarten), 70 percent of black non-Hispanic children spend time in non-parental child care of some sort, compared with 63 percent of white non-Hispanic children, 50 percent of Hispanic children, and 57 percent Asian children.
4. Experts say a woman providing care in her home for four children can expect to gross just $30,000 to $35,000 a year. But an outside center with 100 children could net close to $250,000.
5. Nearly two thirds (63%) of children under five have some kind of regular childcare arrangement (regular is defined as being used at least once a week), according to a U.S. Census Bureau study in winter 2002. Four in 10 (40%) are cared for by relatives, 35% are cared for by non-relatives, and 11% are cared for by both.
6. Nearly a quarter of preschoolers (23%) are cared for by their grandparents, and 14% get daycare from their fathers.
7. Nearly nine in 10 preschoolers (89%) whose moms work participate in at least one form of childcare on a regular basis, compared with 31% of preschoolers whose moms don't work.
8. Nearly a quarter (22%) of preschoolers with employed moms have more than one type of regular childcare arrangement, compared with 7% of kids with non-employed moms.
9. Preschool children spend an average of 32 hours a week in childcare, but kids of working moms spend twice as much time (36 hours) as those with stay-at-home moms (18 hours).
10. Black and Hispanic moms who work are more likely to utilize grandparents (29% of Blacks and 37% of Hispanics) than fathers (18% of Blacks and 24% of Hispanics) as regular providers of childcare, while non-Hispanic White moms are about equally likely to utilize fathers (30%) and grandparents (27%). Asian moms are more likely than moms of other races/ethnicities to utilize their older children as childcare providers for their preschoolers.
11. According to the Census Bureau, in 1999 more than one-fifth of children under age 5 were cared for in a daycare center. Nearly one-fifth more were enrolled in family daycare -- care provided outside the home by a non-relative.

5.2 Industry Trends

We will determine the trends that are impacting our consumers and indicate ways in which our customers' needs are changing and any relevant social, technical or other changes that will impact our target market. Keeping up with trends and reports will help management to carve a niche for our business, stay ahead of the competition and deliver products that our customers need and want.

IBISWorld posits that the larger chains will try to capitalize on this preference for day care educational enrichment by offering "personalized development services for children." These services are projected to bolster marketing efforts but also contribute to expanding day care business revenues, which are estimated to rise by an average annual rate of 2.8% from 2012 to 2019, reaching $53.8 billion by 2019.

In addition to slowly improving economic conditions, recent upticks in birthrates and positive research findings on the benefits of early education are also contributing to growing demand for daycare services. The net result is that daycare industry employment is estimated to increase 2.8% per year on average to 1.9 million.

Other trends include:
1. The revolutionary increase in mothers' labor force participation during the past half-century led to enormous increases in non-parental care of young children. 2. Between 1992 and 2005, the labor force participation rate for women between the ages of 25 and 54 increased from 75% to 83%.
2. Ongoing demographic trends suggest that, in the coming decades, early childhood programs will be serving a population of children which is increasingly diverse in economic resources, racial and ethnic background, and family structure.
3. Broad demographic trends as well as efforts to reform the welfare system are likely to increase rates of labor force participation by mothers with young children, further expanding the demand for non-parental child care.
4. The diversity in the characteristics and needs of the nation's children has also increased, particularly in terms of their economic circumstances, their racial and ethnic backgrounds, and their family living arrangements. Child care policies and programs must be designed to respond to the differing needs of the many children who use them.
5. Child care centers have mostly transitioned to centers for early education, where young tots are involved with early learning. This trend to learning centers is partly due to high parent and school expectations; it's also attributable to research that shows that kids are capable of learning early academics and other skills that previously were not taught until later.
6. More Companies will offer on-site childcare for their employees. Companies are showing dramatic increase in providing on-site childcare from just over 100 firms in 1978 to 4,177 in 1989 to now over 8,000. This trend is continuing as more businesses are discovering that employer-assisted child care is an effective way to attract and retain quality workers. Eighty-five percent of employers report that providing child care services improved employee recruitment and almost two-

thirds of employers found that providing child care services reduced turnover.
7. Corporate child care is raising the bar in terms of quality child care. An increasing number of companies are either offering (or considering) in-house child care centers as a perk for attracting and retaining top employees.
8. In addition, more companies are partnering with child care centers to offer discounted rates or even special hours for employees.
9. Parents today can consider a wider menu of child care choices, and many families are choosing to use a variety of care options based on current needs. Some families may use a nanny for an infant, an in-home provider for a toddler, and then switch to a care center for a preschooler. Some families use one type of care during the school year and then another for summer months. Occasional care service options can include babysitters, drop-in care, specified parent night out nights, and even child care co-ops.
10. Drop-in child care is on the grow and these facilities typically offer high-quality, safe, and affordable care options.
11. Many families, especially those who have moved to a new community, rely on the internet to find quality child care. Many websites offer free listings of child care; most states have a child care site for review as well. Web-based babysitting and child care services are on the increase, and parents can type in a zip code and find providers who meet the specifications designated.
12. An increasing number of facilities offer parents the peace of mind of being able to check on their child while at daycare as desired through video-streaming of classroom activities throughout the day. Other providers regularly take photos of children and send to parents, post daily or weekly blogs or e-newsletters online for parents to view, or even exchange emails or text messages throughout the day. The technology provides parents and providers with another tool for staying "in touch" and bonding with activities and events planned for youngsters.
13. Most child care providers are increasing measures to protect children in their charge. Increased security concerning picking up of children, additional background checks and screenings being done on prospective employees, and more surveillance and monitoring (both overt as well as the covert varieties) are helping to increase safety. Training and more thorough checklists is also helping to keep kids safer on field trips and outings.
14. Child care providers are using a variety of tools to provide parents with ongoing information about their child's day. Some providers create websites where they post monthly menus, weekly day-by-day activities, and even behavioral reports. Others provide parents with a daily update that is then emailed.
15. More and more child care centers are offering enrichment options for tots to participate in while still at child care. Parents nowadays are busier than ever, yet want their child to participate in an array of activities at the same time. The solution for some is to sign kids up for optional fee-based ballet, karate, soccer and gymnastics classes that kids participate in during the week while still in care. The instructor comes to the facility rather than the other way around. This type of option may not be for everyone, but it works for those who are very busy or have long commutes each day.
16. Many resorts and tourist-based communities have added on-site or close

proximity child care. While some facilities may have pricey fees for kids to participate, others are free and include crafts, special movie nights, field trips and more.
17. IRS Child and Dependent Care Credit: If you paid someone to care for a child under age 13 or a qualifying spouse or dependent so you could work or look for work, you may be able to reduce your tax by claiming the Child and Dependent Care Credit on your federal income tax return. To qualify, your spouse, children age 13 or older, and other dependents must be physically or mentally incapable of self-care.
18. Businesses that provide child care and early education services report declining enrollments as families cut costs amid a tough economy.
19. Day care centers are adding half-day pre-kindergarten programs to help parents save money.
20. More states are taking aim at transitioning from registered day cares to licensed facilities, and requiring regular inspections.
21. More providers are offering flexible hours, keeping rates the same or even reducing them in some cases, and working out pay arrangements for struggling families to encourage families to stay. Special programs or fees are also being scrutinized as providers scramble to find ways to lessen costs while maintaining a quality care program for kids.
22. More resorts and other types of travel destinations are offering on-site day care services.
23. More small-businesses are looking to bring more parents in the door by offering free or discounted child care to patrons, and may want to outsource this function.

Resources:
http://childcare.about.com/od/evaluations/tp/trends.htm
http://www.sbdcnet.org/small-business-research-reports/daycare-business-2012

5.3 Key Industry Terms

We will use the following term definitions to help our company to understand and speak the common language of our industry, and aid efficient communication.

Accreditation
A process through which child care programs voluntarily meet specific standards to receive endorsement from a professional agency, such as the National Association for the Education of Young Children or the National Association for Family Day Care.

Day Care Centers
A nonresidential facility in which more than twelve children receive care during all or part of the day. In this type of care, children are grouped by age and developmental stage. Because day care centers provide care for large numbers of children, their hours of operation may be less flexible than other arrangements. All centers, with the exception of religious and school-based programs, must meet state licensing requirements for health

and safety, staff-to-child ratios, caregiver qualifications, and curriculum.
Chain Centers
Offer standardized programs and curriculum for children. They are growing rapidly and are profit oriented.
Cooperative Childcare
Daycare run by a group of parents who hire staff to care for their children, allowing parents to decide what services are provided and who is hired.
Corporate Day Care Centers
Corporations may either fund or subsidize child care for their employee's children. Parents employed by these corporations are able to enroll their children in local day care centers in which the corporation has purchased spaces or in an on-site center. These centers must meet state licensing requirements.
Family Daycare (or Home Daycare)
Childcare provided by individual caregivers in their own homes. Usually taking in small groups of children, family daycare is licensed by local authorities. Family daycare providers provide care for groups of 6 or 8 children in smaller daycares and up to 14 children for larger daycares. Family daycare is usually less expensive than daycare centers, preschools and in-home childcare options like nannies and au pairs. If parents choose to put their child in family daycare, they can expect to pay on average $300 to $800 per month per child. The cost of family daycare can be higher or lower depending on a combination of factors. Children in family home care are usually mixed in age. The small group size and home-based setting of family home care appeal particularly to parents of infants and toddlers.
Group Daycare
A common option for families where there are two working parents and a popular option for single parents. There are five types of group childcare: private childcare centers, workplace childcare, cooperative childcare, nonprofit childcare, and chain centers.
Learning Center
In an early childhood program, this is an area that contains materials, such as blocks, pretend household items or art supplies, where children can explore their own interests at their own pace.
Licensed Child Care
Child care programs operated in homes or in facilities that fall within the regulatory system of a state or community and comply with those regulations. Many states have different levels of regulatory requirements and use different terms to refer to these levels (e.g., licensing, certification, registration).
Nonprofit Daycare
Usually for low income families and is funded by government agencies and private donations
On-site Child Care
Child care programs that occur in facilities where parents are on the premises. For example, a child care center at the parents' place of employment.
Preschools
The primary function is the education of its charges. Most are required to meet state childcare standards, although some preschools may not fall under state regulation. Most dedicated preschools only run part-time or partial day programs. Preschools follow a

curriculum that has standards and measurable cognitive and developmental outcomes. Quality preschools require teachers to have a minimum of a bachelor's degree, achieve their state teaching certificate in Early Childhood Education, have a continuing education requirement, and several years of teaching experience. Classes in quality preschools are often smaller and teacher compensation more closely resembles that of a private school teacher, so turnover is often lower than what is experienced in childcare facilities. The cost of attending a quality preschool is substantially higher than a childcare focused facility because the higher compensation and smaller class sizes.

Private Daycare Center
Involves childcare outside the licensee's own home and is usually located in commercial buildings. Daycare centers which are facilities dedicated to providing childcare to larger groups of children encompassing a fairly large range of ages (usually from babies through pre-schoolers). Quality daycare centers are state-licensed and often have other types of accreditation from non-profit childcare organizations. Children are placed in smaller groups and receive the attention of pre-specified caregivers. Childcare staff must have completed courses in Child Development or Early Childhood Education. There is no limit to how many children a center may accept, as long as staff-child ratios and other licensing requirements are met.

Resource and Referral Agency
A local organization who gives parents information about local child care centers or family child care homes when researching child care options. They also may provide training for child care providers, administer child care subsidy, and/or work with the community to increase public awareness of the need for child care services.

Staff-to-Child Ratio
The number of qualified caregivers caring for a specified number of children in a child care program. Required ratios vary depending on ages and abilities of the children in care.

Workplace Childcare Centers
Provided by employers. One of the most rapidly growing options, corporate daycare is gaining popularity because employers are recognizing that providing onsite daycare is not only a nice benefit for employees but makes good business sense. Employers that provide daycare find they improve employee morale, productivity and retention.

5.4 Industry Leaders

We plan to study the best practices of industry leaders and adapt certain selected practices to our business model concept. Best practices are those methods or techniques resulting in increased customer satisfaction when incorporated into the operation.

Top of the World Private Preschool
451 Lake Forest Dr., McKinney, Texas 75070
972-529-1466   topoftheworldpreschool.com

Challenger Schools
Locations in California, Utah, Nevada and Idaho

challengerschool.com

Childrens' Creative Learning Centers (CCLC)
Locations Nationwide   cclc.com

KinderCare Learning Centers
Locations Nationwide   kindercare.com

Knowledge Beginnings Learning Centers
Locations Nationwide
1-888-525-2780   knowledgebeginnings.com

La Petite Academy
Locations Nationwide
877-861-5078   lapetite.com

Tutor Time Child Care and Learning Centers
Locations Nationwide
1-877-684-1613   tutortime.com

Child Time Learning Centers
Locations Nationwide
1-866-CHILDTIME   childtime.com

Kids Klub Child Development Centers
380 S. Raymond Ave., Pasadena, CA 91105
626-795-2501   kidsklubcdc.com

Bright Horizons Family Solutions
200 Talcott Avenue South, Watertown, MA 02472
617-673-8000   brighthorizons.com

In the early 2000s, **KinderCare Learning Centers** was the nation's largest for-profit childcare organization; it cared for over 129,000 children, ages 6 weeks to 12 years old, in 39 states as well as two sites in the United Kingdom. The average weekly tuition was approximately $135. Along with its KinderCare Learning Centers and Mulberry Child Care Centers, KinderCare also operated on-site at nearly 50 corporate sites under the banner KinderCare at Work. In 2002 the company reported a net income of $16.5 million on sales of $829.4 million.

With an enrollment of some 74,600 children, **La Petite** was the second largest for-profit provider of childcare services, with approximately 720 centers in 36 states and Washington, D.C. J.P. Morgan Partners owned a controlling share of the organization. In fiscal year 2002 (ending in June) La Petite reported revenues of $384.8 million, resulting in a net loss of $6.3 million.

Bright Horizons was another large childcare center chain, specializing in on-site child care. It operated centers over 400 centers for more than 300 employers. Some of its clients were Allstate Insurance, Apple Computer, AT&T, Dunkin' Donuts, DuPont Company, Ernst & Young, Fidelity Investments, Hewlett Packard, IBM, Mattel Toys, MCA/Universal City Studios Inc., Merck & Co., Motorola Inc., Paramount Pictures, Procter & Gamble, Prudential Insurance Co., Sony Pictures Entertainment, Time Warner, United Nations, Women & Infants Hospital, and Xerox.

Children's Lighthouse Learning Centers
Early childhood learning centers that offer quality preschool education and after-school programs for children. Centers are state-of-the-art, with key code entry and cameras in each room so a parent can view their child from anywhere in the world.

www.franchiseopportunities.com/Zor_107270/Children_s_Lighthouse_Learning.htm

Goddard Systems Inc.
The Goddard School offers year-round programs for children from six weeks to six years old including after-school enrichment and summer programs.Each school is a licensed childcare facility with an on-site owner, an Education Director and a faculty trained in Early Childhood Education or Childhood Development. GSI provides continuing education for all teachers as well as a corporate Quality Assurance program. The King of Prussia, Pa., company added 25 new franchises in 2010. What makes Goddard popular is the added value they offer parents by combining child care with educational services. They offer their FLEX Learning Program, a play-based curriculum developed by early childhood education experts. Goddard schools teach everything from potty training for toddlers to computer skills for preschoolers to yoga for kindergarteners. Franchisees do not need to have a background in education. Goddard's dual-management system encourages them to focus on the business side of the franchise while an accredited educational director tackles the teaching.

6.0 Strategy and Implementation Summary

Resource:
www.childcarenetwork.org/dnn/portals/0/training/admin2/Marketing%20Strategies%20That%20Work%20in%20Child%20Care.pdf

Our sales strategy is based on serving our niche markets better than the competition and leveraging our competitive advantages. These advantages include superior attention to understanding and satisfying customer needs and wants, creating a one-stop solution, and value pricing.

The objectives of our marketing strategy will be to recruit new customers, retain existing customers, get good customers to spend more and return more frequently. Establishing a loyal customer base is very important because such core customers will not only generate the most lifetime sales, but also provide valuable referrals.

We will generate word-of-mouth buzz through direct-mail campaigns, exceeding customer expectations, developing a Web site and getting involved in community events and with local businesses, and donating our services at charity functions, in exchange for press release coverage. Our sales strategy will seek to convert potential and first-time customers into long-term relationships and referral agents.

The target customers are dual income, middle-class families who value a quality education and child care provided for their children ages 4 months to 12 years. The combination of our competitive advantages, targeted marketing campaign and networking activities, will enable _____ (company name) to continue increasing our market share.

Resources:
www.firstchildrensfinance.org/businessresourcecenter/centers-2/marketing/marketing-tools/
www.firstchildrensfinance.org/businessresourcecenter/family-2/marketing-2/marketing-tools/

We will perfect the art of giving facility tours to parents by adhering to the following guidelines:

1. Offer tours at one or two specific times of the day, such as mid-morning after teachers and kids have had a chance to settle into the day's routine

2. Have the same person conduct all of our tours to create a consistent process and allow the benchmarking of trends over time.

3. Provide reminders by calling a day or two in advance to remind parents about upcoming appointments to reduce the risk of no-shows.

4. Present the same three biggest selling points during every tour, such as state-of-the-art security system, accredited by the National Association for the Education of Young Children, and all meals prepared in-house.
5. Start by uncovering and then addressing the parents' specific concerns during the tour.
6. Give a parting age-appropriate gift to send the parent home with the school logo, such as a small toy or book with the child's name on a write-in sticker, etc.
7. Close well by knowing your ideal outcome, such as same day registration, before the tour starts.
8. Proactively follow up with them, such as with a phone call a few days later to thank them for coming and ask if they have any additional questions you can answer for them or send a handwritten thank-you note.

6.1.0 Promotion Strategy

We will depend on client referrals, community involvement and direct mail campaigns as our primary ways to reach new clients. Our promotional strategies will also make use of the following tools:

- **Advertising**
    - Yearly anniversary parties to celebrate the success of each year.
    - Multiple Yellow Pages ads in the book and online.
    - Flyers promoting pre-enrollment drives.
    - Doorknob hangers, if not prohibited by neighborhood associations.
- **Local Marketing / Public Relations**
    - Client raffle for gift certificates or discount coupons
    - Participation in local civic groups.
    - Press release coverage of our sponsoring of events at the local community center for families and residents.
    - Article submissions to magazines describing the importance of early child development programs.
    - Sales Brochure to convey our curriculum content and theme to prospective clients.
- **Local Media**
    - Direct Mail - We will send quarterly direct mailings to residents with a ___ (7?) mile radius of our center. It will contain an explanation of our child care service programs and a newsletter with a listing of open house events.
    - Radio Campaign - We will make "live on the air" presentations of our discount coupons to the disk jockeys, hoping to get the promotions

>   broadcasted to the listening audience.
>   o Newspaper Campaign - Placing several ads in local community newspapers to launch our initial campaign. We will include a discount coupon in the ad to track the return on investment.
>   o Website – We will collect email addresses for a monthly newsletter.

6.1.1 Grand Opening

Our Grand Opening celebration will be a very important promotion opportunity to create word-of-mouth advertising results.

We will do the following things to make the open house a successful event:
1. Enlist local business support to contribute a large number of door prizes.
2. Use a sign-in sheet to create an email/mailing list.
3. Create free children ID cards.
4. Schedule appearance by local celebrities.
5. Create a festive atmosphere with balloons, beverages and music.
6. Get the local radio station to broadcast live from the event and handout fun gifts.
7. Offer an application fee waiver.
8. Giveaway our logo imprinted T-shirts as a contest prize.
9. Allow potential customers to view your facility and ask questions.
10. Print promotional flyers and pay a few kids to distribute them locally.
11. Arrange for face painting, storytelling, clowns, and snacks for everyone.
12. Arrange for local politician to do the official opening ceremony so all the local newspapers came to take pictures and do a feature story.
13. Arrange that people can tour our day care on the open day in order to see our facilities, collect sales brochures and find out more about our services.
14. Arrange the layout of all equipment in every room in order to show the day care to best effect.
15. Allocate staff members specific rooms and business cards and instruct them to deal with any questions or queries.
16. Organize a drawing with everyone writing their name and phone numbers on the back of business cards and give a voucher to the day care as a prize to start a marketing list.

6.1.2 Value Proposition

Our value proposition will summarize why a consumer should use our daycare services. We will offer uniquely premium child care services, as substantiated by our curriculum and activities offered, the experience and educational level of our instructors and our community involvement.

It will convince prospects that our services will add more value or better solve their need for a convenient, one-stop daycare service. We will use this value proposition statement to target customers who will benefit most from using our daycare services. These are parents who are concerned about education and the development of social and motor skills. Our value proposition will be concise and appeal to the customer's strongest decision-making drivers, which are convenience, security, availability, child development and quality of personal relationships.

Recap of Our Value Proposition:

Trust – We are known as a trusted partner with strong customer and vendor endorsements. We have earned a reputation for quality, integrity, safety, and delivery of comprehensive day care solutions.

Quality – We offer child day care experience and extensive professional backgrounds at competitive rates.

Experience – Our ability to bring people with years of child care experience with deep technical knowledge of successful learning environments is at the core of our success.

True Vendor Partnerships – Our true vendor partnerships enable us to offer the resources of much larger organizations with greater flexibility.

Customer Satisfaction and Commitment to Success – Through partnering with our customers and delivering quality solutions, we have been able to achieve an impressive degree of repeat and referral business. Since _____ (year), more than ____% of our business activity is generated by existing customers. Our philosophy is that "our clients' peace of mind is our success." Our success is measured in terms of our customer's appreciation for the attentive care we provide their children.

6.1.3 Positioning Statement

It is the objective of _____ (company name) to become the local leader in quality child care services in the _____ area. The educational aspect of our child care service will allow us to pursue a differentiation business strategy and not have to focus intently on low cost leadership.

We also plan to develop specialized services that will enable us to pursue a niche focus on specific interest based programs, such as tutoring, drop-off child care and after school enrichment activities.

These objectives will position us at the _____ (high-end of the market?) and will allow the company to realize a healthy profit margin in relation to its low-end, discount rivals and achieve long-term growth.

Market Positioning Recap

Price: The strategy is to offer competitive prices that are lower that the market leader, yet set to indicate value and worth. .

Quality: The day care service quality will have to be very good as the finished service results will be apparent in highly visible situations and venues.

Service: Highly individualized and customized service will be the key to success in this type of business. Personal attention to the needs of the children will result in higher sales and word of mouth advertising.

6.1.4 Unique Selling Proposition (USP)

Our unique selling proposition will answer the question why a customer should choose to do business with our company versus any and every other option available to them in the marketplace. Our USP will be a description of a unique important benefit that our child day care center offers to customers, so that price is no longer the key to our sales.

Our USP will include the following:
Who our target audience is: _____
What we will do for them: _____
What qualities, skills, talents, traits do we possess that others do not: _____
What are the benefits we provide that no one else offers: _____
Why that is different from what others are offering: _____
Why that solution matters to our target audience: _____

Our unique selling point is attached to the fact all of the kiddies will be treated and related to on an individual basis.

6.1.5 Distribution Strategy

Customers can contact the _____ (company name) by telephone, fax, internet and by dropping in. Our nearest competitors' are ___ (#) miles away in either direction.

Our customers will have the following access points:
1. **Order by Phone**
   Customers can contact us 24 hours a day, 7days a week at _____.
   Our Customer Service Representatives will be available to assist customers Monday through Friday from ___ a.m. to ___ p.m. EST.
2. **Order by Fax**
   Customers may fax their registrations to _____ anytime.
   They must provide: Account number, Billing and shipping address, Purchase order number, if applicable, Name and telephone number, class number/description.
3. **Order Online**
   Customers can register online at www._____.com. Once the account is activated, customers will be able to place orders, browse the schedule, check class availability and pricing, check status and view transaction history.
4. **In-person at Our Facility**

All customers can be serviced in person at our facilities Monday through Friday from ___ a.m. to ___ p.m. EST.

We will utilize the following distribution channels:
1. Retail   via our facility selling to final consumer buyers.
2. Wholesale   selling through agents to our commercial accounts.
3. Direct Mail   using catalogs and flyers to sell directly to consumer buyers at retail prices.
4. Telemarketing   selling directly to consumer buyers at retail via phones.
5. Cybermarketing   selling directly to consumer buyers at retail prices, or business-to-business services via computer networks
6. Sales Force   using independent commissioned representatives to sell services to corporate accounts.
7. TV and Cable   direct marketing of our services to consumers.

6.2   Competitive Advantages

A **competitive advantage** is the thing that differentiates a business from its competitors. It is what separates our business from everyone else. It answers the questions: "Why do customers buy from us versus a competitor?", and "What do we offer customers that is unique?". We will make certain to include our key competitive advantages into our marketing materials. We will use the following competitive advantages to set us apart from our competitors. The distinctive competitive advantages which __(company name) brings to the marketplace are as follows: (Note: Select only those you can support)

1. With our experienced staff and innovative programs, we provide your child with an unsurpassed learning experience. Your child will discover that learning is fun, while making new friends and building strong relationships with teachers who partner with you in your child's development.
2. We regularly update our curricula to align with national and state accreditation standards and are developing new enrichment program offerings to meet the needs of families.
3. We conduct pre-hire background screenings and drug testing on all individuals before they are hired.
4. We have a low teacher-to-student ratio.
5. We accept all forms of Public Aid Programs
6. We offer a Young Parents Program.
7. We have built a custom designed facility.
8. We offer a curriculum that features innovative learning programs.
9. We developed a specialized training program for the staff so they will be proficient at teaching our specific programs.
10. We teach skills, not in isolation, but together, so that children are able to better assimilate the new task into their skill set.
11. We offer a wide range of business hours to accommodate the needs of working

parents.
12. Children are engaged throughout the day, learning new skills and reinforcing already acquired ones in an environment that promotes the vital development of socialization skills.
13. We offer a unique combination of educational program and child care services.
14. Our educational approach is unique.
15. Our staff has over _____ (#) years of child care expertise and over ___ (#) years of _____ (technology?) savvy.
16. We offer transportation to select _____ Elementary Schools.
17. We offer foreign Language Studies (Spanish and French).
18. Our Creative Curriculum is taught by trained faculty.
19. We create a portfolio-based record of each child's progress and communicate that information to parents on a monthly basis
20. We provide home-cooked lunches and snacks daily.
21. Our facility has well-equipped, center-based classrooms that inspire exploration.
22. The Creative Curriculum promotes the highest level teaching theory for developmentally appropriate practice (DAP) in an early childhood setting.
23. We offer quality education for young children through a creative and nurturing environment.

6.2.1   Branding Strategy

Our branding strategy involves what we do to shape what the customer immediately thinks our business offers and stands for. The purpose of our branding strategy is to reduce customer perceived purchase risk and improve our profit margins by allowing use to charge a premium for our Child Day Care Center products and services.

We will invest $____ every year in maintaining our brand name image, which will differentiate our child day care business from other companies. The amount of money spent on creating and maintaining a brand name will not convey any specific information about our products, but it will convey, indirectly, that we are in this market for the long haul, that we have a reputation to protect, and that we will interact repeatedly with our customers. In this sense, the amount of money spent on maintaining our brand name will signal to consumers that we will provide products and services of consistent quality.

We will invest $____ every year in maintaining our personal brand name image, which will differentiate our child day care business from other companies. The amount of money spent on creating and maintaining a brand name will not convey any specific information about our products, but it will convey, indirectly, that we are in this market for the long haul, that we have a reputation to protect, and that we will interact repeatedly with our customers. In this sense, the amount of money spent on maintaining our brand name will signal to consumers that we will provide products and services of consistent quality.

We will use the following ways to build trust and establish our personal brand:
1. Build a consistently published blog and e-newsletter with informational content.
2. Create comprehensive social media profiles.
3. Contribute articles to related online publications.
4. Earn Career Certifications

Resources:
https://www.abetterlemonadestand.com/branding-guide/

Our key to marketing success will be to effectively manage the building of our brand platform in the marketplace, which will consist of the following elements:
- **Brand Vision** - our envisioned future of the brand is to be the local source for child day care solutions to manage the complications of child care for dual income or single parent families.
- **Brand Attributes** - Partners, problem solvers, responsive, reliable, safe, secure, progressive curriculum, comprehensive, reliable, flexible and easy to work with.
- **Brand Essence** - the shared soul of the brand, the spark of which is present in every experience a customer has with our products, will be "Problem Solving" and "Responsive" This will be the core of our organization, driving the type of people we hire and the type of behavior we expect.
- **Brand Image** - the outside world's overall perception of our organization will be that we are the 'child care' pros who are alleviating the complications of matching the right child day care resources for the right family needs.
- **Brand Promise** - our concise statement of what we do, why we do it, and why customers should do business with us will be, "To realize solid child day care return on investment with the help of our responsive and well-trained staff"

We will use the following methodologies to implement our branding strategy:
1. Develop processes, systems and quality assurance procedures to assure the consistent adherence to our quality standards and mission statement objectives.
2. Develop business processes to consistently deliver upon our value proposition.
3. Develop training programs to assure the consistent professionalism and responsiveness of our employees.
4. Develop marketing communications with consistent, reinforcing message content.
5. Incorporate testimonials into our marketing materials that support our promises.
6. Develop marketing communications with a consistent presentation style. (Logo design, company colors, slogan, labels, packaging, stationery, etc.)
7. Exceed our brand promises to achieve consistent customer loyalty.
8. Use surveys, focus groups and interviews to consistently monitor what our brand means to our customers.
9. Consistently match our brand values or performance benchmarks to our customer requirements.
10. Focus on the maintenance of a consistent number of key brand values that are tied to our company strengths.
11. Continuously research industry trends in our markets to stay relevant to customer needs and wants.

12. Attach a logo-imprinted product label and business card to all products, marketing communications and invoices.
13. Develop a memorable and meaningful tagline that captures the essence of our brand.
14. Prepare a one page company overview and make it a key component of our sales presentation folder.
15. Hire and train employees to put the interests of customers first.
16. Develop a professional website that is updated with fresh content on a regular basis.
17. Use our blog to circulate content that establishes our niche expertise and opens a two-way dialogue with our customers.
18. Attractive and tasteful uniforms will also help our staff's morale. The branding will become complete with the addition of our corporate logo, or other trim or accessories which echo the style and theme of our establishment.
19. Create an effective slogan with the following attributes:
    a. Appeals to customers' emotions.
    b. Shows off how our service benefits customers by highlighting our customer service or care.
    c. Has 8 words or less and is memorable
    d. Can be grasped quickly by our audience.
    e. Reflects our business' personality and character.
    f. Shows sign of originality.
20. Create a Proof Book that contains before and after photos, testimonial letters, our mission statement , copies of industry certifications and our code of ethics.
21. Make effective use of trade show exhibitions and email newsletters to help brand our image.

Resources:
https://blog.crowdspring.com/2010/07/tagline-slogan-marketing/

The communications strategy we will use to build our brand platform will include the following items:

Website - featuring curriculum information, research, testimonials, cost benefit analysis, frequently asked questions, and policy information. This website will be used as a tool for both our caregivers, sales team and our customers.

Presentations, brochures and mailers geared to the consumer, explaining the benefits of our learning programs as part of a comprehensive child development plan.

Presentations and brochures geared to the family decision maker explaining the benefits of our child development programs in terms of positive child outcomes, reduced cost from complications, and reduced risk of negative survey results.

A presentation and recruiting brochure geared to prospective sales people that emphasizes the benefits of joining our organization.

Training materials that help every employee deliver our brand message in a consistent manner.

Resource: http://marketingangels.com.au/kidskorner/

6.2.2 Brand Positioning Statement

We will use the following brand positioning statement to summarize what our brand means to our targeted market:
To _____ (target market) _____ (company name) is the brand of _____ (product/service frame of reference) that enables the customer to _____ (primary performance benefit) because ____ (company name) _____ (products/services) _____ (are made with/offer/provide) the best _____ (key attributes)

6.3 Business SWOT Analysis

Definition: SWOT Analysis is a powerful technique for understanding your Strengths and Weaknesses, and for looking at the Opportunities and Threats faced.

Strategy: We will use this SWOT Analysis to uncover exploitable opportunities and carve a sustainable niche in our market. And by understanding the weaknesses of our business, we can manage and eliminate threats that would otherwise catch us by surprise. By using the SWOT framework, we will be able to craft a strategy that distinguishes our business from our competitors, so that we can compete successfully in the market.

Strengths (select)
What day care products and services are we best at providing?
What unique resources can we draw upon?
1. Experienced management team from the _____ (?) industry.
2. Strong networking relationships with many different organizations.
3. Excellent sales staff who are experienced, highly trained and very customer attentive.
4. Wide diversity of product/service bundled offerings.
5. High customer loyalty.
6. Remarkable introduction of creativity into the learning process.
7. Our staff is well trained and educated about child education, social development and toddler psychology.
8. We are a licensed daycare provider monitored by the government.
9. We provide an environment that is consistently clean and well ventilated.
10. _____

Weaknesses
In what areas could we improve?
Where do we have fewer resources than others?
1. New comer to the area.
2. Lack of marketing experience.

3. The struggle to build brand equity.
4. A limited marketing budget to develop brand awareness.
5. Finding dependable and people oriented staff.
6. Staff turnover is high.
7. Our hours are less flexible than other types of daycare.
8. Children are often exposed to more illness.
9. Our care is less individualized because there is a higher staff/child ratio.
10. Management expertise gaps.
11. Inadequate monitoring of competitor strategies and responses.
12. _____

Opportunities
What opportunities are there for new and/or improved services?
What trends could we take advantage of?
1. Could take market share away from existing competitors.
2. Greater need for mobile home services by time starved dual income families.
3. Growing market with a significant percentage of the target market still not aware that _____ (company name) exists.
4. The ability to develop many long-term customer relationships.
5. Expanding the range of product/service packaged offerings.
6. Greater use of direct advertising to promote our services.
7. Establish referral relationships with local businesses serving the same target market segment.
8. Networking with non-profit organizations.
9. Development of after school enrichment programs.
10. As the number of children served grows, fixed costs are spread over a larger customer base.
11. The use of lower penetration registration fees to jumpstart enrollment.
12. _____

Threats
What trends or competitor actions could hurt us?
What threats do our weaknesses expose us to?
1. Another child daycare business could move into this area.
2. Further declines in the economic forecast.
3. Inflation affecting operations for gas, labor, and other operating costs.
4. Keeping trained efficient staff and key personnel from moving on or starting their own business venture.
5. Imitation competition from similar indirect service providers.
6. Price differentiation is a significant competition factor.
7. Unfounded public scares regarding childcare
8. Must prevent the spreading of illnesses or epidemics among the children.
9. _____

Recap:

We will use the following strengths to capitalize on recognized opportunities:
1. _____
2. _____

We will take the following actions to turn our weaknesses into strengths and prepare to defend against known threats.
1. _____
2. _____

6.4.0 Marketing Strategy

Marketing in the child care industry primarily depends on reputation and referral. We will seek to build our reputation by having an involved commitment to those we serve. The company will rely heavily on word-of-mouth referrals for business.

Our marketing strategy will also revolve around two different types of media, sales brochures and a website. These two tools will be used to make customers aware of our broad range of service offerings. One focus of our marketing strategy will be to drive customers to our website for information about our programs and online registration.

A combination of local media and event marketing will be utilized. _____ (company name) will create an identity oriented marketing strategy with executions particularly in the local media. Our marketing strategy will utilize prime time radio spots, print ads, press releases, yellow page ads, flyers, facility tours and newsletter distribution. We will make effective use of direct response advertising, and include coupons in all print ads. We will also place small display ads in local free parenting magazines.

We will use comment cards, newsletter sign-up forms and surveys to collect customer email addresses and feed our client relationship management (CRM) software system. This system will automatically send out, on a predetermined schedule, follow-up materials, such as article reprints, seminar invitations, email messages, surveys and e-newsletters. We will offset some of our advertising costs by asking our suppliers and other local merchants to place ads in our newsletter.

Current Situation

We will study the current marketing situation on a weekly basis to analyze trends and identify sources of business growth. As onsite owners, we will be on hand daily to insure customer service. Our services include products of the highest quality and a prompt response to feedback from customers. Our extensive and highly detailed financial statements, produced monthly, will enable us to stay competitive and exploit presented opportunities.

Marketing Budget

Our marketing budget will be a flexible $_____ per quarter. The marketing budget can be allocated in any way that best suits the time of year.

Marketing budget per quarter:

Newspaper Ads	$_____	Radio advertisement	$_____
Web Page	$_____	Customer contest	$_____
Direct Mail	$_____	Sales Brochure	$_____
Trade Shows	$_____	Seminars	$_____
Superpages	$_____	Google Adwords	$_____
Giveaways	$_____	Vehicle Signs	$_____
Business Cards	$_____	Flyers	$_____
Labels/Stickers	$_____	Videos/DVDs	$_____
Samples	$_____	Newsletter	$_____
Bandit Signs	$_____	Email Campaigns	$_____
Sales Reps Comm.	$_____	Restaurant Placemats	$_____
Press Releases	$_____	Billboards	$_____
Movie Theater Ads	$_____	Fund Raisers	$_____
Infomercials	$_____	Speeches	$_____
Postcards	$_____	Proof Books	$_____
Social Networking	$_____	Charitable Donations	$_____
Other	$_____		

Total: $_____

Our objective in setting a marketing budget has been to keep it between ____ (3?) and ____ (5?) percent of our estimated annual gross sales.

The following represents a recap of our marketing programs:
- Promotion expenses (free gifts for coming in the shop)
- Printed materials (sales brochures, pamphlets, fliers, postcards)
- Media advertisements (radio, newspapers, outdoor billboards)
- Facility Tours
- Donations (door prizes, charities)
- Referral Program Brochure
- Website Development

Marketing Mix

Clients will primarily come from word-of-mouth and our referral program. The overall market approach involves creating brand awareness through targeted advertising, public relations, co-marketing efforts with select alliance partners, direct mail, email campaigns (with constant contact.com), seminars and a website.

Advertising

_____ (company name) will rely on the recommendations of satisfied customers and preferred vendors as a means of attracting customers away from the competition. Past experience has also proven that many customers come on the recommendations of others. Although word-of-mouth is an effective way of increasing market share, it is also extremely slow. To accelerate the process of expanding the customer base, the business will maintain an advertising budget of $_____ for the first year. The bulk of this budget will be spent on listings in the _____ (city) yellow pages, complimentary discount coupons, and direct mailings to ad respondents.

Video Marketing

We will link to our website a series of YouTube.com based video clips that talk about our range of Child Day Care Center products and services, and demonstrate our expertise with certain brands and age groups. We will create business marketing videos that are both entertaining and informational, and improve our search engine rankings.

The video will include:
- **Client testimonials** - We will let our best customers become our instant sales force because people will believe what others say about us more readily than what we say about ourselves.
- **Product Demonstrations** - We will train and pre-sell our potential clients on our most popular products and services by talking about and showing them. Often, our potential clients don't know the full range and depth of our products and services because we haven't taken the adequate time to explain them.
- **Include Business Website Address**
- **Video tour of the facility.**
- **Post commercial created for DVD distribution.**
- **Owner Interview:** Discussion of company mission statement, value proposition and competitive advantages.
- **Frequently Asked Questions** - We will answer questions that we often get, and anticipate objections we might get and give great reasons to convince potential clients that we are the best day care center in the area.
- **Include a Call to Action** - We have the experience and the know-how to supply your next family or business event. So call us, right now, and let's get started.
- **Seminar** - Include a portion of a seminar on how to make learning a fun experience.
- **Comment on industry trends and product news** - We will appear more in-tune and knowledgeable in our market if we can talk about what's happening in our industry and marketplace.

Resources:
www.businessvideomarketing.tv
www.hotpluto.com
www.hubspot.com/video-marketing-kit
www.youtube.com/user/mybusinessstory
https://www.youtube.com/watch?v=A_oI_QAV-Ig
Analytics Report
http://support.google.com/youtube/bin/static.py?hl=en&topic=1728599&guide=1
    714169&page=guide.cs
Note: Refer to Video Marketing Tips in rear marketing worksheets section.
Example:
http://www.youtube.com/watch?v=HZVUV7VHh5c

Top 10 places where we will share our videos online:

YouTube www.youtube.com
This very popular website allows you to log-in and leave comments and ratings on the videos. You can also save your favorite videos and allows you to tag posted videos. This makes it easier for your videos to come up in search engines.

Google Video http://video.google.com/
A video hosting site. Google Video is not just focused on sharing videos online, but this is also a market place where you can buy the videos you find on this site using Google search engine.

Yahoo! Video http://video.yahoo.com/
Uploading and sharing videos is possible with Yahoo Video!. You can find several types of videos on their site and you can also post comments and ratings for the videos.

Revver http://www.revver.com/
This website lets you earn money through ads on your videos and you will have a 50/50 profit split with the website. Another great deal with Revver is that your fans who posted your videos on their site can also earn money.

Blip.tv http://blip.tv/
Allows viewers to stream and download the videos posted on their website. You can also use Creative Commons licenses on your videos posted on the website. This allows you to decide if your videos should be attributed, restricted for commercial use and be used under specific terms.

Vimeo http://www.vimeo.com/
This website is family safe and focuses on sharing private videos. The interface of the website is similar to some social networking sites that allow you to customize your profile page with photos from Flickr and embeddable player. This site allows users to socialize through their videos.

Metacafe http://www.metacafe.com/
This video sharing site is community based. You can upload short-form videos and share it to the other users of the website. Metacafe has its own system called VideoRank that ranks videos according to the viewer reactions and features the most popular among the viewers.

ClipShack http://www.clipshack.com/
Like most video sharing websites you can post comments on the videos and even tag some as your favorite. You can also share the videos on other websites through the html code from ClipShack and even sending it through your email.

Veoh http://www.veoh.com/
You can rent or sell your videos and keep the 70% of the sales price. You can upload a range of different video formats on Veoh and there is no limit on the size and length of the file. However when your video is over 45 minutes it has to be downloaded before the viewer can watch it.

Jumpcut http://download.cnet.com/JumpCut/3000-18515_4-10546353.html
Jumpcut allows its users to upload videos using their mobile phones. You will have to attach the video captured from your mobile phone to an email. It has its own movie making wizard that helps you familiarize with the interface of the site.

New Homeowners / Movers

We will reach out to new movers in our immediate neighborhood. Marketing to new movers will help bring in more long-term customers. And, because new movers are five times more likely to become loyal, this marketing program, will generate new, fresh customers who are likely to turn in to the regular customers. The value of a new loyal customer will be significant, as a new loyal customer who comes in ___ (#) times a month can be worth up to $_____ a year for standard services. Furthermore, many studies suggest that new movers typically stay in their new homes for an average of 5.6 years. We will also participate in local Welcome Wagon activities for new residents, and assemble a mailing list to distribute sales literature from county courthouse records and Realtor supplied information. We will use a postcard mailing to promote a special get-acquainted offer to new residents.

We will adhere the following routine when marketing to new local homeowners:
1. Send out a friendly welcome letter / flyer / brochure welcoming each new family to the community along with information on our pest control services.
2. Include a gift certificate or a new client discount coupon / certificate to entice the new family to try our service, risk free with no obligation.
3. Send out a new client discount or offer an initial free evaluation.
4. Send out a postcard with a discount or coupon.

Resources:
Welcome Wagon   www.WelcomeWagon.com
Welcome Mat Services   www.WelcomeMatServices.com
Welcomemat Services uses specialized, patent-pending technology to store and log customer demographics for use by the local companies it supports.

Networking
Networking will be a key to success because referrals and alliances formed can help to improve our community image and keep our business growing. We will strive to build long-term mutually beneficial relationships with our networking contacts and join the following types of organizations:
1. We will form a LeTip Chapter to exchange business leads.
2. We will join the local BNI.com referral exchange group.
3. We will join the Chamber of Commerce to further corporate relationships.
4. We will join the Rotary Club, Kiwanis Club, Church Groups, etc.
5. We will become an active member of the National Association for the Education of Young Children, The Child Care Action Campaign, and The National Association for Family Child Care (NAFCC).
6. We will participate in child care conventions and seminars. (ChildcareExchange.com provides a national calendar of child care conferences and conventions for child care professionals.)

We will use our metropolitan _____ (city) Chamber of Commerce to target prospective business contacts. We will mail letters to each prospect describing our daycare services. We will follow-up with phone calls.

We will also network with other child daycare providers. We will introduce ourselves to other providers in our area and use each other for referrals. We will keep in contact with each other. If one provider is full and receives a phone call, they will be able to refer the family to a provider with an opening and vice-versa.

Newsletter

We will develop a monthly e-newsletter to stay in touch with our clients and use it to market to local businesses. We will include the following types of information:
1. Success case studies
2. New Service Introductions/ Staff Changes
3. Featured employee/client of the month.
4. Child care industry trends.
5. Client endorsements/testimonials.
6. Classified ads from local sponsors and suppliers.
7. Nutrition / recipes.
8. Announcements / Upcoming events.

Resources: Microsoft Publisher   AWeber

We will adhere to the following newsletter writing guidelines:
1. We will provide content that is of real value to our subscribers.
2. We will provide solutions to our subscriber's problems or parent questions.
3. We will communicate regularly on a weekly basis.
4. We will create HTML Messages look professional and allow us to track how many people click on our links and/or open our emails.
5. We will not pitch our business opportunity in our Ezine very often.
6. We will focus our marketing dollars on building our Ezine subscriber list.
7. We will focus on relationship building and not the conveying of a sales message.
8. We will vary our message format with videos, articles, checklists, quotes, pictures and charts.
9. We will recommend occasionally affiliate products in some of our messages to help cover our marketing costs.
10. We will consistently follow the above steps to build a database of qualified prospects.

Examples:
http://www.childcarelounge.com/director-articles/newsletter-samples.php
http://www.kidscountrychildcare.com/Monthly_Newsletter
Resources:
http://www.childcarelounge.com/director-articles/write-newsletter.php

Resources:
www.constantcontact.com
www.mailchimp.com
http://lmssuccess.com/10-reasons-online-business-send-regular-newsletter-customers/
www.smallbusinessmiracles.com/how/newsletters/
www.fuelingnewbusiness.com/2010/06/01/combine-email-marketing-and-social-media-for-ad-agency-new-business/

Vehicle Signs

We will place magnetic and vinyl signs on our passenger vans and include our company name, phone number, company slogan and website address, if possible. We will create a cost-effective moving billboard with high-quality, high-resolution vehicle wraps. We will wrap a portion of the vehicle or van to deliver excellent marketing exposure.

Resource:
http://www.fastsigns.com/

Design Tips:
1. Avoid mixing letter styles and too many different letter sizes.
2. Use the easiest to recognize form of your logo.
3. The standard background is white.
4. Do not use a background color that is the same as or close to your vehicle color.
5. Choose colors that complement your logo colors.
6. Avoid the use too many colors.
7. Use dark letter colors on a light background or the reverse.
8. Use easy to read block letters in caps and lower case.
9. Limit content to your business name, slogan, logo, phone number and website-address.
10. Include your license number if required by law.
11. Magnetic signs are ideal for door panels (material comes on 24" wide rolls).
12. Graphic vehicle window wraps allow the driver to still see out.
13. Keep your message short so people driving by can read it at a glance.
14. Do not use all capital letters.
15. Be sure to include your business name, phone number, slogan and web address.

Vehicle Wraps

Vehicle wrapping will be one of our preferred marketing methods. According to company research, wrapped vehicles have more impact than billboards, create a positive image for the company and prompt the public to remember the words and images featured in the company's branding. Vehicle wrapping is also an inexpensive marketing strategy. A typical truck wrap costs about $2,500, and is a one-time payment for an ad that spans the life of a truck's lease.

DVD Presentation

We plan to create a DVD that will provide a tour of our facility and present testimonials from some our satisfied clients. We will include this DVD in our sales presentation folder and direct mail package.

Advertising Wearables

We will give all preferred club members an eye-catching T-shirt or sweatshirt with our company name and logo printed across the garment to wear about town. We will also give them away as a thank you for customer referral activities. We will also ask all employees to wear our logo-imprinted shirts in the play area and at sponsored events. We will also sell the garments in our facility at cost.

Charitable Donations

We will use these coupon donation opportunities to demonstrate our new services, meet and greet many new potential clients and distribute lots of sales brochures and business cards to event sponsors and attendees.

Sales Promotion/Information Package/Kit

Our promotional sales presentation kit will contain the following items:

- Owner/Key Staff Resumes
- Hours Sheet
- DVD Presentation
- FAQs
- Press Release Clippings
- Testimonials
- Policy Statement
- Child Care Agreement
- Referral Program Form
- Sample Child Progress Report Form
- Administrative Procedures
- Rate Sheet/Payment Policies
- Child Care Article Reprints
- Sales Brochure
- Business Card
- Community Service Awards
- Substitute Care Statement
- Sample Program/Daily Schedule
- Medical/Emergency Form
- Client Satisfaction Survey
- Authorization to Release Info

Stage Events

We will stage events to become known in our community. This is essential to attracting referrals. We will schedule regular events, such as seminar talks, catered open house events, BBQ cook-offs, art days, carnivals, and fundraisers. These events will provide the public a low-pressure way to get to know our center while spending quality time with their family. We will make sure we have plenty of business cards, flyers and registration forms available should parents express interest. We will ask that all guests sign in with their name and email address so we can follow up after the event. We will use event registration forms, our website and an event sign-in sheet to collect the names and email addresses of all attendees. This database will be used to feed our automatic customer relationship follow-up program and newsletter service.

Resource:
www.eventbrite.com

Events will help our day care center to connect with our clientele by showing them what we are all about and engaging parents and children in fun family activities. Open houses will be good marketing tools. We will also host an art day, kids vs. parents activity day or other special family bonding events.

We will open up the center in the evenings for a discounted "family movie night". We will also offer arts and crafts classes on the weekends, and host a lecture series for parents on topics that are of interest to them, and provide childcare services while the parents are being educated.

We will make sure we have take-away information on-hand, demonstrations or a way to schedule private appointments and/or collect name, address and demographic information so we can capture leads.

We will use the following types of events as marketing opportunities and issue press releases to improve exposure:
- Birthday Parties
- Christmas Parade
- Christmas Show
- Graduation Program
- Holiday Specials
- Creating Special Days in our center for family members: examples (Cousin's Day, Auntie's Day, Grand Parent's Day) and invite them out to attend and get a small refreshment while visiting with the children.

Sales Brochures

Our brochure will provide prospects with specific unique benefits that speak to how we will transform the lives of children and families. Our sales brochure will include the following contents and become a key part of our direct mail package:

- Contact Information
- Customer Testimonials/Reviews
- Competitive Advantages
- Trial Coupon
- Call to Action
- Company Description
- List of Services/Benefits
- Owner Resume
- Vendor List

We will use the following incentives to get parents to "Come visit us" as our call to action:
1. Free gift valued at $_____ just for taking a tour of our daycare.
2. Visit us within 7 days of receiving this brochure and save $1_____ additional on enrollment fees.
3. Free child Pre-K assessment valued at $_____ just for visiting us.
4. Free Trial Day of care if registered before _____ (date)
5. Free 2-hour session of learning if you bring a friend on the tour.

Resource: www.childcare-marketing.com/child-care-marketing/child-care-brochures/

Sales Brochure Design
1. Speak in Terms of Our Prospects Wants and Interests.
2. Focus on all the Benefits, not Just Features.
3. Put the company logo and Unique Selling Proposition together to reinforce the fact that your company is different and better than the competition.
4. Include a special offer, such as a discount, a free report, a sample, or a free trial to increase the chances that the brochure will generate sales.

We will incorporate the following Brochure Design Guidelines:
1. Design the brochure to achieve a focused set of objectives (marketing of programs) with a target market segment (residential vs. commercial).
2. Tie the brochure design to our other marketing materials with colors, logo, fonts and formatting.
3. List capabilities and how they benefit clients.
4. Demonstrate what we do and how we do it differently.
5. Define the value proposition of our engineering installing services
6. Use a design template that reflects your market positioning strategy.
7. Identify your key message (unique selling proposition)
8. List our competitive advantages.
9. Express our understanding of client needs and wants.
10. Use easy to read (scan) headlines, subheadings, bullet points, pictures, etc.
11. Use a logo to create a visual branded identity.
12. The most common and accepted format for a brochure is a folded A3 (= 2 x A4), which gives 4 pages of information.
13. Use a quality of paper that reflects the image we want to project.
14. Consistently stick to the colors of our corporate style.
15. Consider that colors have associations, such as green colors are associated with the environment and enhance an environmental image.
16. Illustrations will be appropriate and of top quality and directly visualize the product assortment, product application and production facility.
17. The front page will contain the company name, logo, the main application of your product or service and positioning message or Unique Selling Proposition.
18. The back page will be used for testimonials or references, and contact details.

Resource:
http://graphicdesign.stocklayouts.com/2010/05/11/give-new-life-baby-child-day-care-brochure-newsletter-designs/

Sales Presentation Folder Contents

1.	Resumes	2.	Facility Photos
3.	Contract/Application	4.	Frequently Asked Questions
5.	Sales Brochure	6.	Business Cards
7.	Testimonials/References	8.	Program Descriptions
9.	Informative Articles	10.	Referral Program
11.	Company Overview	12.	Operating Policies
13.	Article Reprints	14.	Press Releases

Employee Personal Marketing

We will develop a training program and business cards to help employees to market themselves as sales agents and get new people interested in our _____ business. Employee personal marketing is the ability to showcase employee talents and present them in a fashion that our customers and prospects will recognize them. We will need to be able to back up and actually do what we say we can do. This type of marketing will also be very important for the customers we already have. We will develop an employee certification program to make sure our customers are aware of all the ways our products and services can benefit them, and that every customer gets served properly.

Coupons

We will use coupons with limited time expirations to get prospects to try our service programs. We will also accept the coupons of our competitors to help establish new client relationships. We will run ads directing people to our Web site for a $___ coupon certificate. This will help to draw in new clients and collect e-mail addresses for the distribution of a monthly newsletter. We will use "dollars off" and not "discount" percentages, as customers are not impressed with "10 to 20 percent off" coupons today. They are very impressed with "$10 off a $50 value" or one free week or the waiving of the registration fee. Research indicates that we can use our coupons to spark online searches of our website and drive sales. This will help to draw in new clients and collect e-mail addresses for the distribution of a monthly newsletter. We will include a coupon with each sale, or send them by mail to our mailing list.

We will use coupons selectively to accomplish the following:
1. To introduce a new product or service.
2. To attract loyal customers away from the competition
3. To prevent customer defection to a new competitor.
4. To help celebrate a special event.

Examples:
https://www.retailmenot.com/coupons/childcare
https://www.valpak.com/coupons/printable/a-b-child-care-learning-center/104377

Types of Coupons:
1. Courtesy Coupons   Rewards for repeat business
2. Cross-Marketing Coupons Incentive to try other products/services.
3. Companion Coupon   Bring a friend incentive.

Websites like Groupon.com, LivingSocial, Eversave, and BuyWithMe sell discount vouchers for services ranging from custom _____ to ____ consultations. Best known is Chicago-based Groupon. To consumers, discount vouchers promise substantial savings — often 50% or more. To merchants, discount vouchers offer possible opportunities for price discrimination, exposure to new customers, online marketing, and "buzz." Vouchers are more likely to be profitable for merchants with low marginal costs, who can better accommodate a large discount and for patient merchants, who place higher value on consumers' possible future return visits.

Examples:
https://www.groupon.com/local/child-care
https://www.groupon.com/deals/mommy-time-montessori-1

Cross-Promotions
We will develop and maintain partnerships with local businesses that cater to the needs of

children, such as clothing stores, fun centers, toy stores, dentists. and pediatricians, and conduct cross-promotional marketing campaigns.

Premium Giveaways
We will distribute logo-imprinted promotional products at events, also known as giveaway premiums, to foster top-of-mind awareness (www.promoideas.org). These items include business cards with magnetic backs, frisbees with daycare name and contact phone number and calendars that feature important date reminders. We will distribute them in public places, such as parks, where they will be found by families with young children.

During a parent's initial call to our center, we will find out the names and ages of their children. This will enable us to personalize the tour accordingly. It will also let us select an age-appropriate gift to send the parent home with for the child(ren). Examples might include a onesie with our school logo on it, a small toy or book with the child's name on a write-in sticker and our contact label or stamp inside the book, etc. These touches will be inexpensive but invaluable when it comes to making prospective families feel appreciated and welcome.
Source:
http://www.childcareofchoice.com/8-secrets-to-successful-child-care-tours/

Book Donations
We will donate books to businesses with a waiting room such as doctor's offices, dentist's office or hair salons. We will place a large sticker on the inside front cover that says "This book donated by..." with the name, address and phone number of our daycare.

Local Newspaper Ads
We will use these ads to announce the opening of our child day care center and get our name established. We will adhere to the rule that frequency and consistency of message are essential. We will include a list of our top brand names and specialty services. We will include a coupon to track the response in zoned editions of 'Shopper' Papers, Theater Bills, and Community Newsletters and Newspapers. We will use the ad to announce any weekly or monthly price specials.

Our newspaper ads will utilize the following design tips:
1. We will start by getting a media kit from the publisher to analyze their demographic information as well as their reach and distribution.
2. Don't let the newspaper people have total control of our ad design, as we know how we want our company portrayed to the market.
3. Make sure to have 1st class graphics since this will be the only visual distinction we can provide the reader about our business.
4. Buy the biggest ad we can afford, with full-page ads being the best.
5. Go with color if affordable, because consumers pick color ads over black 82% of the time.
6. Ask the paper if they have specific days that more of our type of buyer reads their

paper.
7. If we have a hit ad on our hands, we will make it into a circular or door-hanger to extend the life of the offer.
8. Don't change an ad because we are getting tired of looking at it.
9. We will start our headline by telling our story to pull the reader into the ad.
10. We will use "Act Now" to convey a sense of urgency to the reader.
11. We will use our headline to tell the reader what to do.
12. The headline is a great place to announce a free offer.
13. We will write our headline as if we were speaking to one person, and make it personal.
14. We will use our headline to either relay a benefit or intrigue the reader into wanting more information.
15. Use coupons giving a dollar amount off, not a percentage, as people hate doing the math.

Local Publications

We will place low-cost classified ads in neighborhood publications to advertise our day care services. We will also submit public relations and informative articles to improve our visibility and establish our expertise and trustworthiness. These publications include the following:
1. Neighborhood Newsletters and Church Bulletins
2. Local Restaurant Association Newsletter
3. Local Chamber of Commerce Newsletter
4. Realtor Magazines
5. Homeowner Association Newsletters

Resources:
Hometown News   www.hometownnews.com
Pennysaver   www.pennysaverusa.com
Examples:
www.pennysaverusa.com/classifieds/services/personal-services/child-care-
         services/usa/california/los-angeles/glendale/91201/child-daycare-34410848.html

Publication Type	Ad Size	Timing	Circulation	Section	Fee

Magazine Ads

We plan on purchasing the names of local subscribers to national parenting magazines and make a direct mailing. We will use these display ads to get our name in front of our likely prospects and track the return on investment to determine if we should expand or restrict this marketing strategy.

Publication Type	Ad Size	Timing	Circulation	Section	Fee

Business Journal Display Ads
We will consider placing display ads in business journals read by professionals and possibly rent a list of their local subscribers for a planned direct mailing. The mailing will describe our educational programs and teaching method. We will use empirical data to prove how our programs can actually foster child development.

Resource: The Business Journals   http://www.bizjournals.com/
The premier media solutions platform for companies strategically targeting business decision makers. Delivers a total business audience of over 10 million people via their 42 websites, 62 publications and over 700 annual industry leading events. Their media products provide comprehensive coverage of business news from a local, regional and national perspective.

Publication Type	Ad Size	Timing	Circulation	Section	Fee

Doorhangers
Our doorhangers will feature a calendar of Open House Events. The doorhanger will include a list of all our service programs and info about our pick-up and drop-off options. We will also attach our business card to the doorhanger and distribute the doorhangers multiple times to the same subdivision.

Article Submissions
We will pitch articles to consumer magazines, local newspapers, business magazines and internet articles directories to help establish our specialized expertise and improve our visibility. Hyperlinks will be placed within written articles and can be clicked on to take the customer to another webpage within our website or to a totally different website. These clickable links or hyperlinks will be keywords or relevant words that have meaning to our Child Day Care Center. In fact, we will create a position whose primary function is to link our child care services with opportunities to be published in local publications.

Publishing requires an understanding of the following publisher needs:
1. Review of good work.
2. Editor story needs.
3. Article submission process rules
4. Quality photo portfolio
5. Exclusivity requirements.
6. Target market interests

Our Article Submission Package will include the following:
1. Well-written materials
2. Good Drawings
3. High-quality Photographs
4. Well-organized outline.

Examples of General Publishing Opportunities:
1. Document a new solution to old problem
2. Publish a research study
3. Mistake prevention advice
4. Present a different viewpoint

5.	Introduce a local angle on a hot topic.	6.	Reveal a new trend.
7.	Share specialty niche expertise.	8.	Share health benefits

Examples of Specific Article Titles:
1. New Trends in Child Daycare Services.
2. How to Interview Daycare Providers.
3. Understanding Daycare Contracts and Legislation.
4. How to Qualify for Child Care Tax Credits and Subsidies
5. How to Choose Between a Nanny and a Daycare Center
6. How To Investigate Potential Day Care Providers
7. How to Save On Child Care Costs
8. Understanding How Parents Choose a Child Day Care
9. Sixteen Tips to Help Your Child Adjust to Their First Day of Day Care
   Ex: https://www.care.com/c/stories/3433/16-tips-for-the-first-day-of-day-care/

Sample Content
1. **Atmosphere:** Parents would like to see and feel a happy and nurturing environment, that is, happy children, caring and happy staff, friendly environment, and a clean place. Wall decorations, children's artwork posted on the walls, toys, books, freshly painted room colors, and etc. are all factors that can contribute to a positive atmosphere.
2. **Location and convenience:** Parents will select a daycare that is relatively near their residence and/or their place of work. Even parking or ingress / egress access can be a decision factor for most parents.
3. **Value driven:** Depending on the demography, financial constraints play a considerable role in the decision-making process of the parent. A daycare that offers quality at a value-price could be the clinching factor in parents' decision to enroll their child there.
4. **Programming.** Weekly lesson plans, parent involvement activities, programming, and the availability of different kinds of learning materials are critical in establishing a good learning environment for the child. A daycare center that includes enrichment programs such as heritage activities, language lessons or math programs can be a decision factor for some parents.
5. **Facilities:** The equipment available, cleanliness and general appearance of the facilities will differentiate a daycare center from other daycare centers. Examples include playground, play structure, indoor gymnasium, security, air conditioning and etc.
6. **Check licensing, accreditation, staff training:** Whether online or in person, check whether the facility is properly licensed and accredited by local and state authorities.

Write Articles With a Closing Author Resource Box or Byline
1.	Author Name with credential titles.	2.	Explanation of area of expertise.
3.	Mention of a special offer.	4.	A specific call to action
5.	A Call to Action Motivator	6.	All possible contact information

7. Helpful Links   8. Link to Firm Website.

Article Objectives:
   Article Topic   Target Audience   Target Date

_____

Article Tracking Form
Subject Publication   Target   Business   Resources   Target
                      Audience   Development   Needed   Date

_____

Possible Magazines to submit articles include:
1. Parents Magazine   2. Good Housekeeping Magazine
3. Parenting Magazine   4. Parenting Early Years Magazine
5. Parenting School Years   6. Parent and Child Magazine
7. Kiwi Magazine   8. Family Fun Magazine
9. American Baby Magazine   10. Pregnancy and Newborn Magazine

Resources:
Writer's Market   www.writersmarket.com
Directory of Trade Magazines   www.techexpo.com/tech_mag.html

Internet article directories include:
http://ezinearticles.com/   http://www.mommyshelpercommunity.com
http://www.wahm-articles.com   http://www.ladypens.com/
http://www.articlecity.com   http://www.amazines.com
http://www.articledashboard.com   http://www.submityourarticle.com/articles
http://www.webarticles.com   http://www.articlecube.com
http://www.article-buzz.com   http://www.free-articles-zone.com
www.articletogo.com   http://www.content-articles.com
http://article-niche.com   http://superpublisher.com
www.internethomebusinessarticles.com http://www.site-reference.com
http://www.articlenexus.com   www.articlebin.com
http://www.articlefinders.com   www.articlesfactory.com
http://www.articlewarehouse.com   www.buzzle.com
http://www.easyarticles.com   www.isnare.com
http://ideamarketers.com/   //groups.yahoo.com/group/article_announce
http://clearviewpublications.com/   www.ebusiness-articles.com
http://www.goarticles.com/   www.authorconnection.com/
http://www.webmasterslibrary.com/   www.businesstoolchest.com
http://www.connectionteam.com   www.digital-women.com/submitarticle.htm
http://www.MarketingArticleLibrary.com www.searchwarp.com
http://www.dime-co.com   www.articleshaven.com
http://www.allwomencentral.com   www.marketing-seek.com
http://www.reprintarticles.com   www.articles411.com
http://www.articlestreet.com   www.articleshelf.com

http://www.articlepeak.com
http://www.simplysearch4it.com
http://www.mainstreetmom.com
http://www.valuablecontent.com
http://www.article99.com

www.articlesbase.com
www.articlealley.com
www.LinkGeneral.com
www.articleavenue.com
www.virtual-professionals.com

Online Classified Ad Placement Opportunities

The following free classified ad sites, will enable our Child Day Care Center to thoroughly describe the benefits of our using our services:

1. **Craigslist.org**
2. Ebay Classifieds
3. Classifieds.myspace.com
4. KIJIJI.com
5. //Lycos.oodle.com
6. Webclassifieds.us
7. USFreeAds.com
8. www.oodle.com
9. Backpage.com
10. stumblehere.com
11. Classifiedads.com
12. **gumtree.com**
13. Inetgiant.com
14. www.sell.com
15. Freeadvertisingforum.com
16. Classifiedsforfree.com
17. www.olx.com
18. www.isell.com
19. Base.google.com
20. www.epage.com
21. Chooseyouritem.com
22. www.adpost.com
23. Adjingo.com
24. Kugli.com

Example:
www.gumtree.com.au/s-ad/lakelands/childcare-nanny/happy-home-family-daycare/1058663023

Sample Classified Ad:
Looking for a Quality Day Care Center with Reasonable Weekly Rates? We have been serving the _____ area since _____ (year). _____ (company name) is a licensed child care/center in the _____ area. We enroll children starting at 6 months of age. As founder, I have a Master's Degree in Early Childhood Development. We cover multiple subjects which will prepare your children for School. We prepare children for success in kindergarten by providing developmentally appropriate activities such as music lessons three times a week. Children are also given opportunities to play in a safe outdoor activity area. We have a separate quiet sleeping room for kids. We offer healthy, homemade hot meals daily. Visits to the center are welcome. Please call any time to set up an appointment. References from parents can be provided. I am willing to work with the parents when it comes to the price. Please give me a call and set up an appointment where you can see the daycare. I also offer an after-school program for students in the _____ area, as well as a babysitting program. We are located at _____ (address). Visit us at _____ (Website) for our class schedule and parent testimonials. Please feel free to call us at _____ with questions you may have or to schedule a visit. We encourage parents to visit our facility to observe our family daycare and meet our staff; We are offering special this Month!

Licensed Child Daycare Competitive Advantages:
*CPR, First AID, and SIDS Certified

* Non-smoking environment
*Provides healthy food (Meals and snacks)
* Provides educational curriculum
*Age-appropriate activities promote cognitive and social development.

Two-Step Direct Response Classified Advertising
We will use 'two-step direct response advertising' to motivate readers to take a step or action that signals that we have their permission to begin marketing to them in step two. Our objective is to build a trusting relationship with our prospects by offering a free unbiased, educational report in exchange for permission to continue the marketing process. This method of advertising has the following benefits:

1.	Shorter sales cycle.	2.	Eliminates need for cold calling.
3.	Establishes expert reputation.	4.	Better qualifies prospects
5.	Process is very trackable.	6.	Able to run smaller ads.

Sample Two Step Lead Generating Classified Ad:
FREE Report Reveals "The Child Development Benefits of Day Care Centers"
Or….. "How to Evaluate and Compare Day Care Centers".
Call 24 hour recorded message and leave your name and address.
Your report will be sent out immediately.
Note: The respondent has shown they have an interest in our service specialty. We will also include a section in the report on our other services and our complete contact information, along with a time limited discount trial coupon.

Yellow Page Ads
Research indicates that the use of the traditional Yellow Page Book is declining, but that new residents or people who don't have many personal acquaintances will look to the Yellow Pages to establish a list of potential businesses to call upon. Even a small 2" x 2" boxed ad can create awareness and attract the desired target client, above and beyond the ability of a simple listing. We will use the following design concepts:
1. We will use a headline to sell people on what is unique about our day care service.
2. We will include a service guarantee to improve our credibility.
3. We will include a coupon offer and a tracking code to monitor the response rate and decide whether to increase or decrease our ad size in subsequent years.
4. We will choose an ad size equal to that of our competitors, and evaluate the response rate for future insertion commitments.
5. We will include our hours of operation, motto or slogan and logo.
6. We will include our competitive advantages.
7. We will list under the same categories as our competitors.
8. We will use some bold lettering to make our ad standout.
9. We will utilize yellow books that also offer an online dimension.
Resource: www.superpages.com   www.yellowpages.com
Examples: www.yellowpages.com/miami-fl/child-care
Ad Information:
    Book Title: _____   Coverage Area: _____

Yearly Fee: $_____   Ad Size: _____ page
Renewal date: _____   Contact: _____

Cable Television Advertising

Cable television will offer us more ability to target certain market niches or demographics with specialty programming. We will use our marketing research survey to determine which cable TV channels our customers are watching. It is expected that many watch the Home & Garden TV channel, and that people with surplus money watch the Disney Channel and the ABC Family Network. Our plan is to choose the audience we want, and to hit them often enough to entice them to take action. We will also take advantage of the fact that we will be able to pick the specific areas we want our commercial to air. Ad pricing will be dependent upon the number of households the network reaches, the ratings the particular show has earned, contract length and the supply and demand for a particular network.

Resource:
Spot Runner   www.spotrunner.com
Television Advertising   http://televisionadvertising.com/faq.htm

Ad Information:
    Length of ad "spot": ___ seconds   Development costs: $____ (onetime fee)
    Length of campaign: __ (#) mos.   Runs per month: Three times per day
    Cost per month.: $_____   Total campaign cost: $_____.

Radio Advertising

We will use non-event based radio advertising. This style of campaign is best suited for non-retail businesses, such as our child day care center. We will utilize a much smaller schedule of ads on a consistent long-range basis (48 to 52 weeks a year) with the objective of continuously maintaining top-of-mind-awareness. This will mean maintaining a sufficient level of awareness to be either the number one or number two choice when a triggering-event, such as a relocation, moves the consumer into the market for services and forces "a consumer choice" about which day care company in the consumer's perception might help them the most. This consistent approach will utilize only one ad each week day (260 days per year) and allow our company to cost-effectively keep our message in front of consumers once every week day. The ad copy for this non-event campaign, called a positioning message, will not be time-sensitive. It will define and differentiate our business' "unique market position", and will be repeated for a year. Note: On the average, listeners spend over 3.5 hours per day with radio.

Radio will give us the ability to target our audience, based on radio formats, such as news-talk, classic rock and the oldies. Radio will also be a good way to get repetition into our message, as listeners tend to be loyal to stations and parts of the day.

1.   We will use radio advertising to direct prospects to our Web site, advertise a limited time promotion or call for an informational brochure about child care.
2.   We will try to barter our services for radio ad spots.
3.   We will use a limited-time offer to entice first-time customers to use our services.
4.   We will explore the use of on-air community bulletin boards to play our public

announcements about community sponsored events.
5. We will also make the radio station aware of our expertise in the child development field and our availability for interviews.
6. Our choice of stations will be driven by the market research information we collect via our surveys.
7. We will capitalize on the fact that many stations now stream their programming on the internet and reach additional local and even national audiences, and if online listeners like what they hear in our streaming radio spot, they can click over to our website.
8. Our radio ads will use humor, sounds, compelling music or unusual voices to grab attention.
9. Our spots will tell stories or present situations our target audience can relate to.
10. We will make our call to action, a website address or vanity phone number, easy to remember and tie it in with our company name or message.
11. We will approach radio stations about buying their unsold advertising space for deep discounts. (Commonly known at radio stations' as "Run of Station")
On radio, this might mean very early in the morning or late at night. We will talk to our advertising representatives and see what discounts they can offer when one of those empty spaces comes open.

Resources: Radio Advertising Bureau   www.RAB.com
            Radio Locator   www.radio-locator.com
            Radio Directory   www.radiodirectory.com

Ad Information:
Length of ad "spot": ___ seconds   Development costs: $____ (onetime fee)
Length of campaign: __ (#) mos.   Runs per month: Three times per day
Cost per month.: $_____   Total campaign cost: $_____.

Press Release Overview:

We will use market research surveys to determine the media outlets that our demographic customers read and then target them with press releases. We will draft a cover letter for our media kit that explains that we would like to have the newspaper print a story about the start-up of our new local business or a milestone that we have accomplished. And, because news releases may be delivered by feeds or on news services and various websites, we will create links from our news releases to content on our website. These links which will point to more information or a special offer, will drive our clients into the sales process. They will also increase search engine ranking on our site. We will follow-up each faxed package to the media outlet with a phone call to the lifestyle section editor.

Resource:
www.childcareofchoice.com/how-to-write-a-great-press-release-for-your-child-care-center/

Media Kit
We will compile a media kit with the following items:

1. A pitch letter introducing our company and relevant impact newsworthiness for their readership.
2. A press release with helpful newsworthy story facts.
3. Biographical fact sheet or sketches of key personnel.
4. Listing of product and service features and benefits to customers.
5. Photos and digital logo graphics
6. Copies of media coverage already received.
7. Frequently Asked Questions (FAQ)
8. Customer testimonials
9. Sales brochure
10. Media contact information
11. URL links to these online documents instead of email attachments.
12. Our blog URL address.

Public Relations Opportunities
We will use well-written press releases to not only catch a reader's attention, but also to clearly and concisely communicate our business' mission, goals and capabilities.
The following represents a partial list of some of the reasons we will issue a free press release on a regular basis:
1. Announce Grand Opening Event and the availability of services.
2. Planned Open House Event
3. Addition of new product releases or service line.
4. Support for a Non-profit Cause or other local event.
5. Presentation of a free maintenance seminar or workshop.
6. Report Survey Results
7. Publication of an article on auto parts industry trends.
8. Addition of a new staff member.
9. Notable Successes/Case Studies
10. Other Milestone Accomplishments.

Examples:
http://www.cclc.com/About-Us/Press-Releases/
http://www.rainbowccc.com/blog/?cat=6
http://www.drdaycare.com/press-releases/

Green Public Relations
We will create a positive image for our _____ by creating newsworthy stories that tout our green qualities using the following tactics:
1. We will host an environmental film screening or a tasting featuring organic and locally-grown foods. We will also hold a fundraiser or a community gathering that focuses on the environment.
2. We will ask other business to join in initiating a recycling or composting program.
   We will also partner with another eco-friendly business by offering our customers coupons for that business and asking them to do the same for our _____.
3. We will help with community programs, such as the hosting of school field trips or environmental educational classes for kids. This kind of community

involvement will not only encourage environmentally responsible behavior in the next generation, but it will also get the community interested in our business as an established green leader in the community.

We will use the following techniques to get our press releases into print:
1. Find the right contact editor at a publication, that is, the editor who specializes in family, child development and lifestyle issues.
2. Understand the target publication's format, flavor and style and learn to think like its readers to better tailor our pitch.
3. Ask up front if the journalist is on deadline.
4. Request a copy of the editorial calendar--a listing of targeted articles or subjects broken down by month or issue date, to determine the issue best suited for the content of our news release or article.
5. Make certain the press release appeals to a large audience by reading a couple of back issues of the publication we are targeting to familiarize ourselves with its various sections and departments.
6. Customize the PR story to meet the magazine's particular style.
7. Avoid creating releases that look like advertising or self-promotion.
8. Make certain the release contains all the pertinent and accurate information the journalist will need to write the article and accurately answer the questions "who, what, when, why and where".
9. Include a contact name and telephone number for the reporter to call for more information.

PR Distribution Checklist
We will send copies of our press releases to the following entities:
1. Send it to clients to show accomplishments.
2. Send to prospects to help prospects better know who you are and what you do.
3. Send it to vendors to strengthen the relationship and to influence referrals.
4. Send it to strategic partners to strengthen and enhance the commitment and support to our firm.
5. Send it to employees to keep them in the loop.
6. Send it to Employees' contacts to increase the firm's visibility exponentially.
7. Send it to elected officials who often provide direction for their constituents.
8. Send it to trade associations for maximum exposure.
9. Put copies in the lobby and waiting areas.
10. Put it on our Web site, to enable visitors to find out who we are and what our firm is doing, with the appropriate links to more detailed information.
11. Register the Web page with search engines to increase search engine optimization.
12. Put it in our press kit to provide members of the media background information about our firm.
13. Include it in our newsletter to enable easy access to details about company activities.
14. Include it in our brochure to provide information that compels the reader to contact our firm when in need of legal counsel.

15. Hand it out at trade shows and job fairs to share news with attendees and establish credibility.

Media List
    Journalist   Interests   Organization   Contact Info

Distribution: www.1888PressRelease.com   www.ecomwire.com
    www.prweb.com   www.WiredPRnews.com
    www.PR.com   www.eReleases.com
    www.24-7PressRelease.com   www.NewsWireToday.com
    www.PRnewswire.com   www.onlinePRnews.com
    www.PRLog.org   **www.onlinepressreleases.com**
    www.businesswire.com   www.marketwire.com
    www.primezone.com   www.primewswire.com
    www.xpresspress.com/   www.ereleases.com/index.html
    www.digitaljournal.com   www.Mediapost.com
    www.falkowinc.com/inc/proactive_report.html

Journalist Lists: www.mastheads.org   www.easymedialist.com
    www.helpareporter.com

Media Directories
    Bacon's – www.bacons.com/   AScribe – www.ascribe.org/
    Newspapers – www.newspapers.com/ Gebbie Press – www.gebbieinc.com/

Support Services
    PR Web - http://www.prweb.com
    Yahoo News – http://news.yahoo.com/
    Google News – http://news.google.com/

Direct Mail/Postcards

1. We will use personalized postcards to stay-in-touch with prior customers.
2. Postcards will offer cheaper mailing rates, staying power and attention grabbing graphics, but require repetition, like most other advertising methods.
3. We will develop an in-house list of potential clients for routine communications from open house events, seminar registrations, direct response ads, etc.
4. We will use postcards to encourage users to visit our website, and take advantage of a special offer.
5. We will grab attention and communicate a single-focus message in just a few words.
6. The visual elements of our postcard (color, picture, symbol) will be strong to help get attention and be directly supportive of the message.
7. We will facilitate a call to immediate action by prominently displaying our phone number and website address.
8. We will include a clear deadline, expiration date, limited quantity, or consequence of inaction that is connected to the offer to communicate immediacy

and increase response.
Resource:
www.Postcardmania.com

Flyers
1. We will seek permission to post flyers describing the benefits of our child day care center in the following places frequented by parents:
   - Local Retail businesses
   - Clinic waiting rooms
   - Laundromats
   - Lamaze classes
   - Public and private schools
   - Public libraries
   - Pediatrician offices
   - Corporate training centers.
   - Supermarkets and Pharmacies
   - Condo Associations
   - Community centers
   - Toy and Party Supply Stores
   - Pediatric hospitals
   - Shopping centers
   - Grocery stores
   - Newspaper Offices
   - Centers of worship
   - Colleges and universities
   - Parent Teacher Associations
   - Baby Boutiques

2. We will also insert flyers into our direct mailings.
3. We will use our flyers as part of a handout package at open house events.
4. The flyers will feature a one week free coupon.
5. We will circulate flyers to the following local agencies and organizations:
   - YWCA
   - Churches and Synagogues
   - Nat'l Council of Jewish Women
   - Junior League
   - YMCA
   - Parent Support Groups
   - National Org. for Women
   - United Way

Resources:
www.marketingv2.com/stepping-stones-child-care-center/
http://graphicdesign.stocklayouts.com/2012/03/06/daycare-advertisements-flyers-for-small-business-marketing/
http://detroitprintshop.com/blog/marketing-materials-for-day-care-centers/

Referral Program
We will ask our current Daycare Parents to spread the word and to make referrals. We will offer a finder's fee or a coupon worth a deduction in their daycare fees to motivate our families to help generate qualified leads. We understand the importance of setting up a formal referral program with the following characteristics:
1. Give a premium reward based simply on people giving referral names.
2. Send an endorsed testimonial letter from a loyal client to the referred prospect.
3. Include a separate referral form as a direct response device.
4. Provide a space on the response form for leaving positive comments that can be used to build a testimonial letter, that will be sent to each referral.
5. We will clearly state our incentive rewards, and terms and conditions.
6. We will distribute a newsletter to stay in touch with our clients and include

articles about our referral program success stories.
Resource:
National Association of Child Care Resource and Referral Agencies www.naccrra.org/

Sources:
1. Referrals from other educators, particularly those of other niche specialties.
2. Give speeches on a complicated niche area that other practitioners may feel is too narrow for them to handle, thus triggering referrals.
3. Structured Client Referral Program.
4. Newsletter Coupons.

Methods:
1. Always have ready a 30-second elevator speech that describes what you do and who you do it for.
2. Use a newsletter to keep our name in front of referrals sources.
3. Repeatedly demonstrate to referral sources that we are also thinking about their practice or business.
4. Regularly send referrals sources articles on unique yet important topics that might affect their businesses.
5. Use Microsoft Outlook to flag our contacts to remind us it is time to give them some form of personal attention.
6. Ask referral sources for referrals.
7. Get more work from a referral source by sending them work.
8. Immediately thank a referral source, even for the mere act of giving his name to a third party for consideration.
9. Remember referral sources with generous gift baskets and gift certificates.
10. Schedule regular lunches with former school classmates and new contacts.

We will offer an additional donation of $ _____ to any organization whose member use a referral coupon to become a client. The coupon will be paid for and printed in the organization's newsletter.

Referral Tracking Form

Referral Source Name	Presently Referring Yes/No	No. of Clients Referred	Anticipated Revenue	Actions to be Taken	Target Date

Sample Referral Program
We want to show our appreciation to established customers and business network partners for their kind referrals to our business. ____ (company name) wants to reward our valued and loyal customers who support our ____ Programs by implementing a new referral program. Ask any of our team members for referral cards to share with your family and friends to begin saving towards your next ____ (product/service) purchase. We will credit your account $___ (?) for each new customer you refer to us as well as

give them 10% off their first enrollment. When they come for their first visit, they should present the card upon arrival. We will automatically set you up a referral account.

The Referral Details Are As Follows:
1. You will receive a $__ (?) credit for every customer that you refer for _____ (products/services). Credit will be applied to your referral account on their initial visit.
2. We will keep track of your accumulated reward dollars and at any time we can let you know the amount you have available for use in your reward account.
3. Each time you visit _____ (company name), you can use your referral dollars to pay up to 50% of your total charge that day
4. Referral dollars are not applicable towards the purchase of _____ products.
5. All referral rewards are for __products and cannot be used towards __ services.

Referral Coupon Template
Company Name: _____
Address: _____
Phone: _____ Website: _____
Print and present this coupon with your first order and the existing customer who referred you will receive a credit for $_____ towards _____.

Examples:
Parent Referral Program
Receive One Week Free Tuition
Take advantage of our referral reward program by recommending a friend, relative or family member to Children of America.
THERE ARE NO LIMITS ON REFERRALS

Our referral program is based on a ONE WEEK FREE per family referred credit. It has no monetary value. The credit will be issued to your oldest child attending Children of America. The referral credit will be issued after the referred child has completed 30 days of childcare.
Note: Referred family's child must attend COA for 30 days before credit is issued.
Source:
http://www.childrenofamerica.com/parent-referral.cfm

Current Enrolled Family   **Referred Attendee**
Name: _____   Name: _____
Address: _____   Address: _____
Phone: _____   Phone: _____
Email: _____   Email: _____
Date referred: _____

Office use only
Credit memo number:_____

Credit issued date: _____   Credit applied by: _____

Invite-A-Friend
We will setup an aggressive invite-a-friend referral program. We will encourage new members or newsletter subscribers, during their initial registration process, to upload and send an invitation to multiple contacts in their email address books. We will encourage them by providing an added incentive, such as a free _____.

Circular Inserts
The Company plans to advertise through circulars which will be inserted in newspapers or mailed directly to consumers' residences.

Bandit and Yard Signs
We plan to use sign holders or bandit signs placed strategically along key roads close to our business or in our front yard to promote special events.

E-mail Marketing
We will use the following email marketing tips to build our mailing list database, improve communications, boost customer loyalty and attract new and repeat business.
1. Define our objectives as the most effective email strategies are those that offer value to our subscribers: either in the form of educational content or promotions. To drive sales, a promotional campaign is the best format. To create brand recognition and reinforce our expertise in our industry we will use educational newsletters.
2. A quality, permission-based email list will be a vital component of our email marketing campaign. We will ask customers and prospects for permission to add them to our list at every touch-point or use a sign-in sheet.
3. We will listen to our customers by using easy-to-use online surveys to ask specific questions about customers' preferences, interests and satisfaction.
4. We will send only relevant and targeted communications.
5. We will reinforce our brand to ensure recognition of our brand by using a recognizable name in the "from" line of our emails and including our company name, logo and a consistent design and color scheme in every email.

Every ___ (five?) to ___ (six?) weeks, we will send graphically-rich, permission-based, personalized, email marketing messages to our list of customers who registered on our website or in our center. The emails will alert clients to promotions as well as other local events sponsored by our nonprofit business This service will be provided by either ExactTarget.com or ConstantContact.com. The email will announce a special event and contain a short sales letter. The message will invite recipients to click on a link to our website to checkout more information about the event. The software offered by these two companies will automatically personalize each email with the customer's name. The software also provides detailed click-through behavior reports that will enable us to

evaluate the success of each message. The software will also allow our nonprofit to dramatically scale back its direct mail efforts and associated costs. We will send a promotional e-mail about a promotion that the client indicated was important to them in their preferred membership application. Each identified market segment will get notified of new services, and offers based on past buying patterns and what they've clicked on in our previous e-newsletters or indicated on their surveys. The objective is to tap the right customer's need at the right time, with a targeted subject line and targeted content. Our general e-newsletter may appeal to most customers, but targeted mailings that reach out to our various audience segments will build even deeper relationships, and drive higher sales. We also develop an email list for routine communications about program specials, frequent buyer programs, the referral program, and special events and seminars, and push users to our website for free newsletter sign-up.
Resource: www.ezcare2.com/childcare-software/childcare-center-marketing.asp

Google Reviews
We will use our email marketing campaign to ask people for reviews. We will ask people what they thought of our business or services and encourage them to write a Google Review if they were impressed. We will incorporate a call to action (CTA) on our email auto signature with a link to our Google My Review page.
Source:
https://superb.digital/how-to-ask-your-clients-for-google-reviews/

Resources:
https://support.google.com/business/answer/3474122?hl=en
https://support.google.com/maps/answer/6230175?co=GENIE.Platform
    %3DDesktop&hl=en

Example:
We will tell our customers to:
1.   Go to https://www.google.com/maps
2.   Type in your business name, select the listing
3.   There's a "card" (sidebar) on the left-hand side. At the bottom, they can click '**Be the First to Write a Review'** or '**Write a Review'** if you already have one review.
Source:
https://www.reviewjump.com/blog/how-do-i-get-google-reviews/

Facebook.com
We will use Facebook to move our businesses forward and stay connected to our customers in this fast-paced world. Content will be the key to staying in touch with our customers and keeping them informed. The content will be a rich mix of information, before and after photos, interactive questions, current trends and events, industry facts, education, promotions and specials, humor and fun. We will use the following step system to get customers from Facebook.com:
1.   We will open a free Facebook account at Facebook.com.
2.   We will begin by adding Facebook friends. The fastest way to do this is to allow

Facebook to import our email addresses and send an invite out to all our customers.
3. We will post a video to get our customers involved with our Facebook page. We will post a video called "How Day Care Centers Promote Child Development". The video will be first uploaded to YouTube.com and then simply be linked to our Facebook page. Video will be a great way to get people active and involved with our Facebook page.
4. We will send an email to our customers base that encourages them to check out the new video and to post their feedback about it on our Facebook page. Then we will provide a link driving customers to our Facebook page.
5. We will respond quickly to feedback, engage in the dialogue and add links to our response that direct the author to a structured mini-survey.
6. We will optimize our Facebook profile with our business keyword to make it an invaluable marketing tool and become the "go-to" expert in our industry
7. On a monthly basis, we will send out a message to all Facebook fans with a special offer, as Fan pages are the best way to interact with customers and potential customers on Facebook,
8. We will use Facebook as a tool for sharing success stories and relate the ways in which we have helped our customers.
9. We will use Facebook Connect to integrate our Facebook efforts with our regular website to share our Facebook Page activity. This will also give us statistics about our website visitors, and add social interaction to our site.
10. We will use a company called Payvment (www.payvment.com) that has a 0 storefront application for Facebook, that requires a Facebook fan page set up for our dealership. We will install the application on our page, set up the look and feel of the storefront using the tools that Payvment provides, enter information about our dealership, and then start loading products.

Resources:
http://www.facebook.com/advertising/
www.socialmediaexaminer.com/how-to-set-up-a-facebook-page-for-business/
www.socialmediaexaminer.com/how-to-build-a-better-target-audience-for-your-facebook-ads/
http://smallbizsurvival.com/2009/11/6-big-facebook-tips-for-small-business.html

Examples:
www.facebook.com/pages/Senses-of-a-Child-Day-Care-Center-School-No2-Inc/104586192954927

Facebook Profiles represent individual users and are held under a person's name. Each profile should only be controlled by that person. Each user has a wall, information tab, likes, interests, photos, videos and each individual can create events.

Facebook Groups are pretty similar to Fan Pages but are usually created for a group of people with a similar interest and they are wanting to keep their discussions private. The members are not usually looking to find out more about a business - they want to discuss a certain topic.

Facebook Fan Pages are the most viral of your three options. When someone becomes a fan of your page or comments on one of your posts, photos or videos, that is spread to all of their personal friends. This can be a great way to get your information out to lots of people...and quickly! In addition, one of the most valuable features of a business page is that you can send "updates" about new products and content to fans and your home building brand becomes more visible.

Facebook Live lets people, public figures and Pages share live video with their followers and friends on Facebook.
Source:
https://live.fb.com/about/
Resource:
http://smartphones.wonderhowto.com/news/facebook-is-going-all-live-video-streaming-your-phone-0170132/

Small Business Promotions
This group allows members to post about their products and services and is a public group designated as a Buy and Sell Facebook group.
Source: https://www.facebook.com/groups/smallbusinesspronotions/
Resource:
https://www.facebook.com/business/a/local-business-promotion-ads
https://www.facebook.com/business/learn/facebook-create-ad-local-awareness
www.socialmediaexaminer.com/how-to-use-facebook-local-awareness-ads-to-target-customers/

Facebook Ad Builder
https://waymark.com/signup/db869ac4-7202-4e3b-93c3-80acc5988df9/?partner=fitsmallbusiness

Best social media marketing practices:
1. Assign daily responsibility for Facebook to a single person on your staff with an affinity for dialoguing .
2. Set expectations for how often they should post new content and how quickly they should respond to comments – usually within a couple hours.
3. Follow and like your followers when they seem to have a genuine interest in your area of health and wellness expertise.
4. Post on the walls of not only your own Facebook site, but also on your most active, influential posters with the largest networks.
5. Periodically post a request for your followers to "like" your page.
6. Monitor Facebook posts to your wall and respond every two hours throughout your business day.

We will use Facebook in the following ways to market our Child Day Care:
1. Promote our blog posts on our Facebook page
2. Post a video of our service people in action.

3. Make time-sensitive offers during slow periods
4. Create a special landing page for coupons or promotional giveaways
5. Create a Welcome tab to display a video message from our owner. Resource: Pagemodo.
6. Support a local charity by posting a link to their website.
7. Thank our customers while promoting their businesses at the same time.
8. Describe milestone accomplishments and thank customers for their role.
9. Give thanks to corporate accounts.
10. Ask customers to contribute success stories.
11. Use the built-in Facebook polling application to solicit feedback.
12. Use the Facebook reviews page to feature positive comments from customers, and to respond to negative reviews.
13. Introduce customers to our staff with resume and video profiles.
14. Create a photo gallery of child accomplishments to showcase our expertise.

We will also explore location-based platforms like the following:
- FourSquare
- GoWalla
- Facebook Places
- Google Latitude

As a child day care serving a local community, we will appreciate the potential for hyper-local platforms like these. Location-based applications are increasingly attracting young, urban influencers with disposable income, which is precisely the audience we are trying to attract. People connect to geo-location apps primarily to "get informed" about local happenings.

Foursquare.com

A web and mobile application that allows registered users to post their location at a venue ("check-in") and connect with friends. Check-in requires active user selection and points are awarded at check-in. Users can choose to have their check-ins posted on their accounts on Twitter, Facebook, or both. In version 1.3 of their iPhone application, foursquare enabled push-notification of friend updates, which they call "Pings". Users can also earn badges by checking in at locations with certain tags, for check-in frequency, or for other patterns such as time of check-in.]
Resource:
https://foursquare.com/business/

Instagram

Instagram.com is an online photo-sharing, video-sharing and social networking service that enables its users to take pictures and videos, apply digital filters to them, and share them on a variety of social networking services, such as
Facebook, Twitter, Tumblr and Flickr. A distinctive feature is that it confines photos to a square shape, similar to Kodak Instamatic and Polaroid images, in contrast to the 16:9 aspect ratio now typically used by mobile device cameras. Users are also able to record and share short videos lasting for up to 15 seconds.

We will use Instagram in the following ways to help amplify the story of our brand, get

people to engage with our content when not at our store, and get people to visit our child daycare center or site:
1. Let our customers and fans know about specific day care service availability.
2. Tie into trends, events or holidays to drive awareness.
3. Let people know we are open and our center ambiance is spectacular.
4. Run a monthly contest and pick the winning hashtagged photograph to activate our customer base and increase our exposure.
5. Encourage the posting and collection of happy onsite or offsite customer photos.

Examples:
https://www.instagram.com/explore/tags/childcare/

Note: Commonly found in tweets, a hashtag is a word or connected phrase (no spaces) that begins with a hash symbol (#). They're so popular that other social media platforms including Facebook, Instagram and Google+ now support them. Using a hashtag turns a word or phrase into a clickable link that displays a feed (list) of other posts with that same hashtag. For example, if you click on #____ in a tweet, or enter #____ in the search box, you'll see a list of tweets all about _____.
Ex: http://iconosquare.com/tag/childcare

MySpace Advertising

MySpace.com offers a self-service, graphical "display" advertising platform that will enable our company to target our marketing message to our audience by demographic characteristics. With the new MySpace service, we will be able to upload our own ads or make them quickly with an online tool, and set a budget of $25 to $10,000 for the campaigns. We can choose to target a specific gender, age group and geographic area. We will then pay MySpace each time someone clicks on our ad. Ads can link to other MySpace pages, or external websites. MyAds will let us target our ads to specific groups of people using the public data on MySpace users' profiles, blogs and comments. MySpace will enable our company to target potential customers with similar interests to our existing customer base, as revealed via our marketing research surveys. Also the bulletin function on MySpace will allow us to update customers on company milestone achievements and coming events. We will also post a short video to our home page and encourage the sharing of the video with other MySpace users.

LinkedIn.com

LinkedIn ranks high in search engines and will provide a great platform for sending event updates to business associates. To optimize our LinkedIn profile, we will select one core keyword. We will use it frequently, without sacrificing consumer experience, to get our profile to skyrocket in the search engines. Linkedin provides options that will allow our detailed profile to be indexed by search engines, like Google. We will make use of these options so our business will achieve greater visibility on the Web. We will use widgets to integrate other tools, such as importing your blog entries or Twitter stream into your profile, and go market research and gain knowledge with Polls. We will answer questions in Questions and Answers to show our expertise, and ask questions in Questions and

Answers to get a feel for what customers and prospects want or think. We will publish our LinkedIn URL on all our marketing collateral, including business cards, email signature, newsletters, and web site. We will grow our network by joining industry and alumni groups related to our business. We will update our status examples of recent work, and link our status updates with our other social media accounts. We will start and manage a group or fan page for our product, brand or business. We will share useful articles that will be of interest to customers, and request LinkedIn recommendations from customers willing to provide testimonials. We will post our presentations on our profile using a presentation application. We will ask our first-level contacts for introductions to their contacts and interact with LinkedIn on a regular basis to reach those who may not see us on other social media sites. We will link to articles posted elsewhere, with a summary of why it's valuable to add to our credibility and list our newsletter subscription information and archives. We will post discounts and package deals. We will buy a LinkedIn direct ad that our target market will see. We will find vendors and contractors through connections.
Example: http://www.linkedin.com/company/boelieboe-child-daycare
Resource: https://www.linkedin.com/company/childcare-marketing

Podcasting

Podcasting is a way of publishing audio broadcasts via the internet through MP3 files, which users can listen to using PCs and i-Pods. Our podcasts will provide both information and advertising. Our podcasts will allow us to pull in a lot of customers. Our monthly podcasts will be heard by ___ (#) eventual subscribers. Podcasts can now be downloaded for mobile devices, such as an iPod. Podcasts will give our company a new way to provide information and an additional way to advertise. Podcasting will give our business another connection point with customers. We will use this medium to communicate on important issues, what is going on with a planned event, and other things of interest to our health conscious customers. The programs will last about 10 minutes and can be downloaded for free on iTunes. The purpose is not to be a mass medium. It is directed at a niche market with an above-average educational background and very special interests. It will provide a very direct and a reasonably inexpensive way of reaching our targeted audience with relevant information about our day care products and services.
Resources:
www.apple.com/itunes/download/.
www.cbc.ca/podcasting/gettingstarted.html
http://www.daycarebusinesspodcast.com/
http://elearningfeeds.com/why-you-should-write-a-child-care-center-blog-tips-for-success/

Blogging

We will use our blog to keep customers and prospects informed about products, events and services that relate to our child care services business, new releases, contests, and specials. Our blog will show readers that we are a good source of expert information that they can count on. With our blog, we can quickly update our customers anytime our company releases a new product, the holding of a contest or are placing items on special pricing. We will use our blog to share customer testimonials and meaningful child development success stories. Our visitors will be able to subscribe to our RSS feeds and be instantly updated without any spam filters interfering. We will also use the blog to solicit product usage recommendations and future product addition suggestions. Additionally, blogs are free and allow for constant ease of updating.

Our blog will give our company the following benefits:
1. An cost-effective marketing tool.
2. An expanded network.
3. A promotional platform for new after school programs.
4. An introduction to people with similar interests.
5. Builds credibility and expertise recognition.

We will use our blog for the following purposes:
1. To share customer testimonials, experiences and meaningful success stories.
2. Update our clients anytime our company releases a new service.
3. Supply advice on _____ options.
4. Discuss research findings.
5. To publish helpful content.
6, To welcome feedback in multiple formats.
7. Link together other social networking sites, including Twitter.
8. To improve Google rankings.
9. Make use of automatic RSS feeds.

We will consider using the following specific day care content ideas in our blogs:
1. Parenting tips
2. Baby behavior tips
3. Babysitting and child care tips
4. Humorous stories or video of children
5. Parenting news and trends
6. Child product and toy reviews and recalls
7. How to cope with daycare as a parent
8. Information on childhood nutrition, sleep, etc
9. Proven day care/child care strategies

We will adhere to the following blog writing guidelines:
1. We will blog at least 2 or 3 times per week to maintain interest.
2. We will integrate our blog into the design of our website.
3. We will use our blog to convey useful information and not our advertisements.
4. We will make the content easy to understand.
5. We will focus our content on the needs of our targeted audience.

Our blog will feature the following on a regular basis:
1. Useful articles and assessment coupons.
2. Give away of a helpful free report in exchange for email addresses

3. Helpful information for our professional referral sources, as well as clients, and online and offline community members.
5. Use of a few social media outposts to educate, inform, engage and drive people back to our blog for more information and our free report.

To get visitors to our blog to take the next action step and contact our firm we will do the following:
1. Put a contact form on the upper-left hand corner of our blog, right below the header.
2. Put our complete contact information in the header itself.
3. Add a page to our blog and title it, "Become My patient.", giving the reader somewhere to go for the next sign-up steps.
4. At the end of each blog post, we will clearly tell the reader what to do next; such as subscribe to our RSS feed, or to sign up for our newsletter mailing list.

Resources:
www.blogger.com
www.blogspot.com
www.wordpress.com
www.tumblr.com
www.typepad.com
Example:
http://kitchenerhomedaycare.webs.com/apps/blog/

Twitter

We will use 'Twitter.com' as a way to produce new business from existing clients and generate prospective clients online. Twitter is a free social networking and micro-blogging service that allows its users to send and read other users' updates (otherwise known as tweets), which are text-based posts of up to 140 characters in length. Updates are displayed on the user's profile page and delivered to other users who have signed up to receive them. The sender can restrict delivery to those in his or her circle of friends, with delivery to everyone being the default. Users can receive updates via the Twitter website, SMS text messaging, RSS feeds, or email. We will use our Twitter account to respond directly to questions, distribute news, solve problems, post updates, and offer special discounts on new services.

We will provide the following instructions to register as a 'Follower' of _____ (company name) on Twitter:
1. In your Twitter account, click on 'Find People' in the top right navigation bar, which will redirect to a new page.
2. Click on 'Find on Twitter' which will open a search box that says 'Who are you looking for?'
3. Type '_____ (company name) / _____ (owner name)' and click 'search'. This will bring up the results page.
4. Click the blue '_____' name to read the bio or select the 'Follow' button.

Examples:
htttps://twitter.com/losfelizdaycare?lang=en
http://twitter.com/#!/yourbabyland

Testimonial Marketing

We will either always ask for testimonials immediately after a completed project or contact our clients once a quarter for them. We will also have something prepared that we would like the client to say that is specific to a service we offer, or anything relevant to advertising claims that we have put together. For the convenience of the client we will assemble a testimonial letter that they can either modify or just sign off on. Additionally, testimonials can also be in the form of audio or video and put on our website or mailed to potential clients in the form of a DVD or Audio CD. A picture with a testimonial is also excellent. We will put testimonials directly on a magazine ad, slick sheet, brochure, or website, or assemble a complete page of testimonials for our sales presentation folder.

Examples:
http://www.kindercare.com/our-centers/testimonials/parent-teacher-testimonials

We will collect customer testimonials in the following ways:
1. Our website – A page dedicated to testimonials (written and/or video).
2. Social media accounts – Facebook fan pages offer a review tab, which makes it easy to receive and display customer testimonials.
3. Google+ also offers a similar feature with Google+ Local.
4. Local search directories – Ask customers to post more reviews on Yelp and Yahoo Local.
5. Customer Satisfaction Survey Forms

We will pose the following questions to our customers to help them frame their testimonials:
1. What was the obstacle that would have prevented you from buying this product?
2. "What was your main concern about buying this product?"
3. What did you find as a result of buying this product?
4. What specific feature did you like most about this product?
5. What would be three other benefits about this product?
6. Would you recommend this product? If so, why?
7. Is there anything you'd like to add?

Reminder Service

We will use a four-tier reminder system in the following sequence: email, postcard, letter, phone call. We will stress the importance of staying in touch in our messages and keeping their profile updated with their activities. We will also try to determine the reason for the non-response or inactivity and what can be done to reactivate the client. The reminder

service will also work to the benefit of regular clients, that want to be reminded of an agreed upon special date or coming event.
Resource:
http://www.easyivr.com/reminder-service.htm

Business Logo

Our logo will graphically represent who we are and what we do, and it will serve to help brand our image. It will also convey a sense of uniqueness and professionalism. The logo will represent our company image and the message we are trying to convey. Our business logo will reflect the philosophy and objective of the child care services business. Our logo will incorporate the following design guidelines:

1. It will relate to our industry, our name, a defining characteristic of our company or a competitive advantage we offer.
2. It will be a simple logo that can be recognized faster.
3. It will contain strong lines and letters which show up better than thin ones.
4. It will feature something unexpected or unique without being overdrawn.
5. It will work well in black and white (one-color printing).
6. It will be scalable and look pleasing in both small and large sizes.
7. It will be artistically balanced and make effective use of color, line density and shape.
8. It will be unique when compared to competitors.
9. It will use original, professionally rendered artwork.
10. It can be replicated across any media mix without losing quality.
11. It appeals to our target audience.
12. It will be easily recognizable from a distance if utilized in outdoor advertising.

Resources: www.freelogoservices.com/   www.hatchwise.com
            www.logosnap.com   www.99designs.com
            www.fiverr.com   www.freelancer.com

Logo Design Guide:
www.bestfreewebresources.com/logo-design-professional-guide
www.creativebloq.com/graphic-design/pro-guide-logo-design-21221
https://www.graphicsprings.com/category/children-childcare
http://www.websitesfordaycares.com/childcare_logo_design.php

Fundraisers

Community outreach programs involving charitable fundraising and showing a strong interest in the local school system will serve to elevate our status in the community as a "good corporate citizen" while simultaneously increasing store traffic. We will execute a successful fundraising program for our daycare center and build goodwill in the community, by adhering to the following guidelines:
1. Keep It Local
    When looking for a worthy cause, we will make sure it is local so the whole

neighborhood will support it.
2. Plan It
We will make sure that we are organized and outline everything we want to accomplish before planning the fundraiser.
3. Contact Local Media
We will contact the suburban newspapers to do stories on the event and send out press releases to the local TV and radio stations.
4. Contact Area Businesses
We will contact other businesses and have them put up posters in their stores and pass out flyers to promote the event.
5. Get Recipient Support
We will make sure the recipients of the fundraiser are really willing to participate and get out in the neighborhood to invite everyone into our store for the event, plus help pass out flyers and getting other businesses to put up the posters.
6. Give Out Bounce Backs
We will give a "bounce-back" coupon that allows for both a discount and an additional donation in exchange for customer next purchase. (It will have an expiration date of two weeks to give a sense of urgency.)
7. Be Ready with plenty of product and labor on hand for the event.

Fundraiser Action Plan Checklist:
1. Choose a good local cause for your fundraiser.
2. Calculate donations as a percentage for normal sales.
3. Require the group to promote and support the event.
4. Contact local media to get exposure before and after the event.
5. Ask area businesses to put up flyers and donate printing of materials.
6. Use a bounce-back coupon to get new customers back.
7. Be prepared with sufficient labor and product.

Resources:
https://www.justfundraising.com/day-care/
http://www.easy-fundraising-ideas.com/programs/daycare-fundraising/

Online Directory Listings

The following directory listings use proprietary technology to match customers with industry professionals in their geographical area. The local search capabilities for specific niche markets offer an invaluable tool for the customer. These directories help member businesses connect with purchase-ready buyers, convert leads to sales, and maximize the value of customer relationships. Their online and offline communities provide a quick and easy low or no-cost solution for customers to find a daycare center quickly. We intend to sign-up with all no cost directories and evaluate the ones that charge a fee, and consider placing advertisements.

Child Care Directory	http://child-daycare-directory.com/
Day Care Providers	www.daycareproviders.com/

Childcare Directory	www.childcare-directory.com/
National Daycare Directory	www.nationaldaycaredirectory.com/
Daycare Café	http://daycarecafe.com
Top Daycare Centers	www.TopDaycareCenters.com
Daycare Match	www.daycarematch.com/
Metro Daycare	www.metrodaycare.com/pages/search.asp
NAFCC	http://nafcc.org/index.php?option=com_content&view=article&id=390:accredited-provider-search&catid=159:main-menu&Itemid=1186
Great Start to Quality	www.greatstarttoquality.org/
Childcare Seekers	www.ChldcareSeekers.com
Childcare ETC	www.ChildcareETC.com
Child Care Intro	www.childcareintro.com/daycare/usa/il/chicago/
Child Care Central	www.childcarecentral.com
Daycare Leads	www.daycareleads.com
Daycare Bear	www.daycarebear.ca/

Child Care Aware   www.childcareaware.org

Child Care Aware is a non-profit initiative committed to helping parents find the best information on locating quality child care and child care resources in their community by raising visibility for local child care resource and referral agencies nationwide, and by connecting parents with the local agencies best equipped to serve their needs.

We will make certain that our listings contain the following information:

- Business Name
- Phone number
- Email address
- Contact Person: name, phone #, email
- Company logo
- Short Business description
- Specialties
- Twitter Business Page Link
- Address
- Days and Hours of operation
- Website URL
- Facility Photos
- Products/ Services offered
- Affiliations
- Facebook Business Page Link
- LinkedIn Business Page Link

We will also provide answers to the following types of questions:
- Are you in my local area?
- Do you provide transportation?
- What are the nearest schools to your location?
- How can I get in touch with you?
- Do you accept state vouchers?
- What ages of children do you provide care for?

Other General Directories Include:

Listings.local.yahoo.com
YellowPages.com
Bing.com/businessportal
Yelp.com
InfoUSA.com

Switchboard Super Pages
MerchantCircle.com
Local.com
BrownBook.com
iBegin.com

Localeze.com	Bestoftheweb.com
YellowBot.com	HotFrog.com
InsiderPages.com	MatchPoint.com
CitySearch.com	YellowUSA.com
Profiles.google.com/me	Manta.com
Jigsaw.com	LinkedIn.com
Whitepages.com	PowerProfiles.com

Get Listed	http://getlisted.org/enhanced-business-listings.aspx
Universal Business Listing	https://www.ubl.org/index.aspx
	www.UniversalBusinessListing.org

Universal Business Listing (UBL) is a local search industry service dedicated to acting as a central collection and distribution point for business information online. UBL provides business owners and their marketing representatives with a one-stop location for broad distribution of complete, accurate, and detailed listing information.

Day Care Lead Generators
Day Care Leads   http://daycareleads.com/
A leading marketplace connecting families with child care providers.

Google Maps

We will first make certain that our business is listed in Google Maps. We will do a search for our business in Google Maps. If we don't see our business listed, then we will add our business to Google Maps. Even if our business is listed in Google Maps, we will create a Local Business Center account and take control of our listing, by adding more relevant information. Consumers generally go to Google Maps for two reasons: Driving Directions and to Find a Business.
Resource:
http://maps.google.com/

Bing Maps   www.bingplaces.com/
This will make it easy for customers to find our business.

Apple Maps
A web mapping service developed by Apple Inc. It is the default map system of iOS, macOS, and watchOS. It provides directions and estimated times of arrival for automobile, pedestrian, and public transportation navigation.
Resources:
http://www.stallcupgroup.com/2012/09/19/three-ways-to-make-your-pawn-business-
      more-profitable-and-sellable/
http://www.apple.com/ios/maps/
https://en.wikipedia.org/wiki/Apple_Maps

Google Places

Google Places helps people make more informed decisions about where to go for child day care services. Place Pages connect people to information from the best sources across the web, displaying photos, reviews and essential facts, as well as real-time updates and offers from business owners. We will make sure that our Google Places listing is up to date to increase our online visibility. Google Places is linked to our Google Maps listing, and will help to get on the first page of Google search page results when people search for a child care services in our area.
Resource: www.google/com/places

Yelp.com

We will use Yelp.com to help people find our local business. Visitors to Yelp write local reviews, over 85% of them rating a business 3 stars or higher In addition to reviews, visitors can use Yelp to find events, special offers, lists and to talk with other Yelpers. As business owners, we will setup a free account to post offers, photos and message our customers. We will also buy ads on Yelp, which will be clearly labeled "Sponsored Results". We will also use the Weekly Yelp, which is available in 42 city editions to bring news about the latest business openings and other happenings.
Example:
http://www.yelp.com/c/chicago/childcare

Manta.com

Manta is the largest free source of information on small companies, with profiles of more than 64 million businesses and organizations. Business owners and sales professionals use Manta's vast database and custom search capabilities to quickly find companies, easily connect with prospective customers and promote their own services. Manta.com, founded in 2005, is based in Columbus, Ohio.
Resource:
www.manta.com/mb_54_B315F_9VT/child_day_care_services/redford_mi
Example:
http://www.manta.com/c/mt1313t/abc-123-daycare-llc

Pay-Per-Click Advertising

Google AdWords, Yahoo! Search Marketing, and Microsoft adCenter are the three largest network operators, and all three operate under a bid-based model. Cost per click (CPC) varies depending on the search engine and the level of competition for a particular keyword. Google AdWords are small text ads that appear next to the search results on Google. In addition, these ads appear on many partner web sites, including NYTimes.com (The New York Times), Business.com, Weather.com, About.com, and many more. Google's text advertisements are short, consisting of one title line and two content text lines. Image ads can be one of several different Interactive Advertising Bureau (IAB) standard sizes.

Through Google AdWords, we plan to buy placements (ads) for specific search terms through this "Pay-Per-Click" advertising program. This PPC advertising campaign will allow our ad to appear when someone searches for a keyword related to our business, organization, or subject matter. More importantly, we will only pay when a potential customer clicks on our ad to visit our website. For instance, since we operate a day care center in ___ (city), ____ (state), we will target people using search terms such as "child daycare, pre-kindergarten, pre-school, after-school, in ____ (city), ____ (state)". With an effective PPC campaign our ads will only be displayed when a user searches for one of these keywords. In short, PPC advertising will be the most cost-effective and measurable form of advertising for our Child Day Care Center center.

Resources:
http://adwords.google.com/support/aw/?hl=en
www.wordtracker.com

Yahoo Local Listings

We will create our own local listing on Yahoo. To create our free listing, we will use our web browser and navigate to http://local.yahoo.com. We will first register for free with Yahoo, and create a member ID and password to list our business. Once we have accessed http://local.yahoo.com, we will scroll down to the bottom and click on "Add/Edit a Business" to get onto the Yahoo Search Marketing Local Listings page. In the lower right of the screen we will see "Local Basic Listings FREE". We will click on the Get Started button and log in again with our new Yahoo ID and password. The form for our local business listing will now be displayed. When filling it out, we will be sure to include our full web address (http://www.companyname.com). We will include a description of our Child Day Care Center services in the description section, but avoid hype or blatant advertising, to get the listing to pass Yahoo's editorial review. We will also be sure to select the appropriate business category and sub categories.

Examples:
https://local.yahoo.com/info-11394926

Advertorials

An advertorial is an advertisement written in the form of an objective article, and presented in a printed publication—usually designed to look like a legitimate and independent news story. We will use quotes as testimonials to back up certain claims throughout our copy and break-up copy with subheadings to make the material more reader-friendly. We will include the "call to action" and contact information with a 24/7 voicemail number and a discount coupon. The advertorial will have a short intro about a client's experience with our child care services and include quotes, facts, and statistics. We will present helpful information about child development guidelines.

Affiliate Marketing

We will create an affiliate marketing program to broaden our reach. We will first devise a commission structure, so affiliates have a reason to promote our business. We will give them ___ (10)% of whatever sales they generate. We will go after event planner bloggers or webmasters who get a lot of web traffic for our keywords. These companies would then promote our products/services, and they would earn commissions for the sales they generated. We will work with the following services to handle the technical aspects of our program.

ConnectCommerce	www.connectcommerce.com/
Commission Junction	www.cj.com
ShareASale	www.shareasale.com/
Share Results	
LinkShare	www.linkshare.com
Clickbank	www.clickbank.com
Affiliate Scout	http://affiliatescout.com/
Affiliate Seeking	www.affiliateseeking.com/
Clix Galore	www.clixgalore.com/

HotFrog.com

HotFrog is a fast growing free online business directory listing over 6.6 million US businesses. HotFrog now has local versions in 34 countries worldwide.
Anyone can list their business in HotFrog for free, along with contact details, and products and services. Listing in HotFrog directs sales leads and enquiries to your business. Businesses are encouraged to add any latest news and information about their products and services to their listing. HotFrog is indexed by Google and other search engines, meaning that customers can find your HotFrog listing when they use Google, Yahoo! or other search engines.
Resource:
http://www.hotfrog.com/AddYourBusiness.aspx

Local.com

Local.com owns and operates a leading local search site and network in the United States. Its mission is to be the leader at enabling local businesses and consumers to find each other and connect. To do so, the company uses patented and proprietary technologies to provide over 20 million consumers each month with relevant search results for local businesses, products and services on Local.com and more than 1,000 partner sites. Local.com powers more than 100,000 local websites. Tens of thousands of small business customers use Local.com products and services to reach consumers using a variety of subscription, performance and display advertising and website products.
Resource:
http://corporate.local.com/mk/get/advertising-opportunities

Autoresponder

An autoresponder is an online tool that will automatically manage our mailing list and send out emails to our customers at preset intervals. We will write a short article that is helpful to potential child care services buyers. We will load this article into our autoresponder. We will let people know of the availability of our article by posting to newsgroups, forums, social networking sites etc. We will list our autoresponder email address at the end of the posting so they can send a blank email to our autoresponder to receive our article and be added to our mailing list. We will then email them at the

interval of our choosing with special offers. We will load the messages into our autoresponder and set a time interval for the messages to be mailed out.
Resource:
www.aweber.com

Corporate Incentive/Employee Rewards Program

Our Employee Rewards Program will motivate and reward the key resources of local corporations – the people who make their business a success. We will use independent sales reps to market these programs to local corporations. It will be a versatile program, allowing the corporate client to customize it to best suit the following goals:

1. Welcome New Hires
2. Introduce an Employee Discount Program for our child day care services.
3. Reward increases in sales or productivity with an Employee Incentive Program
4. Thank Retirees for their service to the company
5. Initiate a Loyalty Rewards Program geared towards the customers of our corporate clients or their employees.

Database Marketing

Database marketing is a form of direct marketing using databases of customers or potential customers to generate personalized communications in order to promote a product or service for marketing purposes. The method of communication can be any addressable medium, as in direct marketing. As marketers trained in the use of database marketing tools, we will be able to carry out customer nurturing, which is a tactic that attempts to communicate with each customer or prospect at the right time, using the right information to meet that customer's need to progress through the process of identifying a problem, learning options available to resolve it, selecting the right solution, and making the purchasing decision. As marketers we will use our databases to learn more about customers, select target markets for specific campaigns, through customer segmentation, compare customers' value to the company, and provide more specialized offerings for customers based on their transaction histories, demographic profile and surveyed needs and wants.

We will use sign-in sheets, coupons, surveys and newsletter subscriptions to collect the following information from our clients:

1.	Name	2.	Telephone Number
3.	Email Address	4.	Home Address
5.	Birth Date	6.	Other Relevant Dates

We will utilize the following types of contact management software to generate leads and stay in touch with customers to produce repeat business and referrals:

1.	Act	www.act.com
2.	Front Range Solutions	www.frontrange.com
3.	The Turning Point	www.turningpoint.com
4.	Acxiom	www.acxiom.com/products_and_services/

We will utilize contact management software, such as ACT and Goldmine, to track the following:
1. Dates for follow-ups.
2. Documentation of prospect concerns, objections or comments.
3. Referral source.
4. Marketing Materials sent.
5. Log of contact dates and methods of contact.
6. Ultimate disposition.

Cause Marketing

Cause marketing or cause-related marketing refers to a type of marketing involving the cooperative efforts of a "for profit" business and a non-profit organization for mutual benefit. The possible benefits of cause marketing for business include positive public relations, improved customer relations, and additional marketing opportunities. Cause marketing sponsorship by American businesses is rising at a dramatic rate, because customers, employees and stakeholders prefer to be associated with a company that is considered socially responsible. Our business objective will be to generate highly cost-effective public relations and media coverage for the launch of a marketing campaign focused on _____ (type of cause), with the help of the _____ (non-profit organization name) organization.
Resources:
www.causemarketingforum.com/
www.cancer.org/AboutUs/HowWeHelpYou/acs-cause-marketing

Courtesy Advertising

We will engage in courtesy advertising, which refers to a company or corporation "buying" an advertisement in a nonprofit dinner program, event brochure, and the like. Our company will gain visibility this way while the nonprofit organization may treat the advertisement revenue as a donation. We will specifically advertise in the following non-profit programs, newsletters, bulletins and event brochures: _____

BBB Accreditation

We will apply for BBB Accreditation to improve our perceived trustworthiness. BBB determines that a company meets BBB accreditation standards, which include a commitment to make a good faith effort to resolve any consumer complaints. BBB Accredited Businesses pay a fee for accreditation review/monitoring and for support of BBB services to the public. BBB accreditation does not mean that the business' products or services have been evaluated or endorsed by BBB, or that BBB has made a determination as to the business' product quality or competency in performing services. We will place the BBB Accreditation Logo in all of our ads.
Examples:
www.bbb.org/pittsburgh/Business-Reviews/child-care-in-home/open-arms-daycare-

in-pittsburgh-pa-71006399/

Sponsor Events
The sponsoring of events, such as golf tournaments, will allow our company to engage in what is known as experiential marketing, which is the idea that the best way to deepen the emotional bond between a company and its customers is by creating a memorable and interactive experience. We will ask for the opportunity to prominently display our company signage and the set-up of a booth from which to handout sample products and sales literature. We will also seek to capitalize on networking, speech giving and workshop presenting opportunities

Sponsorships
We will sponsor a local team, such as our child's little league baseball team, the local soccer club or a bowling group. We will then place our company name on the uniforms or shirts in exchange for providing the equipment and/or uniforms.

Patch.com
A community-specific news and information platform dedicated to providing comprehensive and trusted local coverage for individual towns and communities. Patch makes it easy to: Keep up with news and events, Look at photos and videos from around town, Learn about local businesses, Participate in discussions and Submit announcements, photos, and reviews.
Example:
http://dalecity.patch.com/listings/muriel-humphrey-child-day-care-center

MerchantCircle.com
The largest online network of local business owners, combining social networking features with customizable web listings that allow local merchants to attract new customers. A growing company dedicated to connecting neighbors and merchants online to help build real relationships between local business owners and their customers. To date, well over 1,600,000 local businesses have joined MerchantCircle to get their business more exposure on the Internet, simply and inexpensively.

Mobile iPhone Apps
We will use new distribution tools like the iPhone App Store to give us unprecedented direct access to consumers, without the need to necessarily buy actual mobile *ads* to reach people. Thanks to Apple's iPhone and the App Store, we will be able to make cool mobile apps that may generate as much goodwill and purchase intent as a banner ad. We will research Mobile Application Development, which is the process by which application software is developed for small low-power handheld devices, such as personal digital assistants, enterprise digital assistants or mobile phones. These applications are either pre-installed on phones during manufacture, or downloaded by customers from various mobile software distribution platforms. iPhone apps make good marketing tools. The bottom line is iPhones and smartphones sales are continually

growing, and people are going to their phones for information. Apps will definitely be a lead generation tool because it gives potential clients easy access to our contact and business information and the ability to call for more information while they are still "hot". Our apps will contain: directory of staffers, publications on relevant issues, office location, videos, etc.

We will especially focus on the development of apps that can accomplish the following:

1. **Mobile Reservations:** Customers can use this app to access mobile reservations linked directly to your in-house calendar. They can browse open slots and book appointments easily, while on the go.
2. **Appointment Reminders:** You can send current customers reminders of regular or special appointments through your mobile app to increase your yearly revenue per customer.
3. **Curriculum Libraries**
   Offer a curriculum library in your app to help customers to pick out a program. Using a simple photo gallery, you can collect photos of various teachers, and have customers browse and select specific programs.
4. **Customer Photos**
   Your app can also have a feature that lets customers take photos of their families and email them to you. This is great for creating a database of customer photos for testimonial purposes, advertising, or just easy reference.
5. **Special Offers**
   Push notifications allow you to drive activity on special promotions, deals, events, and offers. If you ever need to generate revenue during a down time, push notifications allow you to generate interest easily and proactively.
6. **Loyalty Programs**
   A mobile app allows you to offer a mobile loyalty program (buy ten ___, get one free, etc.). You won't need to print up cards or track anything manually – it's all done simply through users' mobile devices.
7. **Referrals**
   A mobile app can make referrals easy. With a single click, a user can post to a social media account on Facebook or Twitter about their experience with your business. This allows you to earn new business organically through the networks of existing customers.
8. **Product Sales**
   You can sell educational products through your mobile app. Customers can browse products, submit orders, and make payments easily, helping you open up a new revenue stream.

Resources: http://www.apple.com/iphone/apps-for-iphone/
http://iphoneapplicationlist.com/apps/business/
Software Development: http://www.mutualmobile.com/
http://www.avenuesocial.com/mob-app.php#

Note: A Finland-based company has now developed an app that allows parents to be in constant touch with the care providers. Developed by While On The Move, the 'Daisy' software of the company is an information system for early childhood education based on near field communications (NFC) technology and provides a mobile application for day care centers and family child care providers. Using the app, the provider can monitor on-line attendance reports and the hours of care provided. The app allows parents to interact with care providers and to book care times.

Resource:
Hi Mama   www.himama.com/blog/5-child-care-marketing-strategies-to-set-you-apart-from-the-competition

We will offer this app for communication, reporting and news updates to give our child care center a distinct advantage.

Voice Broadcasting

A web-based voice broadcast system will provide a powerful platform to generate thousands of calls to clients and customers or create customizable messages to be delivered to specific individuals. Voice broadcasting and voice mail broadcast will allow our company to instantly send interactive phone calls with ease while managing the entire process right from the Web. We will instantly send alerts, notifications, reminders, GOTV - messages, and interactive surveys with ease right from the Web. The free VoiceShot account will guide us through the process of recording and storing our messages, managing our call lists, scheduling delivery as well as viewing and downloading real-time call and caller key press results. The voice broadcasting interface will guide us through the entire process with a Campaign Checklist as well as tips from the Campaign Expert. Other advanced features include recipient targeting, call monitoring, scheduling, controlling the rate of call delivery and customized text to speech (TTS).

Resource:
http://www.voiceshot.com/public/outboundcalls.asp

Transit Ads

According to the Metropolitan Transportation Authority, MTA subways, buses and railroads provide billions of trips each year to residents. Marketing our child day care center in subway cars and on the walls of subway stations will be a great way to advertise our business to a large, captive audience.

Tumblr.com

Tumblr will allow us to effortlessly share anything. We will be able to post text, photos, quotes, links, music, and videos, from our browser, phone, desktop, email, or wherever we happen to be. We will be able to customize everything, from colors, to our theme's HTML.

Examples:
https://www.tumblr.com/tagged/childcare

Gift Certificates

We will offer for sale Gift Certificates via our website. This will provide an excellent way to be introduced to new clients and improve our cash flow position. An e-commerce platform for small businesses. BoomTime protects info with 256-bit SSL encryption when transmitting certain kinds of information, such as financial services information or payment information. An icon resembling a padlock is displayed on the bottom of most browser windows during SSL transactions, which you can also verify by looking at the address bar, which will start with "https://" instead of just "http://". The information you provide will be stored securely on BoomTime servers. BoomTime is PCI DSS compliant, which outlines a standard for security procedures for merchants and service providers that store, process, or transmit cardholder data.

Resources:

    Boom Time   https://ps1419.boomtime.com/lgift
    Gift Cards   www.giftcards.com
    Gift Card Café   www.TheGiftCardCafe.com

    Allows companies to create their own special deals and discount services, and send it to just the contacts in their client database.

thumbtack.com

A directory for finding and booking trustworthy local services, which is free to consumers.

Resource:
www.thumbtack.com/postservice

Examples:
https://www.thumbtack.com/ca/downey/daycare/childcare-provider

Citysearch.com

Citysearch.com is a local guide for living bigger, better and smarter in the selected city. Covering more than 75,000 locations nationwide, Citysearch.com combines in-the-know editorial recommendations, candid user comments and expert advice from local businesses. Citysearch.com keeps users connected to the most popular and undiscovered places wherever they are.

Publish e-Book

Ebooks are electronic books which can be downloaded from any website or FTP site on the Internet. Ebooks are made using special software and can include a wide variety of media such as HTML, graphics, Flash animation and video. We will publish an e-book to establish our child care expertise, and reach people who are searching for ebooks on how to make better use our products and/or services. Included in our ebook will be links back to our website, product or affiliate program. Because users will have permanent access to it, they will use our ebook again and again, constantly seeing a link or banner which directs them to our site. The real power behind ebook marketing will be the viral aspect of it and the free traffic it helps to build for our website. ebook directories include:

    www.e-booksdirectory.com/

Resource:
www.ebookfreeway.com/p-ebook-directory-list.html
www.quantumseolabs.com/blog/seolinkbuilding/top-5-free-ebook-directories-subscribers/
www.free-ebooks.net/

e-books are available from the following sites:
Amazon.com
Lulu.com
BarnesandNoble.com
AuthorHouse.com
Createspace.com
Kobobooks.com
Scribd.com

Business Card Exchanges
We will join our Chamber of Commerce or local retail merchants association and volunteer to host a mixer or business card exchange at our center. We will take the opportunity to invite social and business groups to our store to enjoy beer and wine tastings, and market to local businesses that will be looking for employee and customer holiday gifts in the coming months. We will also build our email database by collecting the business cards of all attendees.

Storefront Banner Advertising
We will use banners as an affordable way to draw attention to our business. We will place one on the side or front of our building, or on a prominent building and have it point to ours. We will use colorful storefront banners with catchy phrases to grab the attention of local foot and vehicle traffic.

Hubpages.com
HubPages has easy-to-use publishing tools, a vibrant author community and underlying revenue-maximizing infrastructure. Hubbers (HubPages authors) earn money by publishing their Hubs (content-rich Internet pages) on topics they know and love, and earn recognition among fellow Hubbers through the community-wide HubScore ranking system. The HubPages ecosystem provides a search-friendly infrastructure which drives traffic to Hubs from search engines such as Google and Yahoo, and enables Hubbers to earn revenue from industry-standard advertising vehicles such as Google AdSense and the eBay and Amazon Affiliates program. All of this is provided free to Hubbers in an open online community.
Resources:
http://hubpages.crabbysbeach.com/blogs/
http://hubpages.com/learningcenter/contents
Examples:
http://child-daycare.hubpages.com/hub/child-daycare-centers

Pinterest.com
The goal of this website is to connect everyone in the world through the 'things' they find interesting. They think that a favorite book, toy, or recipe can reveal a common link

between two people. With millions of new pins added every week, Pinterest is connecting people all over the world based on shared tastes and interests. What's special about Pinterest is that the boards are all visual, which is a very important marketing plus. When users enter a URL, they select a picture from the site to pin to their board. People spend hours pinning their own content, and then finding content on other people's boards to "re-pin" to their own boards. We will use Pinterest for remote personal shopping appointments. When we have a customer with specific needs, we will create a board just for them with items we sell that would meet their needs, along with links to other tips and content. We will invite our customer to check out the board on Pinterest, and let them know we created it just for them.
Example:
http://pinterest.com/dot2dotdaycare/
Resource:
http://www.pinterest.com/shanda214/daycare-marketing-tips-ideas/

Pinterest usage recommendation include:
1. Conduct market research by showing photos of potential programs or test launches, asking the customer base for feedback.
2. Personalize the brand by showcasing staff and what makes the brand different, highlighting new and exciting child development activities through the use of imagery.
3. Add links from Pinterest photos to the company webstore, putting price banners on each photo and providing a link where users can buy the products directly.

Resources:
www.copyblogger.com/pinterest-marketing/
www.shopify.com/infographics/pinterest
www.pinterest.com/entmagazine/retail-business/
www.pinterest.com/brettcarneiro/ecommerce/
www.pinterest.com/denniswortham/infographics-retail-online-shopping/
www.cio.com/article/3018852/e-commerce/how-to-use-pinterest-to-grow-your-business.html

Survey Marketing

We will conduct a door-to-door survey in our target area to illicit opinions to our proposed business. This will provide valuable feedback, lead to prospective clients and serve to introduce our child day care center business, before we begin actual operations.

'Green' Marketing

We will target environmentally friendly customers to introduce new customers to our business and help spread the word about going "green". We will use the following 'green' marketing strategies to form an emotional bond with our customers:
1. We will use clearly labeled 'Recycled Paper' and Sustainable Packaging, such as receipts and storage containers.
2. We will use "green", non-toxic cleaning supplies.

3. We will install a 'green' lighting and heating system to be more eco-friendly.
4. We will use web-based Electronic Mail and Social Media instead of using paper advertisements.
5. We will find local suppliers to minimize the carbon footprint that it takes for deliveries.
6. We will offer produce and pre-made food products that are made with organic ingredients and supplies.
7. We will document our 'Green' Programs in our sales brochure and website.
8. We will be a Certified Energy Star Partner.
9. We will install new LED warehouse lighting, exit signs, and emergency signs.
10. We will install motion detectors in low-traffic areas both inside and outside of warehouses.
11. We will implement new electricity regulators on HVAC units and compressors to lower energy consumption.
12. We will mount highly supervised and highly respected recycling campaigns.
13. We will start a program for waste product to be converted into sustainable energy sources.
14. We will start new company-wide document shredding programs.
15. We will use of water-based paints during the finishing process to reduce V.O.C.'s to virtually zero.

Sticker Marketing

Low-cost sticker, label and decal marketing will provide a cost-effective way to convey information, build identity and promote our company in unique and influential ways. Stickers can be affixed to almost any surface, so they can go and stay affixed where other marketing materials can't; opening a world of avenues through which we can reach our target audience. Our stickers will be simple in design, and convey an impression quickly and clearly, with valuable information or coupon, printed optionally as part of its backcopy. Our stickers will handed out at trade shows and special events, mailed as a postcard, packaged with product and/or included as part of a mailing package. We will insert the stickers inside our product or hand them out along with other marketing tools such as flyers or brochures. Research has found that the strongest stickers are usually less than 16 square inches, are printed on white vinyl, and are often die cut. Utilizing a strong design, in a versatile size, and with an eye-catching shape, that is, relevant to our business, will add to the perceived value of our promotional stickers.

We will adhere to the following sticker design tips:
1. We will strengthen our brand by placing our logo on the stickers and using company colors and font styles.
2. We will include our phone number, address, and/or website along with our logo to provide customers with a call to action.
3. We will write compelling copy that solicits an emotional reaction.
4. We will use die-cut stickers using unusual and business relevant shapes to help draw attention to our business.
5. We will consider that size matters and that will be determined by where they will

be applied and the degree of desired visibility to be realized.
6. We will be aware of using color on our stickers as color can help create contrast in our design, which enables the directing of prospect eyes to images or actionable items on the stickers.
7. We will encourage customers to post our stickers near their phones, on yellow page book covers, on party invitations, on notepads, on book covers, on gift boxes and packaging, etc.
8. We will place our stickers on all the learning materials and products we sell.

Google Calendar   www.google.com/calendar
We will use Google Calendar to organize our child day care center schedule and share events with friends.

USPS Every Door Direct Mail Program
Every Door Direct Mail from the U.S. Postal Service® is designed to reach every home, every address, every time at a very affordable delivery rate. Every business and resident living in the ____ zip code will receive an over sized post card and coupon announcing the _____ (company name) grand opening 7-days before the grand opening.
Source:
www.circlesocialinc.com/marketing-strategies-child-care-centers-works-doesnt-much-cost/
Resources:
https://eddm.usps.com/eddm/customer/routeSearch.action
https://www.usps.com/business/every-door-direct-mail.htm

Seminars
Seminars present the following marketing and bonding opportunities:
1. Signage and branding as a presenting sponsor.
2. Opportunity to provide logo imprinted handouts.
3. Media exposure through advertising and public relations.
4. The opportunity for one-on-one interaction with a targeted group of consumers to demonstrate an understanding of their needs and our matching expert solutions.
5. Use of sign-in sheet to collect names and email addresses for database build.
6. Present opportunity to sell products, such as workbooks.

Possible seminar funding sources:
1. Small registration fee to cover the cost of hand-outs and refreshments.
2. Get sponsorship funding from partner/networking organizations.
3. Sponsorship classified ads in the program guide or handouts.

We will establish our expertise and trustworthiness by offering free seminars on the following topics:
1. How to Locate and Evaluate Child Day Care Centers
2. New Trends in Child Day Care Programs
3. How to Best Invest in Your Child's Development and Well-being

Seminar target groups include the following:
1. Corporations
2. Parenting Clubs
3. Church Groups
4. Pediatricians
5. Teachers and Counselors
6. Women's Clubs

Possible Seminar Handouts:
1. Article Reprints
2. Graphs/Charts
3. Worksheets
4. Research Studies
5. Resource Lists
6. Summary Report
7. Presentation Outline

Seminar marketing approaches include:
1. Posting to website and enabling online registrations.
2. Email blast to in-house database using www.constantcontact.com
3. Include seminar schedule in newsletter and flyer.
4. Classified ads using craigslist.org

Seminar Objectives:

Seminar Topic	Target Audience	Handout	Target Date

Sampling Program
We will start a get acquainted, bring a buddy, one week sampling program to demonstrate to prospects the benefits of our day care program.

ZoomInfo.com
Their vision is to be the sole provider of constantly verified information about companies and their employees, making our data indispensible — available anytime, anywhere and anyplace the customer needs it. Creates just-verified, detailed profiles of 65 million businesspeople and six million businesses. Makes data available through powerful tools for lead generation, prospecting and recruiting.

CitySlick.net
CitySlick.net's unique approach to *online local advertising* helps distribute search traffic for local businesses. We will get more local customers through the internet via CitySlick's local citation network.

Zipslocal.com
Provides one of the most comprehensive ZIP Code-based local search services, allowing visitors to access information through our online business directories that cover all ZIP Codes in the United States. Interactive local yellow pages show listings and display relevant advertising through the medium of the Internet, making it easy for everyone to

find local business information

Hold Biggest Fan Contest
Do you love _____ (company name)? Do you have a great story about how the team at ____ (company Name) helped you "get there" to achieve your goals? Well, then ____ (company name) wants to hear from you!

_____ (company name) has launched the "Biggest Fan Contest" on its Facebook Page at the beginning of ____ (month), inviting current and former customers to share why they are _____'s (company name) "Biggest Fan." Participants are eligible to win a number of prizes including: _____.

To enter, visit www.facebook.com/_____ (company name), "like" the page, and click the "Biggest Fan Contest" tab on the right hand side. Participants are then asked to write a short blurb or upload a photo sharing why they love _____ (company name). If you have a story to tell or photo to share, enter today. Contest ends _____ (date). See contest tab for full details.

Mobile Marketing
We will use the following to leverage our mobile marketing program:
1. Keep parents in the loop regarding their child's status during the day.
2. We will offer customers the opportunity to join a mobile loyalty club and receive special rewards and offers for mobile club members only.
3. We will encourage customers to sign up for the mobile program at the reception counter, on the website and on social media platforms.
4. We will develop compelling up-sell and cross-sell mobile coupon offers, such as a discount on a product when purchasing a service, or up-selling through offering service packages.
5. We will use mobile loyalty programs to stay top of mind with existing customers and drive repeat sales.
6. Our mobile messages will include mobile coupons as well as announcements about new employees or new available services and treatments.
7. We will use mobile messaging on special occasions, such as Mother's Day, and to drive traffic during the slower season.
8. Announce a coming event or a change in the daycare schedule.

Resources:
Mobile Marketing Association   www.mmaglobal.com
BxP Marketing visit   www.bxpmarketing.com.

Resources:
www.instant.ly/blog/2012/12/5-ways-child-focused-businesses-can-use-
    mobile-technology-to-reach-parents/
www.slicktext.com/blog/2013/05/3-ways-day-care-centers-can-use-sms-marketing/

Data.com/connect/index.jsp

A dynamic community with connections to millions of B2B decision makers. It's the fastest way to reach the right people, and never waste time hunting down the wrong person again.
Resource:
http://community.jigsaw.com/t5/How-to-Use-Jigsaw/bd-p/jigsawresourcecenter

BusinessVibes   www.businessvibes.com/about-businessvibes

A growing B2B networking platform for global trade professionals. BusinessVibes uses a social networking model for businesses to find and connect with international partner companies. With a network of over 5000+ trade associations, 20 million companies and 25,000+ business events across 100+ major industries and 175 countries, BusinessVibes is a decisive source to companies looking for international business partners, be they clients, suppliers, JV partners, or any other type of business contact.

Yext.com

Lets companies manage their digital presence in online maps, directories and apps. Over 400,000 businesses make millions of monthly updates across 85+ exclusive global partners, making Yext the global market leader. Digital presence is a fundamental need for all 50 million businesses in the world, and Yext's mission is perfect location information in every hand. Yext is based in the heart of New York City with 350 employees and was named to Forbes Most Promising Companies lists for 2015 and 2017, as well as the Fortune Best Places to Work 2015 list.

Google+

We will pay specific attention to Google+, which is already playing a more important role in Google's organic ranking algorithm. We will create a business page on Google+ to achieve improved local search visibility. Google+ will also be the best way to get access to Google Authorship, which will play a huge role in SEO. Aside from having all the necessary information like hours and contact information, quality photos and visuals will be essential on our Google+ local page. To go above the basics, we will have a local Google photographer visit and create a virtual tour.

Resources:
https://plus.google.com/pages/create
http://www.google.com/+/brands/
https://www.google.com/appserve/fb/forms/plusweekly/
https://plus.google.com/+GoogleBusiness/posts
http://marketingland.com/beyond-social-benefits-google-business-73460
http://searchenginewatch.com/sew/how-to/2124899/seo-for-google-profiles-and-pages

Examples:
https://plus.google.com/+TeddyMeDayCareCenterMorristown/about

Inbound Marketing
Inbound marketing is about pulling people in by sharing relevant child daycare information, creating useful content, and generally being helpful. It involves writing everything from buyer's guides to blogs and newsletters that deliver useful content. The objective will be to nurture customers through the buying process with unbiased educational materials that turn consumers into informed buyers.
Resource:
www.Hubspot.com
http://blog.hubspot.com/marketing/inbound-marketing-for-daycares#sm.
 000070u8ombf3dk2wnh1cjfqjy0gd

Google My Business Profile   www.google.com/business/befound.html
We will have a complete and active Google My Business profile to give our child daycare company a tremendous advantage over the competition, and help potential customers easily find our firm and provide relevant information about our business.

Sampling Program
We will give each sample with a mini-survey to enable customers to rate the product or service, and supply constructive feedback. We will also make certain to always trade free samples for the recipient's contact information. All samples will have a label with our complete contact information.

Reddit.com
An online community where users vote on stories. The hottest stories rise to the top, while the cooler stories sink. Comments can be posted on every story, including stories about startup child daycare companies.
Examples:
https://www.reddit.com/r/ECEProfessionals/

Exterior Signage
We will make effective use of the following types of signage: (select)
1. **Channel Letter**
   Channel letters can be illuminated by LED or neon and come in a variety of colors and sizes. Front-lit signs are illuminated from the letter face, while reverse-lit signs are lit from behind the sign. Open-face channel letters lit by exposed neon work well to create a night presence.
2. **Monument Signs**
   Monument signs are usually placed at the entrance to a parking lot or a building. This sign can easily be installed on a median or lawn. The size for a monument sign is typically based on city regulations for the specific location. These signs can be illuminated or non-illuminated, single- or double-sided.
3. **Pylon Signs**

Also known as pole signs, they soar high above a business location to set the business apart from other businesses. They get attention from highway motorists who are still a distance away.

4. **Cabinet Signs**
Commonly called "wall" or "box" signs, they are a traditional form of signage. They effectively use a large copy area and eye-popping graphics. This type of signage can highlight our business day or night because we have the option to add illumination. The background can be the element that lights up, and the copy can be lit or non-lit.

5. **Sandwich Signs**
This sign will be placed on the sidewalk in front of our business to attract foot traffic.

6.4.1 Strategic Alliances

We will form strategic alliances to accomplish the following objectives:
1. To share marketing expenses.
2. To realize bulk buying power on wholesale purchases.
3. To engage in barter arrangements.
4. To collaborate with industry experts.
5. To set-up mutual referral relationships.

We will seek to form alliances with the following types of businesses to secure drop-off clients:
1. Fitness Clubs
2. Yoga Studios
3. Dance Schools
4. Movie Theaters
5. Fun Centers
6. Toy Stores

We will also see referrals from the following types of businesses:
1. Family Pediatricians
2. Family Physicians
3. Hospitals
4. Large Corporations
5. Dental Practices

We will assemble a sales presentation package that includes sales brochures, business cards, and a DVD seminar presentation. We will print coupons that offer a discount or other type of introductory deal. We will ask to set-up a take-one display for our sales brochures at the business registration counter. We will give the referring business any one or combination of the following reward options:
1. Referral fees
2. Free services
3. Mutual referral exchanges

We will monitor referral sources to evaluate the mutual benefits of the alliance and make certain to clearly define and document our referral incentives prior to initiating our referral exchange program.

6.4.2 Monitoring Marketing Results

To monitor how well _____ (company name) is doing, we will measure how well the advertising campaign is working by taking customer surveys. What we would like to know is how they heard of us and how they like and dislike about our services. In order to get responses to the surveys, we will be give discounts as thank you rewards.

Response Tracking Methods
Coupons: ad-specific coupons that easily enable tracking
Landing Pages: unique web landing pages for each advertisement
800 Numbers: unique 1-800-# per advertisement
Email Service Provider: Instantly track email views, opens, and clicks
Mailing addresses with embedded department codes.

Our financial statements will offer excellent data to track all phases of sales. These are available for review on a daily basis. _____ (company name) will benchmark our objectives for sales promotion and advertising in order to evaluate our return on invested marketing dollars, and determine where to concentrate our limited advertising dollars to realize the best return. We will also strive to stay within our marketing budget.

Key Marketing Metrics
We will use the following two marketing metrics to evaluate the cost-effectiveness of our marketing campaign:
1. The cost to acquire a new customer: The average dollar amount invested to get one new client. Example: If we invest $3,000 on marketing in a single month and end the month with 10 new customers, our cost of acquisition is $300 per new customer.
2. The lifetime value of the average active client. The average dollar value of an average customer over the life of their business with you. To calculate this metric for a given period of time, we will take the total amount of revenue our business generated during the time period and divide it by the total number of customers we had from the beginning of the time period.
3. We will track the following set of statistics on a weekly basis to keep informed of the progress of our business:
    A. Number of total referrals.
    B. Percentage increase of total referrals (over baseline).
    C. Number of new referral sources.
    D. Number of new customers/month.
    E. Number of Leads

Key Marketing Metrics Table

We've listed some key metrics in the following table. We will need to keep a close eye on these, to see if we meet our own forecasted expectations. If our numbers are off in too many categories, we may, after proper analysis, have to make substantial changes to our marketing efforts.

Key Marketing Metrics	2017	2018	2019
Revenue			
Leads			
Leads Converted			
Avg. Transaction per Customer			
Avg. Dollars per Customer			
Number of Referrals			
Number of PR Appearances			
Number of Testimonials			
Number of New Club Members			
Number of Returns			
Number of BBB Complaints			
Number of Completed Surveys			
Number of Blog readers			
Number of Twitter followers			
Number of Facebook Fans			

Metric Definitions
1. Leads: Individuals who step into the store to consider a purchase.
2. Leads Converted: Percent of individuals who actually make a purchase.
3. Average Transactions Per Customer: Number of purchases per customer per month. Expected to rise significantly as customers return for more and more _____ items per month
4. Average $ Per Customer: Average dollar amount of each transaction. Expected to rise along with average transactions.
5. Referrals: Includes customer and business referrals
6. PR Appearances: Online or print mentions of the business that are not paid advertising. Expected to be high upon opening, then drop off and rise again until achieving a steady level.
7. Testimonials: Will be sought from the best and most loyal customers. Our objective is ___ (#) per month) and they will be added to the website. Some will be sought as video testimonials.
8. New Loyalty Club Members: This number will rise significantly as more customers see the value in repeated visits and the benefits of club membership.
9. Number of Returns/BBB Complaints: Our goal is zero.
10. Number of Completed Surveys: We will provide incentives for customers to complete customer satisfaction surveys.

6.4.3 Word-of-Mouth Marketing

We plan to make use of the following techniques to promote word-of-mouth advertising:

1. Repetitive Image Advertising
2. Provide exceptional customer service.
3. Make effective use of loss leaders.
2. Schedule in-store activities, such as demonstrations or special events.
3. Make trial easy with a coupon or introductory discount.
4. Initiate web and magazine article submissions
5. Utilize a sampling program
6. Add a forward email feature to our website.
7. Share relevant and believable testimonial letters
8. Publish staff bios.
9. Make product/service upgrade announcements
10. Hold contests or sweepstakes
12. Have involvement with community events.
13. Pay suggestion box rewards
14. Distribute a monthly newsletter
15. Share easy-to-understand information (via an article or seminar).
16. Make personalized marketing communications.
17. Structure our referral program.
18. Sharing of Community Commonalities
19. Invitations to join our community of shared interests.
20. Publish Uncensored Customer Reviews
21. Enable Information Exchange Forums
22. Provide meaningful comparisons with competitors.
23. Clearly state our user benefits.
24. Make and honor ironclad guarantees
25. Provide superior post-sale support
26. Provide support in the pre-sale decision making process.
27. Host Free Informational Seminars or Workshops
28. Get involved with local business organizations.
29. Issue Press Release coverage of charitable involvements.
30. Hold traveling company demonstrations/exhibitions/competitions.
31. Stay in touch with inactive clients.

6.4.4 Customer Satisfaction Survey

We will design a customer satisfaction survey to measure the "satisfaction quotient" of our Child Day Care Center customers. By providing a detailed snapshot of our current customer base, we will be able to generate more repeat and referral business and enhance the profitability of our child day care center.

Our Customer Satisfaction Survey will including the following basics:
1. How do our customers rate our child day care business?
2. How do our customers rate our competition?
3. How well do our customers rate the value of our products or services?
4. What new customer needs and trends are emerging?
5. How loyal are our customers?
6. What can be done to improve customer loyalty and repeat business?
7. How strongly do our customers recommend our business?
8. What is the best way to market our business?
9. What new value-added services would best differentiate our business from that of our competitors?
10. How can we encourage more referral business?
11. How can our pricing strategy be improved?

Our customer satisfaction survey will help to answer these questions and more. From the need for continual new products and services to improved customer service, our satisfaction surveys will allow our organization to quickly identify problematic and underperforming areas, while enhancing our overall customer satisfaction.

Examples:
http://smallbiztrends.com/2007/06/the-small-biz-7-survey.html
www.daycareanswers.com/support-files/daycare-customer-satisfaction-survey.pdf
www.mapleleafchildcare.com/parent-resources/parent-survey/
http://decal.ga.gov/documents/attachments/DECAL2017CustomerSatisfactionReport.pdf
http://www.4qsmartstartdatasystem.com/resources/Parent-Satisfaction-Survey.pdf

Resources:
https://www.survata.com/
https://www.google.com/insights/consumersurveys/use_cases
www.surveymonkey.com
http://www.smetoolkit.org/smetoolkit/en/content/en/6708/Customer-Satisfaction-Survey-Template-
http://smallbusiness.chron.com/common-questions-customer-service-survey-1121.html

6.4.5 Marketing Training Program

Our Marketing Training Program will include both an initial orientation and training, as well as ongoing continuing education classes. Initial orientation will be run by the owner until an HR manager is hired. For one week, half of each day will be spent in training, and the other half shadowing the operations manager.

Training will include:
Learning the entire selection of child day care programs.
Understanding our Mission Statement, Value Proposition, Position Statement and

Unique Selling Proposition.
Appreciating our competitive advantages.
Understanding our core message and branding approach.
Learning our store's policies; returns processing, complaint handling, etc.
Learning our customer services standards of practice.
Learning our customer and business referral programs.
Learning our Membership Club procedures, rules and benefits.
Becoming familiar with our company website, and online ordering options.
Service procedures specific to the employee's role.

Ongoing workshops will be based on customer feedback and problem areas identified by mystery buyers, which will better train employees to educate customers. These ongoing workshops will be held ____ (once?) a month for _____ (three?) hours.

6.5 Sales Strategy

The development of our sales strategy will start by developing a better understanding of our customer needs. To accomplish this task we will pursue the following research methods:
1. Join the associations that our target customers belong to.
2. Contact the membership director and establish a relationship to understand their member's needs, challenges and concerns.
3. Identify non-competitive suppliers who sell to our customer to learn their challenges and look for partnering solutions.
4. Work directly with our customer and ask them what their needs are and if our business may offer a possible solution.

Our sales strategy will be targeted at dual income and single parent households. We will sell our educational theme, services and reputation to differentiate ourselves from traditional daycare-only offerings. We will develop an effective and comprehensive sales process that will involve making the appointment with parents, the interview session, a facilities tour, presentation of our competitive advantages and then closure of the deal.

We will be a one-stop shop for child care services, innovative learning techniques and specialized program offerings. We will also be very active in the community, building a solid reputation with parents and community leaders.

Our clients will be primarily obtained through word-of-mouth referrals, but we will also advertise introductory offers, such as the waiving of the registration fee, to introduce people to our programs. The combination of the perception of higher quality, exceptional technical support and the recognition of superior value should turn referral leads into satisfied customers.

The company's sales strategy will be based on the following elements:

Advertising in the Yellow Pages - two inch by three inch ads describing our services will be placed in the local Yellow Pages.
Placing classified advertisements in the regional editions of auto magazines.
Word of mouth referrals - generating sales leads in the local community through customer referrals.

One of the ways we will differentiate our sales strategy will be in how calls are handled when people are looking for information. As the first conversation begins, a record will be created, tracking the caller's name, the name and age of the child (or children), what the parent is looking for in the way of child-care services, and any other information that's discussed. When the parent comes in to tour the facility, the administrator will make it a point to refer to the child by name and will be able to focus on the aspects of the center that are consistent with what the parent wants or expressed a prior interest in.

Our basic sales strategy is to:
Develop a website for lead generation by _____ (date).
Provide exceptional customer service.
Accept payment by all major credit cards, cash, PayPal and check.
Survey our customers regarding services they would like to see added.
Sponsor charitable and other community events.
Provide tours of the facility so parents can personally witness the learning process and build a trust bond with our operations.
Motivate employees with a pay-for-performance component to their straight salary compensation package, based on profits and customer satisfaction rates.
Build long-term customer relationships by putting the interests of customers first.
Establish mutually beneficial relationship with local businesses serving the needs of children.

By succeeding at these programs, we expect to see an operational net profit in month ____ (#) of the _____ (first?) year.

6.5.1 Customer Retention

We will use the following techniques to improve customer retention and the profitability of our business:
1. Keep the facility sparkling clean and well-organized.
2. Use only well-trained instructors, and the highest quality equipment.
3. Ask the customers for feedback and promptly act upon their inputs.
4. Tell customers how much you appreciate their business.
5. Call regular customers by their first names.
6. Send thank you notes.
7. Offer free new product and service samples.
8. Change displays and sales presentations on a regular basis.
9. Practice good phone etiquette

10. Respond to complaints promptly.
11. Reward referrals.
12. Publish a monthly newsletter.
13. Develop and publish a list of frequently asked questions.
14. Issue Preferred Customer Membership Cards.
15. Hold informational seminars and workshops.
16. Run contests.
17. Develop service contracts.
18. Provide an emergency hotline number.
19. Publish code of ethics and our service guarantees.
20. Publish all customer reviews.
21. Help customers to make accurate competitor comparisons.
22. Build a stay-in-touch (drip marketing) communications calendar.
23. Keep marketing communications focused on our competitive advantages.
24. Offer repeat user discounts and incentives.
25. Be supportive and encouraging, and not judgmental.
26. Measure customer retention and look at recurring revenue and customer surveys.
27. Keep parents involved with a photo sharing program.
    Resource: http://blog.kinderlime.com/2013/01/17/using-photo-sharing-to-market-your-childcare-and-retain-your-parents/
28. Ensure that all caregivers have a close rapport with the kids.
29. Make birthdays and special holidays memorable for the kids.
30. Make use of effective customer relationship management (CRM) software to effectively manage our clientele base.
31. Ensures that we carry parents along when making decisions that directly affect them.
32. Keep parents posted as to facility or equipment malfunctions and the forecasted repair schedule.
33. Put on an annual show where the kids can demonstrate the progress they have made.

We will also consider the following Customer Retention Programs:

Type of Program	Customer Rewards
Frequency Purchase Loyalty Program	Special Discounts
	Free Product or Services
Rebate Loyalty Programs	Credit Based on Percent of Incremental Sales from Prior Period.
'Best Customer' Program	Special Recognition/Treatment/Offers
Affinity Programs	Sharing of Common Interests
	Accumulate Credit Card Points
Customer Community Programs	Special Event Participation
Auto-Knowledge Building Programs	Purchase Recommendations based On Past Transaction History
Profile Building Programs	Recommendations Based on Stated Customer Profile Information.

6.5.2 Sales Forecast

Our sales projections are based on the following:
1. Actual sales volumes of local competitors
2. Interviews with child daycare owners and managers
3. Observations of sales and traffic at competitor establishments.
4. Government and industry trade statistics
5. Local population demographics and projections.
6. Discussions with suppliers.

Our sales forecast is an estimated projection of expected sales over the next three years, based on our chosen marketing strategy and assumed competitive environment.

Sales are expected to be below average during the first year, until a regular customer base has been established. It has been estimated that it takes the average daycare business a minimum of one year to establish a significant customer base. After the customer base is built, sales will grow at an accelerated rate from word-of-mouth referrals and continued networking efforts.

We expect sales to steadily increase as our marketing program and contact management system are executed. By using advertising, especially discounted introductory coupons, as a catalyst for this prolonged process, _____ (company name) plans to attract more customers sooner.

Throughout the first year, it is forecasted that sales will incrementally grow until profitability is reached toward the end of year _____ (one?). Year two reflects a conservative growth rate of _____ (15?) percent. Year three reflects a growth rate of _____ (15?) percent. We expect to be open for business on _____ (date), and start with an initial enrollment of _____ (#) students. With our unique product and service offerings, along with our thorough and aggressive marketing strategies, we believe that sales forecasts are actually on the conservative side.

Table: Sales Forecast

Unit Sales	2017	Annual Sales 2018	2019
Full-time students			
After School Care			
Summer Camp			
Part-time students			
Drop-ins			
Transportation Services			
Miscellaneous			
Total Unit Sales			

Unit Prices
Full-time students
After School Care
Summer Camp
Part-time students
Drop-ins
Transportation Services
Miscellaneous
Sales:
Full-time students
After School Care
Summer Camp
Part-time students
Drop-ins
Transportation Services
Miscellaneous
Total Sales

Direct Unit Costs:
Full-time students
After School Care
Summer Camp
Part-time students
Drop-ins
Transportation Services
Miscellaneous

Direct Cost of Sales:
Full-time students
After School Care
Summer Camp
Part-time students
Drop-ins
Transportation Services
Miscellaneous
Subtotal Direct Cost of Sales

6.6 Merchandising Strategy

Merchandising is that part of our marketing strategy that is involved with promoting the sales of our merchandise, as by consideration of the most effective means of selecting, pricing, displaying, and advertising items for sale in our child care business.

We will develop a merchandising strategy to sell educational products to our clients. We will strive to feature merchandise that is not found in competitor stores and use proper and informative signage to help sell merchandise. We plan to group similar types of merchandise together for maximum visual appeal. Product presentation will be designed to lead the customers through the entire display area.

We will monitor our sales figures and data to confirm that products in demand are well-stocked and slow moving products are phased-out. We will improve telephone skills of employees to boost phone orders.

To illustrate our cost competitiveness on selected educational products, we will use shelf signs to compare our prices to those of the local discount store. This will also help to develop the client's trust in the competitive pricing of all of our products and services.

We will encourage impulse purchases with the use of descriptive adjectives in our signage. We will attach our own additional business labels to all products to promote our line of services and location.

These are the basics of our merchandising strategy:
1. Products will be placed to maximize cross-selling, plus they are shelved with a vertical merchandising system to showcase more products.
2. We will create a "Power-aisle" with mass displays of impulse items and fast-moving items in the center aisle with "category products" on each side.
3. We will highlight more brand names in product lines.
4. Enhance interior signage to make it easier for customers to find the products they want.
5. Enable customers to have a panoramic view of our merchandise by opening up the floor space.
6. Improve our window displays to encourage customer visits.
7. Facilitate and encourage customer interactivity with displays.
8. Create bundled displays, such as oil and filters, to encourage up-selling.
9. Fixtures will complement each other and match the overall image of our store.
10. Create seating and snack areas that encourage social exchanges among customers.
11. Create clear traffic patterns to encourage complete store navigation by customers.
12. Install lighting that improves merchandise visibility and contributes to the store's overall personality.
13. Update neon signage inside and outside of the store.
14. Make sure sales brochures and flyers are always available at the sales counter.
15. Encourage sales associates to utilize products in demonstrations.

6.7 Pricing Strategy

Our pricing strategy will take into view factors such as our firm's overall marketing objectives, consumer demand, service quality attributes, competitors' pricing, and market and economic trends. We are not interested in being the low price leader.

Our pricing strategy plays a major role in whether we will be able to create and maintain customers for a profit. Our revenue structure must support our cost structure, so the salaries we pay to our certified instructors are balanced by the revenue we collect.

Note: Assuming full-time day care for a 2 year old child on weekdays, according to Runzheimer International, the U.S. national average cost for full-time day care is $611 a month. Large cities such as Boston and New York are most expensive, with average daycare costs of a little more than $1,000 a month.

We will contact our local 'Child Care Resource & Referral Agency' for information about local child care rates. State agencies that administer childcare payment programs also set the rates that they will reimburse providers for care to eligible children. We will also compare prices, hours and services with those of other child care providers in our area.

We will use the following approach to help set our rates and payment policies:
1. Use the Rate Surveys to learn the average rates in our area.
2. Decide how much do you need to earn to breakeven.
3. Make an inventory of the assets of your program. Benefits such as our Education, Parent Aware Rating, Accreditation, many years of experience or other assets may be justification for higher rates.
4. Make an inventory of the deficits of our program. Sometimes a program's location, presence of pets, home arrangement, or hours open may be less than ideal and our rates may need to be adjusted to attract customers.
5. Plan ahead for what services will you offer: full-time care, part-time care, evening, weekend, overnight, drop in … you can set a rate for each service or a flat-rate.
6. Plan ahead for how to handle these situations: a child is sick, provider is sick, child or provider has vacation, parent is late picking up or dropping off child, parent wants you to hold a spot for a child (usually a baby)
7. Decide on a payment schedule: Weekly, biweekly, or whatever works best for our business and our clients.
8. Charge-up front and collect the payment for the last 2 weeks up-front to avoid having parents leave while owing money. If parents cannot pay the last two weeks up front before beginning care, let them pay an extra $10 per week until that balance is reached.
9. Plan ahead for regular rate increases or benefit growth (sometimes extra vacation days are added instead of a fee increase, for example).

Our Proposed Monthly Fee Schedule:

0 - 2 yrs	**Full Days**	**Half Days**
5 days/week	$605/month	$453/month
4 days/week	$555/month	$416/month
3 days/week	$445/month	$333/month
2 days/week	$315/month	$236/month
1 day/week	$165/month	$123/month
Daily/Drop-in	$ 40/day	$ 30/day
Registration	$140/one time	$140/one time

2 yrs & older	**Full Days**	**Half Days**
5 days/week	$505/month	$378/month
4 days/week	$455/month	$341/month
3 days/week	$365/month	$274/month
2 days/week	$265/month	$200/month
1 day/week	$135/month	$101/month
Daily/Drop-in	$ 30/day	$ 26/day
Registration	$115/one	$115/one time

We will offer discounts for the following:
1. Early Bird Payments (Must be paid before the 1st of every month).
2. Multiple Children
3. Children of active military.

Or....Tuition & Fees
Current tuition rates are as follows and subject to change with a two (2) week notice.

Rates
Under 2 years $125/week
Over 2 years $125/week

Note: Some day cares offer a sliding scale for tuition that's based on gross family income.

Pick Up Late Fee
The center closes at 6:00 pm. A late pick up fee of $ 1.00 per every minute late will apply. You will be expected to pay this fee immediately upon picking up your child. Please notify us as soon as possible if you are running late. If by 6:00 p.m. we have not heard from a parent or designated person, "Emergency Contact" numbers will be called to arrange for an alternate pick up.

Payments

Payments are accepted in cash or check. Payments are due before service is rendered. Due date is Friday before 6:00 pm for the following week. Payments made after 6 p.m. Friday will have a $15 fee added.

If a check is returned, you will be charged $25 plus full tuition, status is considered to be non- payment of fees and child may not attend daycare until payment received. Payment must be met within 72 hours of notification.

If payment is received within 72 hours, child may return to daycare. If payment is not received within 72 hours, child is discharged from daycare. Only cash or certified checks will be accepted for future payments.

Withdrawal and Discharge Policy
A two week notice is required if you plan to withdraw your child from our daycare. This gives the daycare the opportunity to fill your child's spot. Payments already made in excess of two (2) weeks from the date of notice may be refunded.

Our pricing strategy will be guided by the following insights:
1. If more than one child per family is enrolled, we will offer a ___(20?) % discount on the additional family members.
2. We will charge a nominal pre-registration fee of $_____.
3. We will charge separate fees for each of the following:
   - Infant care
   - Meals
   - Field trips
   - Transportation
   - Materials
   - Special Curriculum
4. We will charge $____ (1.00?) overtime fee for each minute of late child pick-up by parents.
5. We will charge a late payment fee of $____ (25?) for each occurrence.
6. We must insure that our price plus service equation is perceived to be an exceptional value proposition.
7. We must refrain from competing on price, but always be price competitive.
8. We must develop value-added services, and bundle those with our products to create offerings that cannot be easily price compared.
9. We must focus attention on our competitive advantages.
10. Development of a pricing strategy based on our market positioning strategy, which is ____ (mass market value leadership/exceptional premium niche value?)
11. Our pricing policy objective, which is to _____ (increase profit margins/ achieve revenue maximization to increase market share/lower unit costs).
12. We will use marketplace intelligence and gain insights from competitor pricing strategy comparisons.
13. We will solicit pricing feedback from customers using surveys and informal interviews.
14. We will utilize limited time pricing incentives to penetrate niche markets
15. We will conduct experiments at prices above and below the current price to determine the price elasticity of demand. (Inelastic demand or demand that does not decrease with a price increase, indicates that price increases may be feasible.)

16. We will keep our offerings and prices simple to understand and competitive, based on market intelligence.

Determining the costs of servicing business is the most important part of covering our expenses and earning profits. We will factor in the following pricing formula:

Materials + Overhead + Labor + Profit = Price
Materials are those items consumed in the delivering of the service.
Overhead costs are the variable and fixed expenses that must be covered to stay in business. Variable costs are those expenses that fluctuate including vehicle expenses, rental expenses, utility bills and supplies. Fixed costs include the purchase of equipment, service ware, marketing and advertising, and insurance. After overhead costs are determined, the total overhead costs are divided among the total number of transactions forecasted for the year.
Labor costs include the costs of performing the services. Also included are Social Security taxes (FICA), vacation time, retirement and other benefits such as health or life insurance. To determine labor costs per hour, keep a time log. When placing a value on our time, we will consider the following: 1) skill and reputation; 2) wages paid by employers for similar skills and 3) where we live. Other pricing factors include image, inflation, supply and demand, and competition.
Profit is a desired percentage added to our total costs. We will need to determine the percentage of profit added to each service. It will be important to cover all our costs to stay in business. We will investigate available computer software programs to help us price our services and keep financial data for decision-making purposes. Close contact with customers will allow our company to react quickly to changes in demand.

We will develop a pricing strategy that will reinforce the perception of value to the customer and manage profitability, especially in the face of rising inflation. To ensure our success, we will use periodic competitor and customer research to continuously evaluate our pricing strategy. We intend to review our profit margins every six months.

6.8 Differentiation Strategies

We will use differentiation strategies to develop and market unique products for different customer segments. To differentiate ourselves from the competition, we will focus on the assets, creative ideas and competencies that we have that none of our competitors has. The goal of our differentiation strategies is to be able to charge a premium price for our unique products and services and/or to promote loyalty and assist in retaining our customers.

Our major source of differentiation will be our emphasis on learning. The children in our care will be given the opportunity to learn at their own pace. We will use a non-regimented model to introduce them to learn the basics of language. science and numbers, while making it a playful learning experience.

We will also be committed to ensuring that all our children receive a broad, relevant, balanced and differentiated curriculum, which is matched to their individual needs. On entering our daycare, children will undergo an initial assessment. If a special need is identified then we will make contact with the parents. Parents will be asked to attend regular review meetings so that they will be informed of the progress of their child and be involved in the planning for future provision. A significant number of children will have special educational needs of some kind at various stages during their early development.

A special educational need (SEN) includes:
- General learning difficulties (which may be sever, profound, multiple or general)
- Specific learning difficulties (such as dyslexia)
- Emotional and behavioral difficulties
- Physical difficulties
- Sensory impairments
- Speech and language difficulties
- Medical condition which impairs learning

We will also seek to address the needs of talented and gifted children.

We will also teach our children the importance of discipline and to better understand the facial expressions and emotions of others and themselves.

Differentiation in our child day care will be achieved in the following types of ways, including:

	Explanation
☐ Product features	
☐ Complementary services	
☐ Technology embodied in design	
☐ Location	
☐ Service innovations	
☐ Superior service	
☐ Creative advertising	
☐ Better supplier relationships	

Source: http://scholarship.sha.cornell.edu/cgi/viewcontent.cgi?article=1295&context=articles

Differentiating will mean defining who our perfect target market is and then catering to their needs, wants and interests better than everyone else. It will be about using surveys to determine what's most important to our targeted market and giving it to them consistently. It will not be about being "everything to everybody"; but rather, "the absolute best to our chosen targeted group".

In developing our differentiation strategy will we use the following form to help define our differences:

1. Targeted customer segments   _____
2. Customer characteristics   _____
3. Customer demographics   _____
4. Customer behavior   _____
5. Geographic focus   _____
6. Ways of working   _____
7. Service delivery approach   _____
8. Customer problems/pain points _____
9. Complexity of customers' problems _____
10. Range of services   _____

We will use the following approaches to differentiate our products and services from those of our competitors to stand apart from standardised offerings:

1. Superior quality
2. Unusual or unique product features
3. More responsive customer service
4. Rapid product or service innovation
5. Advanced technological features
6. Engineering design or styling
7. Additional product features
8. An image of prestige or status

Specific Differentiators will include the following:
1. Being a Specialist in one procedure
2. Utilizing advanced/uncommon technology
3. Possessing extensive experience
4. Building an exceptional facility
5. Consistently achieving superior results
6. Having a caring and empathetic personality
7. Giving customer s WOW experience, including a professional customer welcome package.
8. Enabling convenience and 24/7 online accessibility
9. Calling customers to express interest in their challenges.
10. Keeping to the appointment schedule.
11. Remembering customer names and details like they were family
12. Assuring customer fears.
13. Building a visible reputation and recognition around our community
14. Acquiring special credentials or professional memberships
15. Providing added value services, such as taxi service, longer hours, financing plans, and post-sale services.

Other Differentiation Strategies:
1. We will extend our operating hours to accommodate parents who need to work late.

2. We will offer better quality meals.
3. We will develop a better quality curriculum.
4. We will provide a lower caregiver to child ratio than required and this will permit daily experiences to be tailored to each child's developmental stage and interests.
5. We will endeavor to earn the parents trust and do whatever it takes to ensure that the parents totally trust us. Building trust will mean having to be honest and sharing important information, whatever the consequences are.
6. We will offer an exclusive line of educational products for sale and also use them as part of our lesson plan.
7. We will develop a referral program that turns our clients into commissioned referral agents.
8. We will use regular client satisfaction surveys to collect feedback, improvement ideas, referrals and testimonials.
9. We will promote our "green" practices.
10. We will customize our offerings according to the cultural influences, customs, interests and tastes of our local market to create loyalty and increase sales.
11. We will adapt the learning materials and objectives to the particular ability levels of each child.
12. We will provide web-based, remote video surveillance of the classroom for parents and enable e-mail access to staff, online event calendars and chat rooms. We will use this feature to build an online community both among parents, and between parents and staff.
13. Our low staff turnover rate translates to consistency of one primary caregiver.

Our In-home Daycare will offer the following differentiated benefits:
1. Our mixed age group will provide a better comfort zone for the children because this situation looks similar to the real condition of each child's family.
2. Because there will be fewer children, we will be able to provide more intensive attention and care, and there will less of a chance for the spread of illnesses.
3. The in-home atmosphere will be more familiar and comforting for the children.
4. The children will come from our same neighborhood, which will make it easier for the children to adapt to their new situation.
5. Our in-home daycare prices will be lower than commercial facilities.
6. We will offer more flexibility for the pick-up and dropping off of children, without the charging of excessive late fees.
7. Our In-home daycare have fewer closed holidays than another centre.
8. Our in home daycare providers will be mothers who will have a natural bond with the children through their instinct as a mother.
9. We will offer greater flexibility on food menu choices, and the chance to bring their own food from home, which is rarely allowed by another type of centre.
10. We will customize our hours of service to meet the needs of parents, and focus on the neglected before- and after-school care market.
    Source: https://www.entrepreneur.com/article/246568

Summary

We plan to differentiate our daycare in the following ways:

Differentiation Strategy

1. Outdoor Facilities _____
2. Extra-curricular activities _____
3. Planned daily schedules _____
4. Web-cameras _____
5. Bus transportation _____
6. Price _____
7. Educational philosophy _____
8. Teacher training _____
9. Preparation of environment _____
10. Classroom work _____
11. Staff to Child Ratio _____
12. Program Options _____
13. Payment Options _____
14. Parent Education _____
15. Child Progress Reporting _____
16. Faculty Consistency _____
17. Customized Packages _____
18. Flexible Services _____
19. After school Programs _____
20. Indoor Gym _____
21. Organic Snacks/Lunches _____
22. Onsite Nutritionist _____
23. Safety Measures _____
24. Security System _____
25. Theatrical/Dance Studio _____
26. Equipment Maintenance _____
27. Daily Facilities Cleaning _____

6.9 Milestones

The Milestones Chart is a timeline that will guide our company in developing and growing our business. It will list chronologically the various critical actions and events that must occur to bring our business to life. We will make certain to assign real, attainable dates to each planned action or event.

_____ (company name) has identified several specific milestones which will function as goals for the company. The milestones will provide a target for achievement as well as a mechanism for tracking progress. The dates were chosen based on realistic delivery times and necessary construction times. All critical path milestones will be completed within their allotted time frames to ensure the success of contingent milestones. The following table will provide a timeframe for each milestone.

Table: Milestones

Milestones	Start Date	End Date	Budget	Responsibility
Business Plan Completion				
Secure Permits/Licenses				
Locate & Secure Space				
Obtain Insurance				
Secure Additional Financing				
Get Start-up Supplies Quotes				
Obtain County Certification				
Licensing				
Purchase Office Equipment				
Renovate Facilities				
Define Marketing Programs				
Install Equipment/Displays				
Technology Systems				
Set-up Accounting System				
Finalize Media Plan				
Create Facebook Brand Page				
Open Twitter Account				
Conduct Blogger Outreach				
Develop Personnel Plan				
Curriculum Development				
Develop Staff Training Programs				
Hire Staff				
Train Staff				
Implement Marketing Plan				
Get Website Live				
Conduct SEO Campaign				
Form Strategic Alliances				
Purchase Inventory/Supplies				
Press Release Announcements				
Advertise Grand Opening				
Kickoff Advertising Program				
Join Community Orgs./Network				
Conduct Satisfaction Surveys				
Monitor Social Media Networks				
Respond Positively to Reviews				
Measure Return on Marketing $$$				
Devise Growth Strategy				
Revenues Exceed $_____				
Profitability				

Totals: _____

7.0 Website Plan Summary

_____ (company name) is currently developing a website at the URL address www. (company name).com. We will primarily use the website to advertise services offered, class schedules, curriculum, community activity calendar, instructor resumes and helpful articles. We will use email to communicate with clients wishing to sign-up for email specials and our newsletter.

The job of our childcare website will be to inform parents about every facet of our operation, and to prove to them the benefits of enrolling their children in our daycare center. Our child care website will be designed to inspire confidence in parents, and convince them of the many benefits their children will derive through their centers.

We will also provide multiple incentives to sign-up for various benefits, such as our newsletters and promotional sale notices. This will help us to build an email database, which will supply our automated customer follow-up system. We will create a personalized drip marketing campaign to stay in touch with our customers and prospects.

We will develop our website to be a resource for web visitors who are seeking knowledge and information about child daycare safety procedures, with a goal to service the knowledge needs of our customers and generate leads. Our home page will be designed to be a "welcome mat" that clearly presents our service offerings and provides links through which visitors can gain easy access to the information they seek. We will use our website to match the problems and concerns our customers have with the solutions we offer.
Example: http://localvox.com/blog/child-care-marketing-tips/

We will use the free tool, Google Analytics (http://www.google.com/analytics), to generate a history and measure our return on investment. Google Analytics is a free tool that can offer insight by allowing the user to monitor traffic to a single website. We will just add the Google Analytics code to our website and Google will give our firm a dashboard providing the number of unique visitors, repeat traffic, page views, etc.

Other website analytics include:
1. WebTrends   www.webtrends.com
2. DeepMetrix   www.livestats.com
3. Web Position   www.webpositiongold.com
4. WebSideStory   www.websidestory.com

To improve the readability of our website, we will organize our website content in the following ways.
1. Headlines   2. Bullet points
3. Callout text   4. Top of page summaries

To improve search engine optimization, we will maximize the utilization of the following;

1. Links
2. Headers
3. Bold text
4. Bullets
5. Keywords
6. Meta tags

This website will serve the following purposes:

About Us	How We Work/Our Philosophy
Contact Us	Customer service contact info
Schedule A Visit	Form
Frequently Asked Questions	FAQs
Glossary of Child Care Terms	
Faculty Staff	Resumes
Newsletter Sign-up	Mailing List
Newsletter Archives	
Our Educational Curriculum	
Special Enrichment Programs	Description
Our Competitive Advantages	
Upcoming Events	Community Schedule
Child Care Testimonials	With Client Photos
Monthly Student Spotlight	
Photo Gallery	Facility, Instructors, Clients
Referral Program	Details
Directions	Location directions.
Seminar Calendar	Guest Lectures
Customer Satisfaction Survey	Feedback
Hours of Operation	
Press Releases	Community Involvement
Strategic Alliance Partners	Links
Parent Handbook	Our Policies and Procedures
Parent Resources	Child Care Selection Tips
Child Care Resources	Professional Associations
Our Blog	Center diary/Accept comments
Refer-a-Friend	Viral marketing
YouTube Video Clips	Seminar Presentation/Testimonials
Day Care Contract	Download
Guarantees/Code of Ethics	
Mission Statement	
Career Opportunities	
Classified Ads	

Classified Ads

By joining and incorporating a classified ad affiliate program into our website, we will create the ultimate win-win-win. We will provide our clients with a free benefit, increase our rankings with the search engines by incorporating keyword hyperlinks into our site, attract additional markets to expose to our child day care services, create an additional income source as they upgrade their ads, and provide our prospects a reason to return to our web site again and again

Resources:

App Themes	www.appthemes.com/themes/classipress/
e-Classifieds	http://www.e-classifieds.net/
Noah's Classifieds	http://www.noahsclassifieds.org/
Joom Prod	http://www.joomprod.com/
Flynax	http://www.flynax.com/
Market Grabber	http://www.marketgrabber.com/

7.1 Website Marketing Strategy

Our online marketing strategy will employ the following distinct mechanisms:

1. Search Engine Submission
   This will be most useful to people who are unfamiliar with _____ (company name), but are looking for a local day care center. There will also be searches from customers who may know about us, but who are seeking additional information.

2. Website Address (URL) on Marketing Materials
   Our URL will be printed on all marketing communications, business cards, letterheads, faxes, and invoices and product labels. This will encourage a visit to our website for additional information

3. Online Directories Listings
   We will make an effort to list our website on relevant, free and paid online directories and manufacturer website product locators.
   The good online directories possess the following features:

   Free or paid listings that do not expire and do not require monthly renewal.
   Ample space to get your advertising message across.
   Navigation buttons that are easy for visitors to use.
   Optimization for top placement in the search engines based on keywords that people typically use to find daycare centers.
   Direct links to your website, if available.
   An ongoing directory promotion campaign to maintain high traffic volumes to the directory site. Examples:

Day Care	www.daycare.com
Day Care Directory	www.daycaredirectory.com
Child Care Centers	www.childcarecenters.org
Day Care Match	www.daycarematch.com

4. Strategic Business Partners

We will use a Business Partners page to cross-link to prominent _____ (city) area day care web sites as well as the city Web sites and local recreational sites. We will also cross-link with brand name product suppliers.

5. YouTube Posting
We will produce a video of testimonials from several of our satisfied clients and educate viewers as to the range of our services and products. Our research indicates that the YouTube video will also serve to significantly improve our ranking with the Google Search Engine.

6. Exchange of links with strategic marketing partners.
We will cross-link to non-profit businesses that accept our gift certificate donations as in-house run contest prize awards.

7. E-Newsletter
Use the newsletter sign-up as a reason to collect email addresses and limited profiles, and use embedded links in the newsletter to return readers to website.

8. Create an account for your photos on flickr.com
Use the name of our site on flickr so we have the same keywords.

9. Geo Target Pay Per Click (PPC) Campaign
Available through Google Adwords program. Example keywords include day care center, drop-in, child care, sick care, after school and _____ (city).

10. Post messages on Internet user groups and forums.
Get involved with day care related discussion groups and forums and develop a descriptive signature paragraph. Forums such as those created by Daycare.com, OwnADaycare.com, and About.com will allow our company to discuss related topics, to collaborate, and to share resources.
Ex: www.mothering.com/community/forum/

11. Write up your own MySpace.com bio.
Highlight your background and professional interests.

12. Facebook.com Brand-Building Applications:
As a Facebook member, we will create a specific Facebook page for our business through its "Facebook Pages" application. This page will be used to promote who we are and what we do. We will use this page to post alerts when we have new articles to distribute, news to announce, etc. Facebook members can then become fans of our page and receive these updates on their newsfeed as we post them. We will create our business page by going to the "Advertising" link on the bottom of our personal Facebook page. We will choose the "Pages" tab at the top of that

page, and then choose "Create a Page." We will upload our logo, enter our company profile details, and establish our settings. Once completed, we will click the "publish your site" button to go live. We will also promote our Page everywhere we can. We will add a Facebook link to our website, our email signatures, and email newsletters. We will also add Facebook to the marketing mix by deploying pay-per-click ads through their advertising application. With Facebook advertising, we will target by specifying sex, age, relationship, location, education, as well as specific keywords. Once we specify our target criteria, the tool will tell us how many members in the network meet our target needs.

13. Blog to share our success stories and solicit feedback
    Blogging will be a great way for us to share information, expertise, and news, and start a conversation with our customers, the media, potential partners, suppliers, and any other target audiences. Blogging will be a great online marketing strategy because it keeps our content fresh, engages our audience to leave comments on specific posts, improves search engine rankings and attracts links.
    Resources: www.blogger.com   www.blogspot.com

14. Other Embedded Links
    We will use social networking, article directory postings and press release web sites as promotional tools and to provide good inbound link opportunities.

15. Issue Press Releases
    We will create online press releases to share news about our new website. Resources: Sites that offer free press release services include: www.prweb.com www.1888pressrelease.com and www.pr.com/press-releases.

7.2 Development Requirements

A full development plan will be generated as documented in the milestones. Costs that ____ (company name) will expect to incur with development of its new website include:

Development Costs
    User interface design $_____.
    Site development and testing $_____
    Site Implementation $._____

Ongoing Costs
    Website name registration $_____ per year.
    Site Hosting $_____ or less per month.
    Site design changes, updates and maintenance are considered part of Marketing.

The site will be developed by _____ (company name), a local start-up company. The user interface designer will use our existing graphic art to come up with the website logo and graphics. We have already secured hosting with a local provider, _____ (business name). Additionally, they will prepare a monthly statistical usage report to analyze and improve web usage and return on investment.

The plan is for the website to be live by _____ (date).

Basic website maintenance, including update and data entry will be handled by our staff. Site content, such as images and text will be maintained by _____ (owner name).

In the future, we may need to contract with a technical resource to build the trackable article download and newsletter capabilities.

Resources:
https://www.weebly.com/
http://localvox.com/customers/education-child-care-marketing/
www.webs.com
http://wahm.sitesell.com/
www.metrodaycare.com/How_to_promote_your_child_day_care_center_online_by_metrodaycare.pdf
Inexpensive Options: Wordpress, Weebly and/or Wix

7.3 Sample Frequently Asked Questions

We will use the following guidelines when developing the frequently asked questions for our the ecommerce section of the website:

1. Use a Table of Contents: Offer subject headers at the top of the FAQ page with a hyperlink to that related section further down on the page for quick access.
2. Group Questions in a Logical Way and group separate specific questions related to a subject together.
3. Be Precise With the Question: Don't use open-ended questions.
4. Avoid Too Many Questions: Publish only the popular questions and answers.
5. Answer the Question with a direct answer.
6. Link to Resources When Available: via hyperlinks so the customer can continue with self-service support.
7. Use Bullet Points to list step-by-step instructions.
8. Focus on Customer Support and Not Marketing.
9. Use Real and Relevant Frequently Asked Questions from actual customers.
10. Update Your FAQ Page as customers continue to communicate questions.

The following frequently asked questions will enable us to convey a lot of important information to our clients in a condensed format. We will post these questions and answers on our website and create a hardcopy version to be included on our sales presentation folder.

What is the difference between a daycare and a learning center?
These are marketing labels that provide parents with information about the center's primary purpose. Both daycares and learning centers have to be licensed as childcare facilities in your state. A daycare provides care for your child when you can't, while a learning center has a stronger emphasis on education. While a learning center emphasizes early learning, a daycare center's primary focus is providing childcare.

What qualifications do your teachers have?
Our preschool teachers are four year degreed.

What is the teacher/student ratio in the classroom?
4 year old pre-school class: A typical class of ___ (#) students will have one lead teacher and two assistants.
3 year old pre-school class: A typical class of ___ (#)students will have one lead teacher and two assistants.

Can a preschooler stay all day?
Yes. By using a combination of child development, child development flex, and/or latchkey.

Do you serve lunch?
No. We can provide care over the lunch hour which includes a nap time, but the child must bring a packed lunch.

Do preschoolers go on field trips?
Yes. However, we only take four year olds out of the building. They go on 2 or 3 trips per year and are transported by school bus. The three year olds have resource people, such as Mother Goose, who come into the classroom.

Can my child wear pull-ups?
No. All children must be bathroom independent and be able to care for all of their toileting needs.

Do you provide latchkey for all _____ Elementary Schools?
Yes. Providing we have space available at each grade level.

Must I pay full price for all of my children?
No. We offer a 20% discount for each additional child in the family if that child uses the center for 3 or more days a week.

When is Payment is Expected?
At the beginning each month for all parents with reserved space. Payment in full is expected by the 15th of the month. Part time parents are charged according to how many hours they have reserved for their child, times the rate under the income category that they fall under. This amount is multiplied by 52 weeks and divided by 12 to come up with a monthly rate. Accounts must be paid in full by the end of each month for your child to continue care the following month unless arrangements have been made in

advance.

7.4 Website Performance Summary

We will use web analysis tools to monitor web traffic, such as identifying the number of site visits. We will analyze customer transactions and take actions to minimize problems, such as incomplete sales and abandoned shopping carts.

We will use the following table to track the performance of our website:

Category	2017 Fcst	2017 Act	2018 Fcst	2018 Act	2019 Fcst	2019 Act
No. of Customers						
Bounce Rate						
Percent New Visits						
New Subscribers						
Unique Visitors						
Total Page Views/Visit						
Avg. Time on Site						
No. of Products						
Product Categories						
Number of Incomplete Sales						
Conversion Rate						
Affiliate Sales						
Customer Satisfaction Score						

8.0 Operations Plan

Operations include the business aspects of running our business, such as conducting quality assessment and improvement activities, auditing functions, cost-management analysis, and customer service. Our operations plan will present an overview of the flow of the daily activities of the business and the strategies that support them. It will focus on the following critical operating factors that will make the business a success:

1. We will enjoy the following advantages in the sourcing of our inventory: _____

2. We will utilize the following technological innovations in the customer relationship management (CRM) process: _____

3. We will make use of the following advantages in our distribution process: _____

4. We will develop the following in-house training program to improve caregiver productivity: _____
5. We will utilize the following system to better control inventory carrying costs. _____

6. We will implement the following quality control plan: _____

Quality Control Plan
Our Quality Control Plan will include a review process that checks all factors involved in our operations. The main objectives of our quality control plan will be to uncover defects and bottlenecks, and reporting to management level to make the decisions on the improvement of the whole production process. Our review process will include the following activities:
    Quality control checklist
    Finished product/service review
    Structured walkthroughs
    Statistical sampling
    Testing process

Operations Planning
We will use Microsoft Visio to develop visual maps, which will piece together the different activities in our organization and show how they contribute to the overall "value stream" of our business. We will rightfully treat operations as the lifeblood of our business. We will develop a combined sales and operations planning process where sales and operations managers will sit down every month to review sales, at the same time creating a forward-looking 12-month rolling plan to help guide the product development and manufacturing processes, which can become disconnected from sales. We will approach our operations planning using a three-step process that analyzes the company's

current state, future state and the initiatives it will tackle next. For each initiative, such as launching a new product or service, the company will examine the related financials, talent and operations needs, as well as target customer profiles. Our management team will map out the cost of development and then calculate forecasted return on investment and revenue predictions.

We will develop, document and publish Policy Statements with regard to each of the following:

Payments and Fees
- Enrollment policies and paperwork required
- Monthly/Weekly/Hourly Rates
- Rates for Different Age Groups
- Absences
- Registration Fees
- Vacation and Holiday Policies
- Withdrawal or Termination from Care
- Overtime Charges
- Late Fees
- Types of Payment Accepted (cash, check or money order)
- Returned Check Policy

Food, Clothing, and Supplies
- Number of meals and snacks provided
- Type of food offered
- Treats for special occasions
- Extra clothing and toileting supplies that need to be provided by parents
- Supplies included by the child care program

Health and Safety
- Immunization Requirements and records
- Illness and/or Injury Policy
- Emergency Procedures
- Emergency Care Information
- Mandated Reporting/Child Abuse Policy
- Notification of Parents' Rights
- Medication Policy

Authorizations
- Field Trip Authorization
- Authorization to Provide Transportation
- People Authorized to pick-up Child(ren)
    - Authorization to Give Medication

We will create a plan for each day of the week. It will include the following:
1. Day of the Week
2. Theme
3. Creative Activities
4. Required Special Toys and Games
5. Educational Focus
6. Educational Worksheets
7. Planned Snacks

Registration Procedures
Pre-registration form
A pre-registration form for each child including the registration fee ($___ (50?) per child) must be completed to reserve a space in the program. Forms and fees are required prior to enrollment.

Waiting List
If there is no available space for a child in a classroom, a waiting list is formed. Children on the waiting list will be notified, if space in their age group becomes available, based on the order in which they were put on the list. After being notified, you have 2 weeks for your child to begin attending. If your child does not begin attending in the time given, he/she will be moved to the bottom of the list. Waiting lists will be updated yearly on January 1.

Enrollment Packet
Completed forms checklist – one for each child enrolled:
o Registration Form
o Tuition Agreement
o Immunization Record (Supplied by Physician)
o Permission to give medication form (if needed)
o Emergency Medical Forms
o Signed Agreement of Understanding/ Photo Release
Note: The entire enrollment packet will be due before the child's first day in attendance at the center.

Daily Operations
Hours of Operation
Opening time will be 7:30 a.m. and pickup time is no later than 6:00 p.m. Monday through Friday. Parents will be responsible for putting their child's belongings in their classroom and for taking them home. Children will have individual cubbies with their daily work and notes from the teacher. Parents will pick their child/children up at the door and will walk their child to the car. All children will be required to be in a car seat when they leave

Vacations & Sick Days
1. Tuition payments remain the same when a child is out because of a sickness. There will be no deductions or credits for individual days.
2. Each child or family is allowed two week vacation per year after six (6) months of enrollment. During these weeks, parents will not be responsible for payment.
3. Vacations must be taken in one-week segments, not less than five (5) consecutive

days. Vacation time may be taken prior to six (6) months enrollment but the weekly fee will still need to be paid.

Holidays
The center will be closed to observe the following holidays:
Thanksgiving Day
Christmas Day

Emergency Closings
In the event of school delays and closings, we will do its best to operate as usual. All parents will be contacted no later than 6 a.m. if staff is unable to make it to work.
In the event of power failures or other extenuating circumstances resulting in the need to dismiss the daycare, all reasonable efforts to contact parents will be made.
Tuition payments will not be reduced because of a holiday or closings.

Emergency Procedures
Emergency Plan
We will develop and maintain an emergency file with information provided by the parent on each enrolled child. This file will be accessible to all staff members at all times.
We will develop, implement and maintain a policy and procedures plan for responding to an emergency. This plan will be reviewed with the parents at their orientation and with the staff at their initial orientation and every three months thereafter. In the event of an emergency, staff will follow the procedures as outlined in this plan. Parents will be able to review this plan at any time. This plan will be prominently placed in the classroom and address the following:
- Medical emergencies
- Weather emergencies
- Road Closings
- Fire
- Evacuation plans
- Natural disasters
- Other situations posing a threat to the children

Fire Safety and Evacuation Plan
Our fire safety and evacuation plan will be posted next to the telephone in the center. Fire drills will be conducted at least two (2) times a month during regular hours of operation.

Our Basic Operating Guidelines
1. Ensure that every staff member is properly trained, certified and licensed to give care to multiple children.
2. Make certain that one caregiver does not have more children than they can handle and adhere to the child to caregiver ratio limits imposed by law.
3. Watch for signs that staff may be getting over-worked.
4. If it becomes necessary to hire another caregiver, do so because it's better to pay another employee than risk losing clients because of sub-par care.

5. Purchase equipment for educational and play-related purposes, and make certain that these are age appropriate.
6. Offer a wide variety of items to keep children occupied.
7. Get children on a regular nap schedule at some point during their stay, because a well-rested child is often much easier to handle, and naptimes provide caregivers with a break.
8. Make sure to have a well-planned schedule for nutritious snacks that children will eat.
9. Supply colorful fruits and vegetables to catch the child's attention.
10. Make sure that all toys and equipment are in good repair.
11. Immediately discard anything that might be considered unsafe.
12. Keep age-groups separate to ensure that younger children are not getting a hold of small items.
13. Make sure to have a fully stocked first-aid kit readily available.

Other procedural guidelines include:
1. We will get our children on a regular nap schedule
2. We will a well-planned schedule for nutritious snacks that children will eat.
3. We will make sure that all toys and equipment are in good repair, and immediately discard anything that might be considered unsafe.
4. We will keep age-groups separate to ensure that younger children are not getting a hold of small items.
5. We will have a fully stocked first-aid kit readily available.
6. We will have a system in place to keep our paperwork and records neat and clean.
7. We will create a budget and try to make cuts where we can.
8. We will implement day care scheduling software to maintain accurate recording and scheduling of clients and staff.

Curriculum Development
As part of our focus on providing quality educational experiences, we will create a creative curriculum model that will be designed to harness children's imaginations and encourage learning, geared toward what children are interested in learning.
It will be a play-based program. Throughout each day, teachers will guide children's learning as they interact with them and organize individual and group activities that support early literacy, mathematics, language development, social and emotional development, physical health and development and the arts and sciences.

Pre-employment Screening
We will conduct pre-employment background checks on all potential staff. These checks will safeguard both us and the children in our care. There are two main reasons for performing this step. The first is to verify that the person applying for the position within our child care center is indeed the person they claim to be. The second reason is to research any criminal history that may pose an issue to the children and staff of our daycare facility. Pre-employment background checks will also incorporate a drugs tests to determine if an individual has used recreational drugs.

We will develop an effective fire safety management policy, as fire safety is achieved via this policy combined with adequate fire safety features in our premises. Our goal is to effect whatever measures necessary to minimize the risk of a fire occurring and if a fire does breakout to ensure that staff and children are evacuated swiftly and safely. The fire safety program will detail what fire prevention measures are in place at our day care i.e. the steps we are taking to reduce or eliminate the risks of a fire occurring.

We will use the Client Needs Analysis Worksheet, as provided in the appendix, to precisely document customer needs and specifications, curriculum preferences, and time and budget constraints.

We also plan to develop a list of specific interview questions and a worksheet to evaluate, compare and pre-screen potential suppliers. We will also check vendor references and their rating with the Hoovers.com.

We plan to write and maintain an operations manual and a personnel policies handbook. The Operating Manual will be a comprehensive document outlining virtually every aspect of the business. The operating manual will include management and accounting procedures, hiring and personnel policies, and daily operations procedures, such as opening and closing the store, and how to _____.

The manual will cover the following topics:
- Community Relations
- Media Relations
- Vendor Relations
- Competition Relations
- Environmental Concerns
- Intra Company Procedures
- Banking and Credit Cards
- Computer Procedures
- Quality Controls
- Open/Close Procedures
- Software Documentation

- Customer Relations
- Employee Relations
- Government Relations
- Equipment Maintenance Checklist
- Inventory Controls
- Accounting and Billing
- Financing
- Scheduling Tips
- Safety Procedures
- Security Procedures
- Curriculum

We plan to create the following business manuals:

	Manual Type	Key Elements
1.	Operations Manual	Process flowcharts
2.	Employee Manual	Benefits/Appraisals/Practices
3.	Managers Manual	Job Descriptions
4.	Customer Service Policies	Inquiry Handling Procedures

We will also need a manual to advise parents of the following policies:
- Field Trips: Costs and Approvals.
- Open Times
- Late pick-up Fees
- Authorized pick up adults.

- Required on-site backup clothing and supplies
- Illness handling procedures.
- Vacation and holiday closures
- Meals and Special Diets for allergies
- Approved activities.
- Documented conditions/treatments

Our plan is to automate our sales process, by developing an online registration calculator. We plan to adapt Quickbooks to track product inventory and sales. The plan is to place special emphasis on using technology to make the transaction with customers more efficient and to accept a wide range of automatic credit and debit card options. All systems are computer based and allow for accurate off-premises control of all aspects of our service business.

We plan to purchase a P.O.S. Software Package that will help us to accomplish the following objectives:
1. Speed our order entry and database build processes.
2. Assist in sales forecasting
3. Allow us to provide a higher level of customer service.
4. Lower our inventory costs.
5. Improve overall operational efficiency.

Security Procedures

Security
Our facility will be equipped with up to ___ (#) video cameras on the exterior and interior of the building. These cameras are for the safety of the children and the staff. Exits into our facility will remain locked at all times. Our main entrance will also be locked from the exterior during business hours. To enter visitors will need to knock and be verified by a staff member on the security monitor before gaining access.

Check-in and Check-out
It is required by state law that all parents sign their child in and out each day. For your convenience, a sign in/out sheet, pen, and a clock are located by the door. This will give us a written record of the child's attendance, hours, and the person who brought/picked up the child each day. Pick up persons must be listed on enrollment forms and may be amended at any time. Photo identification will be required for all pick ups.

Open Door policy
We will have an "Open Door" policy. Parents/ guardians are welcome to call or stop by to check in with your child at any time. We will also ask that if the child has separation anxiety at drop off. Parents can call or discreetly check in through the windows.

Daycare Business Software Options
Quickbooks //quickbooks.intuit.com/product/accounting-software/
SDS Software Solutions www.daycaresoftware.com/

My Daycare Software   www.mydaycaresoftware.com/
EZ-CARE2:   Child care management software for record keeping, billing, and
              accounting developed by SofterWare, Inc.
JackRabbit Care: Web-based child care center management and accounts receivables
                     software developed by Jackrabbit Technologies
ProCare: Developed by Professional Solutions
Daycare Information System Plus: Developed by Childcare Seekers One Stop Pro
Childcare Sage: Developed by B & I Computer Consultants, Inc.

9.0 Management Summary

The Management Plan will reveal who will be responsible for the various management functions to keep the business running efficiently. It will further demonstrate how that individual has the experience and/or training to accomplish each function. It will address who will do the planning function, the organizing function, the directing function, and the controlling function. We will also develop an employee retention plan because there are distinct cost advantages to retaining employees. It costs a lot to recruit and train a new employee, and in the early days, new employees are a lot less productive. We will need to make sure that our employees are satisfied in order to retain them and, in turn, create satisfied customers.

At the present time _____ (owner name) will run all operations for _____ (company name). _____ (His/Her) background in _____ (business management?) indicates an understanding of the importance of financial control systems. There is not expected to be any shortage of qualified staff from local labor pools in the market area.

_____ (owner name) will be the owner and operations manager of _____ (company name). His/her general duties will include the following:
1. Oversee the daily operations
2. Ordering inventory and supplies.
3. Develop and implementing the marketing strategy
4. Purchasing equipment.
5. Arranging for the routine maintenance and upkeep of the facility.
6. Teaching advanced students.
7. Hiring, training and supervision of new instructors.
8. Scheduling and planning lessons and special events.
9. Creating and pricing lesson programs and packages.
10. Managing the accounting/financial aspect of the business.
11. Contract negotiation/vendor relations.

The operations manager will take a monthly draw of $_____ month.

9.1 Organizational Structure
I. Owner/President/Executive Director
II. Industry Consultant
III. Business Manager/Director
- After School Instructor
- F/T Substitute
- Arts & Crafts Instructor
- Athletics Instructor
IV. V.P. of Education Operations

9.2 Owner Personal History

The owner has been working in the _____ () industry for over ____ (#) years, gaining personal knowledge and experience in all phases of the industry. _____ (owner name) is the founder and operations manager of _____ (company name). He/she began his/her career as a _____.

Over the last ____ (#) years, _____ (owner name) became quite proficient in a wide range of management activities and responsibilities, becoming an operations manager for _____ (former employer name) from _____ to _____ (dates). There he/she was able to achieve _____.

_____, owner of _____ (company name), has a ____ degree in _____. For ____ years he/she has managed a business similar to _____ (company name). _____ (His/her) duties included _____. Specifically, the owner brings _____ (#) years of experience as a _____ , as well as certification as a _____ from the _____ (National _____ Association).

He/she is an experienced entrepreneur with ____ years of small business accounting, finance, marketing and management experience. Education includes college course work in business administration, banking and finance, investments, and commercial credit management.

The owner will draw an annual salary of $_____ from the business although most of this goes to repay loans to finance business start-up costs. These loans will be paid-in-full by _____ (month) of _____ (year).

9.3 Management Team Gaps

Despite the owner's and manager's experience in the _____ (?) industry, the company will also retain the consulting services of _____ (consultant company name). This company has over ____(#) years of experience in the ____ industry, and has successfully opened dozens of child daycare businesses across the country. The Consultants will be primarily used for certification approval, market research, customer satisfaction surveys and to provide additional input in the evaluation of new business opportunities. The company also expects to retain the services of a local CPA to help the owner manage cash flow. Additionally the business will make use of the following advisory board to provide support for strategic planning and human resource related issues.

The Board of Advisors will provide continuous mentoring support on business matters. Expertise gaps in legal, tax, marketing and personnel will be covered by the Board of Advisors. The owner will actively seek free business advice from SCORE, a national non-profit organization with a local office. This is a group of retired executives and business owners who donate their time to serve as business counselors to new business owners.

Advisory Resources Available to the Business Include:

	Name	Address	Phone
CPA/Accountant			
Attorney			
Insurance Broker			
Banker			
Business Consultant			
Wholesale Suppliers			
Trade Association			
Realtor			
SCORE.org			
Other			

9.4   Management Matrix

Name	Title	Credentials	Functions	Responsibilities

Management Team
The strength of the following management team derives from the combined expertise in both management and technical areas.

Name of Person	Position	Educational Background	Past Industry Experience	Other Companies Served

9.5   Outsourcing Matrix

Company Name	Functions	Responsibilities	Cost

Note: Marketing and public relations will be handled mainly by the owner. If there is a greater need, a marketing consultant will be hired to help issue press releases and generate seminar and website content.

9.6   Personnel Plan

Employee Requirements:
1. **Skills and Abilities**
   In addition to having compassionate and creative personalities, we will require all

staff meet the following requirements prior to working in the daycare:
- 4 year Degree in early childcare or equal experience working with young children
- First Aid & CPR Certification
- Fingerprinted background screenings
- Child Protective services screening
- 12 hours of childcare continuing education coursework per year
- Food handler's license
- Current medical forms completed with TB test
- Participation in a program addressing child abuse and neglect
- SIDS and Shaken Baby Training

2. **Recruitment**
   Experience suggests that personal referrals are an excellent source for experienced technicians.

3. **Training and Supervision**
   Training is largely accomplished through hands-on experience with supplemental instruction. Additional knowledge is gained through our policy and operations manuals, and promotional materials. We will foster professional development and independence in all phases of our business. Supervision is task-oriented and the quantity is dependent on the complexity of the job assignment. Employees are called team members because they are part of Team _____ (company name). To help them succeed, employees will receive assistance with certification. They will also participate in our written training modules.

4. **Salaries and Benefits**
   Employees will be basically paid a wage plus commission. Good training and incentives, such as cash bonuses handed out monthly to everyone for reaching goals, will serve to retain good employees. An employee discount of __ percent on personal sales is offered. As business warrants, we hope to put together a benefit package that includes insurance, and paid vacations. The personnel plan also assumes a 5% annual increase in salaries.

Personnel Plan

1. We will develop a system for recruiting, screening and interviewing employees.
2. Background checks will be performed as well as reference checks and drug tests.
3. We will develop an instructor training course.
4. We will keep track of staff scheduling.
5. We will develop client satisfaction surveys to provide feedback and ideas.
6. We will develop and perform semi-annual employee evaluations.
7. We will "coach" all of our employees to improve their abilities and range of skills.
8. We will employ temporary employees via a local staffing agency to assist with one-time special projects.
9. Each employee will be provided a detailed job description and list of business policies, and be asked to sign these documents as a form of employment contract.
10. Incentives will be offered for reaching quarterly financial and enrollment goals,

completing the probationary period, and passing county inspections.
11. Customer service awards will be presented to those employees who best exemplify our stated mission and exceed customer expectations.
12. We will arrange for a pool of substitute teachers to be called upon to fill vacancies.

9.6.1 Job Description Format

Our job descriptions will adhere to the following format guidelines:

1.	Job Title	2.	Reports to:
3.	Pay Rate	4.	Job Responsibilities
5.	Travel Requirements	5.	Supervisory Responsibilities
6.	Qualifications	7.	Work Experience
8.	Required Skills	10.	Salary Range
11.	Benefits	12.	Opportunities

Job Description -- Assistant Teacher
Key Responsibilities:
1. Assist group supervisor with both long and short range activities in accordance with curriculum objectives, developmentally appropriate practice and program philosophy.
2. Provide input for bi-annual assessment of children's development.
3. Maintain daily open communication with parents.
4. Keep accident reports.
5. Maintain child records.
6. Maintain confidentiality.
7. Report any suspect abuse to supervisor.
8. Arrange a classroom environment in accordance to program goals and philosophy.
9. Maintain a safe and healthy environment.
10. Inspect and replace damaged or lost materials.
11. Attend staff meetings.
12. Keep all appropriate records such as records, attendance and timesheets.
13. Meet all applicable licensing regulations.
14. Organize and store toys and materials to ensure order in activity areas.

Job Description -- Head Teacher
The most basic duties required of a daycare head teacher include:
Develop curriculum and prepare, implement , and supervise age-appropriate activities
Supervise children: Monitor, direct, protect, encourage, and nurture children
Maintain a safe, fun, healthy environment for children
Maintain communication with parents: A daycare head teacher must communicate daily with parents verbally and through daily reports and progress reports. He or she must create and manage client records accurately and efficiently.
Attend staff meetings, required training, and continuing education

Head Daycare Teacher Qualifications
Minimum education qualifications are usually an Associate's Degree in Education or Early Childhood Education or related field, completion of a Child Development Associate Certification, or a certain number of college credits in Early Childhood Development, education or related field along with a plan leading to an Associate's or Bachelor's degree. Candidates must be CPR and First Aid certified and must have passed a recent tuberculosis test. Candidates must also be able to pass a background check and drug screen. Must have at least one year of experience or training in the childcare environment as an educator. Excellent communication skills (written and oral), the ability to lift up to 60 pounds, and the ability to climb stairs are also required.

Desired Characteristics for a Head Daycare Teacher
Head daycare teachers must be enthusiastic, energetic, nurturing, patient, comforting, creative, responsive, compassionate, flexible, encouraging, and culturally sensitive and aware. A lead teacher must also possess great leadership skills in addition to being a good team player and having the ability to work well with others.

Key Responsibilities:
1. Plan both long and short range activities in accordance with curriculum objectives, developmentally appropriate practice and program philosophy.
2. Meet the emotional, social, physical and cognitive needs of each child.
3. Encourage assistants to contribute to curriculum planning.
4. Coordinate field trips.
5. Prepare monthly plan charts.
6. Complete bi-annual assessment of children's development.
7. Report progress of children to parents in bi-annual reports and through parent-teacher conferences.
8. Maintain daily open communication with parents.
9. Keep records on individual children, including daily observations and information about activities, meals served, and medications administered.
10. Instruct children in health and personal habits such as eating, resting, and toilet habits.
11. Read to children, and teach them simple painting, drawing, handicrafts, and songs.
12. Organize and participate in recreational activities, such as games.
13. Assist in preparing food for children and serve meals and refreshments to children and regulate rest periods.
14. Keep accident reports.
15. Maintain child records.
16. Arrange a classroom environment in accordance to program goals and philosophy.
17. Maintain a safe and healthy environment.
18. Inspect and replace damaged or lost materials.
19. Attend staff meetings.
20. Supervise assistants, aides and volunteers in the classroom.
21. Keep all appropriate records such as records, attendance and time sheets.

22. Discipline children and recommend or initiate other measures to control behavior, such as caring for own clothing and picking up toys and books.
23. Identify signs of emotional or developmental problems in children and bring them to parents' or guardians' attention.

Staffing Plan

The personnel plan is included in the following table. It shows the owner's salary and ___ full-time salaries for other key positions. There will be no benefits offered at this time. The following table summarizes our personnel expenditures for the first three years, with compensation costs increasing from $_____ in he first year to about $_____ in the third year, based on ____ (5?) % payroll increases each year and 100% enrollment. The payroll includes tuition reimbursement, pay increases, vacation pay, bonuses and state required certifications.

Table: Personnel

	Number of Employees	Hourly Rate	Annual Salaries 2017	2018	2019
Owner/Executive Director					
Office Clerk					
Industry Consultant					
Facility Director/Bus. Mgr					
Education Ops Director					
Head Teacher					
Assistant Teachers					
After School Instructor					
Arts & Crafts Instructor					
F/T Substitute					
P/T Instructors					
Teaching Assistant					
Sales Manager					
P/T Bookkeeper					
Janitor					
Other					
Total People: Headcount					
Total Annual Payroll					
Payroll Burden (Fringe Benefits)	(+)				
Total Payroll Expense	(=)				

According to the May 2009 National Occupational Employment and Wage Estimates, daycare center owners earned an average of $48,170 annually. The lowest 25 percent of daycare center owners made $32,010 annually while the highest 25 percent made $58,190 annually.

Median annual wages of the largest occupations in child day care services, May 2008
Occupation   Child Day Care   All Industries

Education administrators, preschool and child care center/program	$37,270	$39,940
Child, family, and school social workers	31,210	39,530
First-line supervisors/managers of personal service workers	29,560	34,910
Kindergarten teachers, except special education	28,170	47,100
Office clerks, general	22,320	25,320
Preschool teachers, except special education	22,120	23,870
Janitors and cleaners, except maids and housekeeping cleaners	19,650	21,450
Teacher assistants	19,090	22,200
Cooks, institution and cafeteria	18,970	22,210
Child care workers	17,440	18,970

SOURCE: BLS Occupational Employment Statistics, May 2008.

In 2004, hourly earnings of nonsupervisory workers in the child day care services industry averaged $9.76, much less than the average of $15.67 throughout private industry. On a weekly basis, earnings in child day care services averaged only $299 in 2004, compared with the average of $529 in private industry. Weekly earnings reflect, in part, hours worked—salaried workers in child day care services averaged 30.6 hours a week, compared with about 33.7 throughout private industry.
Source: http://www.collegegrad.com/industries/edhea01.shtml

10.0 Risk Factors

Risk management is the identification, assessment, and prioritization of risks, followed by the coordinated and economical application of resources to minimize, monitor, and control the probability and/or impact of unfortunate events or to maximize the realization of opportunities. For the most part, our risk management methods will consist of the following elements, performed, more or less, in the following order.
1. Identify, characterize, and assess threats
2. Assess the vulnerability of critical assets to specific threats
3. Determine the risk (i.e. the expected consequences of specific types of attacks on specific assets)
4. Identify ways to reduce those risks
5. Prioritize risk reduction measures based on a strategy

Types of Risks:

_____ (company name) faces the following kinds of risks:

1. **Financial Risks**
   Our quarterly revenues and operating results are difficult to predict and may fluctuate significantly from quarter to quarter as a result of a variety of factors. Among these factors are:
   - Changes in our own or competitors' pricing policies.
   - Recession pressures.
   - Fluctuations in expected revenues from advertisers, sponsors and strategic relationships.
   - Timing of costs related to acquisitions or payments.

2. **Legislative / Legal Landscape.**
   Our participation in the child day care arena presents unique risks:
   - Product and other related liability.
   - Federal and State regulations on licensing, privacy and insurance.

3. **Operational Risks**
   For the past __ (#) years the owner has been dealing with computers so he is comfortable with technology and understands a wide array of software applications. However, the biggest potential problem will be equipment malfunction. To minimize the potential for problems, the owner will be taking equipment repair training from the manufacturer and will deal with basic troubleshooting and minor repairs. Beyond that, we have identified a service technician who is located close-by.

   To attract and retain client to the _____ (company name) community, we must continue to provide differentiated and quality services. This confers certain risks including the failure to:
   - Anticipate and respond to consumer preferences for partnerships and service.

- Attract, excite and retain a large audience of customers to our community.
- Create and maintain successful strategic alliances with quality partners.
- Deliver high quality, customer service.
- Build our brand rapidly and cost-effectively.
- Compete effectively against better-established child day care centers.

4. **Human Resource Risks**

   The most serious human resource risk to our business, at least in the initial stages, would be my inability to operate the business due to illness or disability. The owner is currently in exceptional health and would eventually seek to replace himself on a day-to-day level by developing systems to support the growth of the business.

5. **Marketing Risks**

   Advertising is our most expensive form of promotion and there will be a period of testing headlines and offers to find the one that works the best. The risk, of course, is that we will exhaust our advertising budget before we find an ad that works. Placing greater emphases on sunk-cost marketing, such as our storefront and on existing relationships through direct selling will minimize our initial reliance on advertising to bring in a large percentage of business in the first year.

6. **Business Risks**

   A major risk to retail service businesses is the performance of the economy and the small business sector. Since economists are predicting this as the fastest growing sector of the economy, our risk of a downturn in the short-term is minimized. The entrance of one of the major chains into our marketplace is a risk. They offer more of the latest equipment, provide a wider array of products and services, competitive prices and 24-hour service. This situation would force us to lower our prices in the short-term until we could develop an offering of higher margin, value-added services not provided by the large chains. It does not seem likely that the relative size of our market today could support the overhead of one of those operations. Projections indicate that this will not be the case in the future and that leaves a window of opportunity for ___ (company name) to aggressively build a loyal client base. We will also not pursue big-leap, radical change misadventures, but rather strive to hit stepwise performance benchmarks, with a planned consistency over a long period of time.

The Company's start-up quarterly revenues and operating results are difficult to predict and may fluctuate from quarter to quarter as a result of a variety of factors, including changes in pricing to accommodate local market conditions, recession pressures and seasonal patterns of spending.

To combat the usual start-up risks we will do the following:
1. Utilize our industry experience to quickly establish desired strategic relationships.
2. Pursue business outside of our immediate market area.

3. Diversify our range of product and service offerings.
4. Develop multiple distribution channels.
5. Monitor our competitor actions.
6. Stay in touch with our customers and suppliers.
7. Watch for trends which could potentially impact our business.
8. Continuously optimize and scrutinize all business processes.
9. Institute daily financial controls using Business Ratio Analysis.
10. Create pay-for-performance compensation and training programs to reduce employee turnover.

Further, to attract and retain customers the Company will need to continue to expand its market offerings, utilizing third party strategic relationships. This could lead to difficulties in the management of relationships, competition for specific services and products, and/or adverse market conditions affecting a particular partner.

The Company will take active steps to mitigate risks. In preparation of the Company's pricing, many factors will be considered. The Company will closely track the activities of all third parties, and will hold monthly review meetings to resolve issues and review and update the terms associated with strategic alliances.

Additionally, we will develop the following kinds of contingency plans:
Disaster Recovery Plan
Business Continuity Plan
Business Impact and Gap Analysis
Testing & Maintenance

The Company will utilize marketing and advertising campaigns to promote brand identity and will coordinate all expectations with internal and third party resources prior to release. This strategy should maximize customer satisfaction while minimizing potential costs associated with unplanned expenditures and quality control issues.

10.1　　Business Risk Reduction Strategy　　(select)

We plan to implement the following strategies to reduce our start-up business risk:
1. Implement our business plan based on go, no-go stage criteria.
2. Develop employee cross-training programs.
3. Regularly back-up all computer files/Install ant-virus software.
4. Arrange adequate insurance coverage with higher deductibles.
5. Develop a limited number of prototype samples.
6. Test market offerings to determine level of market demand and appropriate pricing strategy.
7. Thoroughly investigate and benchmark to competitor offerings.
8. Research similar franchised businesses for insights into successful prototype business/operations models.
9. Flowchart all structured systems & standardized manual processes.

10. Use market surveys to listen to customer needs and priorities.
11. Purchase used equipment to reduce capital outlays.
12. Use leasing to reduce financial risk.
13. Outsource manufacturing to job shops to reduce capital at risk.
14. Use subcontractors to limit fixed overhead salary expenses.
15. Ask manufacturers about profit sharing arrangements.
16. Pay advertisers with a percent of revenues generated.
17. Develop contingency plans for identified risks.
18. Set-up procedures to control employee theft.
19. Do criminal background checks on potential employees.
20. Take immediate action on delinquent accounts.
21. Only extend credit to established account with D&B rating
22. Get regular competitive bids from alternative suppliers.
23. Check that operating costs as a percent of rising sales are lower as a result of productivity improvements.
24. Request bulk rate pricing on fast moving supplies.
25. Don't tie up cash in slow moving inventory to qualify for bigger discounts.
26. Reduce financial risk by practicing cash flow policies.
27. Reduce hazard risk by installing safety procedures.
28. Use financial management ratios to monitor business vitals.
29. Make business decisions after brainstorming sessions.
30. Focus on the products with biggest return on investment.
31. Where possible, purchase off-the-shelf components.
32. Request manufacturer samples and assistance to build prototypes.
33. Design production facilities to be flexible and easy to change.
34. Develop a network of suppliers with outsourcing capabilities.
35. Analyze and shorten every cycle time, including product development.
36. Develop multiple sources for every important input.
37. Treat the business plan as a living document and update it frequently.
38. Conduct a SWOT analysis and use determined strengths to pursue opportunities.
39. Conduct regular customer satisfaction surveys to evaluate performance.

10.2   Reduce Customer Perceived Risk Tactics

We will utilize the following tactics to help reduce the new customer's perceived risk of starting to do business with our company.

		Status
1.	Publish a page of testimonials.	_____
2.	Secure Opinion Leader written endorsements.	_____
3.	Offer an Unconditional Satisfaction Money Back Guarantee.	_____
4.	Long-term Performance Guarantee (Financial Risk).	_____
5.	Guaranteed Buy Back (Obsolete time risk)	_____
6.	Offer free trials and samples.	_____
7.	Brand Image (consistent marketing image and performance)	_____

8. Patents/Trademarks/Copyrights
9. Publish case studies
10. Share your expertise (Articles, Seminars, etc.)
11. Get recognized Certification
12. Conduct responsive customer service
13. Accept Installment Payments
14. Display product materials composition or ingredients.
15. Publish product test results.
16. Publish sales record milestones.
17. Foster word-of-mouth by offering an unexpected extra.
18. Distribute factual, pre-purchase info.
19. Reduce consumer search costs with online directories.
20. Reduce customer transaction costs.
21. Facilitate in-depth comparisons to alternative services.
22. Make available prior customer ratings and comments.
23. Provide customized info based on prior transactions.
24. Become a Better Business Bureau member.
25. Publish overall customer satisfaction survey results.
26. Offer plan options that match niche segment needs.
27. Require client sign-off before proceeding to next phase.
28. Document procedures for dispute resolution.
29. Offer the equivalent of open source code.
30. Stress your compatibility features (avoid lock-in fear).
31. Create detailed checklists & flowcharts to show processes
32. Publish a list of frequently asked questions/answers.
33. Create a community that enables clients to connect with each other and share common interests.
34. Inform customers as to your stay-in-touch methods.
35. Conduct and handover a detailed needs analysis worksheet.
36. Offer to pay all return shipping charges and/or refund all original shipping and handling fees.
37. Describe your product testing procedures prior to shipping.
38. Highlight your competitive advantages in all marketing materials.

11.0 Financial Plan

The most important factor in our plan is enrollment. Therefore, we must remain focused on the execution of our enrollment plan and maintain budgeted enrollment levels. The over-all financial plan for growth allows for use of the significant cash flow generated by operations. We are basing projected sales on the market research, industry analysis and competitive environment.

_____ (company name) expects a profit margin of over ____ % starting with year one. By year two, that number should slowly increase as the law of diminishing costs takes hold, and the day-to-day activities of the business become less expensive.

Sales are expected to grow at ____ % per year, and level off by year _____. The initial investment in _____ (company name) will be provided by _____ (owner name) in the amount of $ _____. The owner will also seek a ___ (#) year bank loan in the amount of $ _____ to provide the remainder of the required initial funding.

The funds will be used to renovate the space and to cover initial operating expenses. The owner financing will become a return on equity, paid in the form of dividends to the owner. We expect to finance slow and steady growth through cash flow. Salaries and rent are the two major expenses. The owners do not intend to take any profits out of the business until the long-term debt has been satisfied.

Our financial plan includes:
  Moderate growth rate with a steady cash flow.
  Investing residual profits into company expansion.
  Company expansion will be an option if sales projections are met and/or exceeded.
  Marketing costs will remain below ___ (5?) % of sales.
  Repayment of our loan calculated at a high A.P.R. of ___ (10?) percent and at a 10-year-payback on our $_____ loan.

11.1 Important Assumptions

The financial plan depends on important assumptions, most of which are shown in the following table. The Personnel Burden is low because benefits are not paid to our staff.

The following basic assumptions need to be considered:
1. The economy will grow at a steady slow pace, without another major recession.
2. There will be no major changes in the industry, other than those discussed in the trends section of this document.
3. The State will not enact 'impact' legislation on our industry.
4. Sales are estimated at minimum to average values, while expenses are estimated at above average to maximum values..
5. Staffing and payroll expansions will be driven by increased sales.

6. Rent expenses will grow at a slow, predictable rate.
7. Materials expenses will not increase dramatically over the next several years, but will grow at a rate that matches increasing consumption.
8. We assume access to equity capital and financing sufficient to maintain our financial plan as shown in the tables.
9. The amount of the financing needed from the bank will be approximately $_____ and this will be repaid over the next 10 years at $_____ per month.
10. We assume that people in _____ (city) will be interested in learning and will give us the opportunity to provide such support.
11. We assume that the area will continue to grow at present rate of __ % per year.
12. Interest rates and tax rates are based on conservative assumptions.
13. We will not offer consumer credit, but will extend 30 days credit terms to our qualified commercial accounts.
14. We assume the continuing need for motorists to improve gas mileage efficiency and extend the useful life of their vehicles.
15. Total enrollment is critical and is a factor that must be immediately influenced.
16. We will assume a 10% Vacancy Rate.

Revenue Assumptions:

	Year	Sales/Month	Growth Rate
1.			
2.			
3.			

Assumptions	FY2017	FY2018	FY2019
Short-term Interest Rate %	10.00%	10.00%	10.00%
Long-term Interest Rate %	10.00%	10.00%	10.00%
Payment Days Estimator	30	30	30
Collection Days Estimator	45	45	45
Tax Rate %	25.00%	25.00%	25.00%
Expenses in Cash %	10.00%	10.00%	10.00%
Sales on Credit %	15.00%	15.00%	15.00%
Personnel Burden %	15.00%	15.00%	15.00%

Resource:
www.score.org/resources/business-plans-financial-statements-template-gallery

11.2 Break-even Analysis

The Break-even Analysis gives our company an idea of how many students _____ (company name) must teach each month to cover overhead costs. Because _____ (company name) is providing a new customized service, with many students having unique requirements, the estimates of revenue and cost are somewhat arbitrary. We also realize that we may have a slow start, until the word of mouth gets circulated about our business. Furthermore, the company experiences a high degree of seasonality in its contracts which may result in a number of unprofitable summer months.

Fixed costs are based on running costs estimated by the owner(s) of the company and include payroll for all employees. Variable costs are based on a ____% estimate of the average sales per unit. The average revenue estimate is based on the judgment of the owner(s) who have had many years of experience in the industry and on the realistic assumption of the types of contracts the company will get in the beginning and the requirements needed to complete such commitments.

Definition: Break-Even Is the Volume Where All Fixed Expenses Are Covered. Based on projections, we will need an average of __ students each month to breakeven.

Three important definitions used in break-even analysis are:
- **Variable Costs** (Expenses) are costs that change directly in proportion to changes in activity (volume), such as raw materials, labor and packaging.
- **Fixed Costs** (Expenses) are costs that remain constant (fixed) for a given time period despite wide fluctuations in activity (volume), such as rent, loan payments, insurance, payroll and utilities.
- **Unit Contribution Margin** is the difference between your product's unit selling price and its unit variable cost.
  Unit Contribution Margin = Unit Sales Price - Unit Variable Cost

For the purposes of this breakeven analysis, the assumed fixed operating costs will be approximately $ _____ per month, as shown in the following table.

Averaged Monthly Fixed Costs:		Variable Costs:	
Payroll	_____	Cost of Inventory Sold	_____
Rent	_____	Labor	_____
Insurance	_____	Supplies	_____
Utilities	_____	Direct Costs per Student	_____
Security.	_____	Other	_____
Legal/Technical Help	_____		
Other	_____		
Total:	_____	Total	_____

A break-even analysis table has been completed on the basis of average costs/prices. With monthly fixed costs averaging $_____ , $____ in average sales and $_____ in average variable costs, we need approximately $_____ in sales per month to break-even.

Based on our assumed ___ % variable cost, we estimate our breakeven sales volume at around $ _____ per month. We expect to reach that sales volume by our _____ month of operations. Our break-even analysis is shown in further detail in the following table.

Breakeven Formulas:
Break Even Units = Total Fixed Costs / (Unit Selling Price - Variable Unit Cost)
_____ = _____ / (_____ - _____)

·BE Dollars = (Total Fixed Costs / (Unit Price – Variable Unit Costs))/ Unit Price
_____ = (_____ / (_____ - _____)) / _____

·BE Sales = Annual Fixed Costs / (1- Unit Variable costs / Unit Sales Price)
_____ = _____ / (1 - _____ / _____)

Table: Break-even Analysis
Monthly Units Break-even   _____
Monthly Revenue Break-even $ _____
Assumptions:
Average Per-Unit Revenue $ _____
Average Per-Unit Variable Cost $ _____
Estimated monthly Fixed Cost $ _____

Ways to Improve Breakeven Point:
1. Reduce Fixed Costs via Cost Controls
2. Raise unit sales prices.
3. Lower Variable Costs by improving employee productivity or getting lower competitive bids from suppliers.
4. Broaden product/service line to generate multiple revenue streams.

11.3 Projected Profit and Loss

Pro forma income statements are an important tool for planning our future business operations. If the projections predict a downturn in profitability, we can make operational changes such as increasing prices or decreasing costs before these projections become reality.

Our monthly profit for the first year varies significantly, as we aggressively seek improvements and begin to implement our marketing plan. However, after the first ___ months, profitability should be established.

We predict advertising costs will go down in the next three years as word-of-mouth about our day care gets out to the public and we are able to find what has worked well for us and concentrate on those advertising methods, and corporate affiliations generate sales without the need for extra advertising.

Our net profit/sales ratio will be low the first year. We expect this ratio to rise at least _____ (15?) percent the second year. Normally, a startup concern will operate with negative profits through the first two years. We will avoid that kind of operating loss on our second year by knowing our competitors and having a full understanding of our target markets.

Our projected profit and loss is indicated in the following table. From our research of the day care industry, our annual projections are quite realistic and conservative, and we prefer this approach so that we can ensure an adequate cash flow.

Key P & L Formulas:

Gross Margin = Total Sales Revenue - Cost of Goods Sold

Gross Margin % = (Total Sales Revenue - Cost of Goods Sold) / Total Sales Revenue
This number represents the proportion of each dollar of revenue that the company retains as gross profit.

EBITDA =Revenue - Expenses (exclude interest, taxes, depreciation & amortization)

PBIT = Profit (Earnings) Before Interest and Taxes = EBIT
A profitability measure that looks at a company's profits before the company has to pay corporate income tax and interest expenses. This measure deducts all operating expenses from revenue, but it leaves out the payment of interest and tax. Also referred to as "earnings before interest and tax ".

Net Profit = Total Sales Revenues - Total Expenses

Pro Forma Profit and Loss

	Formula	2017	2018	2019
Revenue:				
Food Income				
Subsidies				
Parent Fees				
Product Sales				
Other				
Total Sales Revenue	A			
Direct Cost Food & Beverage	B			
Other Costs of Goods	C			
Total Costs of Goods Sold	B+C=D			
Gross Margin	A-D=E			
Gross Margin %	E / A			
Expenses				
Payroll				
Payroll Taxes				
Temp Labor				
Sales & Marketing				
Depreciation				
License/Permit Fees				
Dues and Subscriptions				
Rent				
Utilities				
Deposits				
Interest				
Repairs and Maintenance				
Janitorial Supplies				
Office Supplies				
Classroom Supplies				
Leased Equipment				
Buildout Costs				
Insurance				
Location Rental				
Van Expenses				
Merchant Fees				
Bad Debts				
Miscellaneous				
Total Operating Expenses	F			
Profit Before Int. & Taxes	E - F = G			
Interest Expenses	H			
Taxes Incurred	I			
Net Profit	G - H - I = J			
Net Profit / Sales	J / A = K			

11.5 Projected Cash Flow

The Cash Flow Statement shows how the company is paying for its operations and future growth, by detailing the "flow" of cash between the company and the outside world. Positive numbers represent cash flowing in, negative numbers represent cash flowing out.

The first year's monthly cash flows are will vary significantly, but we do expect a solid cash balance from day one. We expect that the majority of our sales will be done in cash or by credit card and that will be good for our cash flow position. Additionally, we will stock only slightly more than one month's inventory at any time. Consequently, we do not anticipate any problems with cash flow, once we have obtained sufficient start-up funds. A __ year commercial loan in the amount of $_____, sought by the owner will be used to cover our working capital requirement. Our projected cash flow is summarized in the following table, and is expected to meet our needs. In the following years, excess cash will be used to finance our growth plans.

Cash Flow Management:
We will use the following practices to improve our cash flow position:
1. Become more selective when granting credit.
2. Seek deposits or multiple stage payments.
3. Reduce the amount/time of credit given to clients.
4. Reduce direct and indirect costs and overhead expenses.
5. Use the 80/20 rule to manage inventories, receivables and payables.
6. Invoice as soon as the service has been performed.
7. Generate regular reports on receivable ratios and aging.
8. Establish and adhere to sound credit practices.
9. Use more pro-active collection techniques.
10. Add late payment fees where possible.
11. Increase the credit taken from suppliers.
12. Negotiate extended credit terms from vendors.
13. Use some barter arrangements to acquire goods and service.
14. Use leasing to gain access to the use of productive assets.
15. Covert debt into equity.
16. Regularly update cash flow forecasts.
17. Defer projects which cannot achieve acceptable cash paybacks.
18. Require a 50% deposit upon the signing of the contract and the balance in full, due five days before the event.

Cash Flow Formulas:
Net Cash Flow = Incoming Cash Receipts - Outgoing Cash Payments
Equivalently, net profit plus amounts charged off for depreciation, depletion, and amortization. (also called cash flow).
Cash Balance = Opening Cash Balance + Net Cash Flow
We are positioning ourselves in the market as a medium risk concern with steady cash flows. Accounts payable is paid at the end of each month, while sales are in cash, giving our company an excellent cash structure.

Pro Forma Cash Flow

	Formula	2017	2018	2019

Cash Received
Cash from Operations

Cash Sales	A
Cash from Receivables	B
Subtotal Cash from Operations	A + B = C

Additional Cash Received	
Non Operating (Other) Income	
Sales Tax, VAT, HST/GST Received	
New Current Borrowing	
New Other Liabilities (interest fee)	
New Long-term Liabilities	
Sales of Other Current Assets	
Sales of Long-term Assets	
New Investment Received	
Total Additional Cash Received	D
Subtotal Cash Received	C + D = E

Expenditures

Expenditures from Operations	
Cash Spending	F
Payment of Accounts Payable	G
Subtotal Spent on Operations	F+G = H

Additional Cash Spent	
Non Operating (Other) Expenses	
Sales Tax, VAT, HST/GST Paid Out	
Principal Repayment Current Borrowing	
Other Liabilities Principal Repayment	
Long-term Liabilities Principal Repayment	
Purchase Other Current Assets	
Dividends	
Total Additional Cash Spent	I
Subtotal Cash Spent	H + I = J
Net Cash Flow	**E - J = K**

Cash Balance

11.6 Projected Balance Sheet

Pro forma Balance Sheets are used to project how the business will be managing its assets in the future. As a pure start-up business, the opening balance sheet may contain no values.

Note: The projected balance sheets must link back into the projected income statements and cash flow projections.

_____ (company name) does not project any real trouble meeting its debt obligations, provided the revenue predictions are met. We are very confident that we will meet or exceed all of our objectives in the Business Plan and produce a slow but steady increase in net worth.

All of our tables will be updated monthly to reflect past performance and future assumptions. Future assumptions will not be based on past performance but rather on economic cycle activity, regional industry strength, and future cash flow possibilities. We expect a solid growth in net worth by the year _____.

The Balance Sheet table for fiscal years 2017, 2018, and 2019 follows. It shows managed but sufficient growth of net worth, and a sufficiently healthy financial position.

Excel Resource:
www.unioncity.org/ED/Finance%20Tools/Projected%20Balance%20Sheet.xls

Key Formulas:

Paid-in Capital = Capital contributed to the corporation by investors on top of the par value of the capital stock.

Retained Earnings = The portion of net income which is retained by the corporation rather than distributed to the owners as dividends.

Earnings = **Revenues - (Cost of Sales + Operating Expenses + Taxes)**

Net Worth = Total Assets - Total Liabilities
    Also known as 'Owner's Equity'.

Pro Forma Balance Sheet

	Formulas	2017	2018	2019
Assets				
Current Assets				
Cash				
Accounts Receivable				
Inventory				
Other Current Assets				
Total Current Assets	A			
Long-term Assets				
Long-term Assets	B			
Accumulated Depreciation	C			
Total Long-term Assets	B - C = D			
Total Assets	A + D = E			

Liabilities and Capital

	Formulas	2017	2018	2019
Current Liabilities				
Accounts Payable				
Current Borrowing				
Other Current Liabilities				
Subtotal Current Liabilities	F			
Long-term Liabilities				
Notes Payable				
Other Long-term Liabilities				
Subtotal Long-term Liabilities	G			
Total Liabilities	F + G = H			
Capital				
Paid-in Capital	I			
Retained Earnings	J			
Earnings	K			
Total Capital	I - J + K = L			
Total Liabilities and Capital	H + L = M			
Net Worth	E - H = N			

11.7 Business Ratios

The following table provides significant ratios for the personal services industry. The final column, Industry Profile, shows ratios for this industry as it is determined by the Standard Industrial Classification SIC 8351(Child Day Care Center Services), for comparison purposes.

Our comparisons to the SIC Industry profile are very favorable and we expect to maintain healthy ratios for profitability , risk and return.   Use Business Ratio Formulas provided to assist in calculations.

Key Business Ratio Formulas:

EBIT = Earnings Before Interest and Taxes
EBITA = Earnings Before Interest, Taxes & Amortization. (Operating Profit Margin)

Sales Growth Rate =((Current Year Sales - Last Year Sales)/(Last Year Sales)) x 100
Ex: **Percent of Sales** = (Advertising Expense / Sales) x 100

Net Worth = Total Assets - Total Liabilities

Acid Test Ratio = Liquid Assets / Current Liabilities
Measures how much money business has immediately available. A ratio of 2:1 is good.

Net Profit Margin = Net Profit / Net Revenues
The higher the net profit margin is, the more effective the company is at converting revenue into actual profit.

Return on Equity (ROE) = Net Income / Shareholder's Equity
The ROE is useful for comparing the profitability of a company to that of other firms in the same industry. Also known as "return on net worth" (RONW).

Current Ratio = Current Assets / Current Liabilities
The higher the current ratio, the more capable the company is of paying its obligations. A ratio under 1 suggests that the company would be unable to pay off its obligations if they came due at that point.

Quick Ratio = Current Assets - Inventories / Current Liabilities
The quick ratio is more conservative than the current ratio, because it excludes inventory from current assets.

Pre-Tax Return on Net Worth = Pre-Tax Income / Net Worth
Indicates stockholders' earnings before taxes for each dollar of investment.

Pre-Tax Return on Assets = (EBIT / Assets) x 100
Indicates much profit the firm is generating from the use of its assets.

Accounts Receivable Turnover = Net Credit Sales / Average Accounts Receivable
A low ratio implies the company should re-assess its credit policies in order to ensure the timely collection of imparted credit that is not earning interest for the firm.

Net Working Capital = Current Assets - Current Liabilities
Positive working capital means that the company is able to pay off its short-term liabilities. Negative working capital means that a company currently is unable to meet its short-term liabilities with its current assets (cash, accounts receivable and inventory).

Interest Coverage Ratio = Earnings Before Interest & Taxes /Total Interest Expense
The lower the ratio, the more the company is burdened by debt expense. When a company's interest coverage ratio is 1.5 or lower, its ability to meet interest expenses may be questionable. An interest coverage ratio below 1 indicates the company is not generating sufficient revenues to satisfy interest expenses.

Collection Days = Accounts Receivables / (Revenues/365)
A high ratio indicates that the company is having problems getting paid for services.

Accounts Payable Turnover = Total Supplier Purchases/Average Accounts Payable
If the turnover ratio is falling from one period to another, this is a sign that the company is taking longer to pay off its suppliers than previously. The opposite is true when the turnover ratio is increasing, which means the firm is paying of suppliers at a faster rate.

Payment Days = (Accounts Payable Balance x 360) / (No. of Accounts Payable x 12)
The average number of days between receiving an invoice and paying it off.

Total Asset Turnover = Revenue / Assets
Asset turnover measures a firm's efficiency at using its assets in generating sales or revenue - the higher the number the better.

Sales / Net Worth = Total Sales / Net Worth

Dividend Payout = Dividends / Net Profit

Assets to Sales = Assets / Sales

Current Debt / Totals Assets = Current Liabilities / Total Assets

Current Liabilities to Liabilities = Current Liabilities / Total Liabilities

Business Ratio Analysis

	2017	2018	2019	Industry

Sales Growth _____

Percent of Total Assets
Accounts Receivable
Inventory
Other Current Assets
Total Current Assets
Long-term Assets
Total Assets

Current Liabilities
Long-term Liabilities
Total Liabilities
Net Worth

Percent of Sales
Sales
Gross Margin
Selling G& A Expenses
Advertising Expenses
Profit Before Interest & Taxes

Main Ratios
Current
Quick
Total Debt to Total Assets
Pre-tax Return on Net Worth
Pre-tax Return on Assets

Additional Ratios
Net Profit Margin
Return on Equity

Activity Ratios
Accounts Receivable Turnover
Collection Days
Inventory Turnover
Accounts Payable Turnover
Payment Days
Total Asset Turnover
Inventory Productivity
Sales per sq/ft.
Gross Margin Return on Inventory (GMROI) _____

Debt Ratios
Debt to Net Worth
Current Liabilities to Liabilities

Liquidity Ratios
Net Working Capital
Interest Coverage

Additional Ratios
Assets to Sales
Current Debt / Total Assets
Acid Test
Sales / Net Worth
Dividend Payout

Business Vitality Profile
Sales per Employee
Survival Rate

12.0 Summary

_____ (company name) will be successful. This business plan has documented that the establishment of _____ (company name) is feasible. All of the critical factors, such as industry trends, marketing analysis, competitive analysis, management expertise and financial analysis support this conclusion.

Project Description: (Give a brief summary of the product, service or program.)

Description of Favorable Industry and Market Conditions.
(Summarize why this business is viable.)

Summary of Earnings Projections and Potential Return to Investors:

Summary of Capital Requirements:

Security for Investors & Loaning Institutions:

Summary of expected benefits for people in the community beyond the immediate business concern:

Means of Financing:
A. Loan Requirements: $_____
B. Owner's Contribution: $ $_____
C. Other Sources of Income: $_____
Total Funds Available: $_____

13.0 Potential Exit Scenarios

The following potential exit strategies exist for the investor:

1. **Initial Public Offering. (IPO)**
   We seek to go public within ___ (#) years of operations. The funds used will both help create liquidity for investors as well as allow for additional capital to develop our _____ (international/national?) roll out strategy.

2. **Acquisition Merger with Private or Public Company.**
   Our most desirable option for exit is a merger or buyout by a large corporation. We believe with substantial cash flows and a loyal customer base our company will be attractive to potential corporate investors within five years. Real value has been created through the novel combination of home health care services as well as partnering with key referral groups.

3. **Sale of the Business to a third party.**
   Child daycares usually sell for approximately one to three times earnings given the financial strength of the business. In this event, the business would be sold by a business broker and the business loan sought in this plan would be repaid according to the covenants of the business loan agreement.

Resource: http://www.score.org/article_business_valuation.html

APPENDIX

Purpose: Supporting documents used to enhance your business proposal.

Tax returns of principals for the last three years, if the plan is for new business
A personal financial statement, which should include life insurance and endowment policies, if applicable
A copy of the proposed lease or purchase agreement for building space, or zoning information for in-home businesses, with layouts, maps, and blueprints
A copy of licenses and other legal documents including partnership, association, or shareholders' agreements and copyrights, trademarks, and patents applications
A copy of résumés of all principals in a consistent format, if possible
Copies of letters of intent from suppliers, contracts, orders, and miscellaneous.
In the case of a franchised business, a copy of the franchise contract and all supporting documents provided by the franchisor
Newspaper clippings that support the business or the owner, including something about you, your achievements, business idea, or region
Promotional literature for your company or your competitors
Product brochures of your company or competitors
Photographs of your product. equipment, facilities, etc.
Market research to support the marketing section of the plan
Trade and industry publications when they support your intentions
Quotations or pro-forma invoices for capital items to be purchased, including a list of fixed assets, company vehicles, and proposed renovations
References
All insurance policies in place, both business and personal
Operation Schedules
Organizational Charts
Job Descriptions
Additional Financial Projections by Month
Customer Needs Analysis Worksheet

Helpful Resources:

Associations:
National Association of Family Child Care   www.nafcc.org
The National Association for the Education of Young Children   www.naeyc.org
National After School Association   www.naaweb.org
National Network for Child Care   www.nncc.org
National Assoc. of Child Care Resource & Referral Agencies   www.naccrra.org
 American Society for Testing and Materials (ASTM)
 Child Care Law Center
 Children's Foundation
 National Association for Family Child Care
 National Association of Child Care Professionals
 National Child Care Information Center
 LISC: National Children's Facilities Network and Community Investment
  Collaborative for Kids (CICK)
 National Resource Center for Health and Safety in Child Care

Government Agencies and Related Resources
 Environmental Protection Agency(Note: Contact for a list of restricted chemicals that are unsuitable for use in a child-care environment.)
 U.S. Consumer Product Safety Commission (CPSC)
 U.S. Department of Agriculture, Child and Adult Care Food Program
 Indicators of Quality Day Care   http://aspe.hhs.gov/hsp/ccquality-ind02/

Publications
 Child Care Information Exchange
 Early Childhood Today
 High/Scope
 Young Children
 Safe Ride News

Suppliers:
Daycare Universe   www.daycareuniverse.com
Kazoo Educational Toys   www.kazootoys.com
Mats   www.matsmatsmats.com

For additional information about careers in early childhood education, contact:
- National Association for the Education of Young Children, 1509 16th St. N.W., Washington, DC 20036. Internet: http://www.naeyc.org

For more information about the child care workforce, contact:
- Center for the Child Care Workforce, 555 New Jersey Ave., N.W., Washington, DC 20001. Internet: http://www.ccw.org

For an electronic question-and-answer service on child care, information on becoming a child care provider, and other child care resources, contact:

- National Child Care Information Center, 10530 Rosehaven St, Suite 400, Fairfax, VA 22030. Internet: http://www.nccic.org
  For a database on licensing requirements of child care settings by State, contact:
- National Resource Council for Health and Safety in Child Care, University of Colorado Health and Sciences Center at Fitzsimons, Campus Mail Stop F541, P.O. Box 6508, Aurora, CO 80045-0508. Telephone (toll free): 800-598-5437. Internet: http://nrc.uchsc.edu

Miscellaneous:
Vista Print Free Business Cards	www.vistaprint.com
Free Business Guides	www.smbtn.com/businessplanguides/
Open Office	http://download.openoffice.org/
US Census Bureau	www.census.gov
Federal Government	www.business.gov
US Patent & Trademark Office	www.uspto.gov
US Small Business Administration	www.sba.gov
National Association for the Self-Employed	www.nase.org
International Franchise Association	www.franchise.org
Center for Women's Business Research	www.cfwbr.org

Example: Michigan Day Care Guidelines

1. Decide upon a name for your day care, and register it on the Michigan Business One Stop Shop. Contact the IRS to establish a federal tax identification number for your business, after receiving confirmation of certification of your new day care business name.
Resource: http://www.michigan.gov/business

2. Decide if you want to start a family home day care--caring for up to six children, a group home day care--caring for six to 12 children or a day care center.

3. Michigan law requires that each child has 35 square feet of accessible indoor floor space. You must also have an outdoor play area for the children.

4. Hire staff, keeping in mind that the state requirement is one caregiver for every six children.

5. Each caregiver must be certified in CPR and first aid.

6. Contact local Department of Human Services to schedule licensing orientation for you and your staff. Call a Division of Day Care Licensing representative in Lansing at 866-685-0006 to request a package titled "Licensing Rules for Family and Group Child Care Homes." You may also request "Licensing Rules for Child Care Centers" if you want a large day care facility for children. The representative in Lansing will send you an information packet containing all of the rules about providing day care, departments that you need to contact, and procedures that you must follow to operate a day care in the state. The orientation leader will explain how to fill out the application form, as well as demonstrate how to keep records of all the children's files. The orientation leader will detail the caregiver's responsibilities and required trainings. Fill out the application, listing each staff member along with their driver's license numbers so a background check can be run.
Resources:
www.michigan.gov/dhs/0,1607,7-124-5455_49572_50051---,00.html
http://daycare.com/michigan/
Department of Social Services, Commerce Center, 300 S. Capitol Ave. Lansing MI 48909

7. Present these items when you return your Child Care Application (BCAL-3970): a Supplemental Application Information form (BCAL-3737); a $50 check or money order written out to the State of Michigan; a Fingerprint Clearance for the applicant; a Licensing Record Clearance (BCAL-1326) for everyone over the age of 18 in the home; a Medical Clearance Request (BCAL-3704) or the applicant; a Medical Clearance Request for each assistant caregiver; documentation of a tuberculosis test for everyone in the home over the age of 14; documentation of infant, child and adult CPR as well as blood-borne pathogen training for the

applicant and all assistant caregivers; proof of inspection and approval of your heating system and documentation that radon gases do not exceed 4 picocuries per liter of air in the home.

8. Request the "Child Development and Care Handbook" (DHS Publication 230) as well as "Childcare Changes-How to Talk to Parents" (DHS Publication 129). You may find these resources and others at michigan.gov/daycare, including requirements for day care aides.

9. Take a TB test and receive a physical to make sure you and your staff are physically able to handle all the duties that come with caring for children.

10. Plan your curriculum and activities. Some caregivers like to reference a particular curriculum, such as the Creative Curriculum, which emphasizes children's individual strengths as they learn new skills. It is important to teach young children skills like reading, art and music, but it is just as imperative that they learn how to socialize and interact with others.

11. Schedule an appointment with your local licensing agency by calling the Bureau of Child and Adult Licensing at 866-685-0006 for a six-hour orientation and review of your entire day care plans. The person who schedules your appointment will also ensure that a letter is sent out to you with an explanation of documents you will need to take to the orientation.

12. Secure a Statement of Registration which indicates that you are in compliance with day care rules and the Child Care Organizations Act (1973 PA 116). After orientation, you will be asked to take the Statement of Registration home to ensure that you are in compliance with the law before signing it and returning it.

13. Await the Certificate of Registration. This Certificate of Registration will be good for three years--as long as you comply with the rules and laws that govern day care for children in the state of Michigan. Within 90 days, a licensing consultant will inspect your home to be sure that you are in compliance in your family or group child care home. If you are a child day care center provider, a fire department may also conduct an evaluation for safety.

14. Purchase business cards. You may also print fliers and place a sign in the front of the new facility. Your fliers may be distributed to local stores or to college campuses, where students with children may need care.

15. Primary caregivers need to take 10 training hours in topics such as food sanitation and child abuse and neglect yearly, while assistant caregivers need to complete five hours of training yearly.

Advertising Plan Worksheet

Ad Campaign Title: _____
Ad Campaign Start Date: _____ End Date: _____

What are the features (what product has) and hidden benefits (what product does for consumer) of my products/services?

Who is the targeted audience?

What problems are faced by this targeted audience?

What solutions do you offer?

Who is the competition and how do they advertise?

What is your differentiation strategy?

What are your bullet point competitive advantages?

What are the objectives of this advertising campaign?

What are your general assumptions?

What positioning image do you want to project?
 ___ Exclusiveness ___ Low Cost ___ High Quality
 ___ Speedy Service ___ Convenient ___ Innovative

What is the ad headline?

What is the advertising budget for this advertising campaign?

What advertising methods will be used?
 ___ Radio ___ TV/Cable ___ Yellow Pages
 ___ Coupons ___ Telemarketing ___ Flyers
 ___ Direct Mail ___ Magazines ___ Newspapers
 ___ Press Release ___ Brochures ___ Billboards
 ___ Other

When will each advertising method start and what will it cost?
 Method   Start Date   Frequency   Cost
_____

Indicate how you will measure the cost-effectiveness of the advertising plan.
Formula: Return on Investment (ROI) = Generated Sales / Ad Costs.

Marketing Action Plan

Month: _____

Target Market: _____

Responsibilities: _____

Allocated Budget: _____

Objectives _____

Strategies _____

Implementation _____

Tactics _____

Results
Evaluation _____

_____
_____
_____
_____
_____
_____
_____
_____
_____
_____
_____
_____
_____

Lessons Learned:
_____
_____
_____

New Release Template

News Release

For Immediate Release
(Or Hold For Release Until …(date)….)

Contact:
Contact Person   _____
Contact Title   _____
Company Name   _____
Phone Number   _____
Fax Number   _____
Email Address   _____
Website Address   _____

Date: _____
Attention: _____   (Target Type of Editor)

Headline: Summarize Your Key Message:
                                    _____

Sub-Headline: Optional: _____

Location of the Firm and Date.
_____

Lead Paragraph: A summary of the newsworthy content.
_____
                                   Answers the questions:
                                   Who: _____
                                   What: _____
                                   Where: _____
                                   When: _____

Second Paragraph:
Expand upon the first paragraph and elaborate on the purpose of the Press Release.
_____
_____

Third Paragraph:
Further details with additional quotes from staff, industry experts or satisfied clients.
_____
_____

For Additional Information Contact:

_____

_____

About Your Expertise:
Presentation of your expert credentials

_____

_____

About Your Business:
Background company history on the firm and central offerings.

_____

_____

Enclosures: Photographs, charts, brochures, etc.

Special Event Release Format   Notes

1. Type of Event   _____
2. Sponsoring Organization   _____
3. Contact Person Before the Event   _____
4. Contact Person At the Event   _____
5. Date and Time of the Event   _____
6. Location of the Event   _____
7. Length of Presentation Remarks   _____
8. Presentation Topic   _____
9. Question Session (Y/N)   _____
10. Speaker or Panel   _____
11. Event Background   _____
12. Noteworthy Expected Attendees   _____
13. Estimated Number of Attendees   _____
14. Why readers s/b interested in event.   _____
15. Specifics of the Event.   _____
16. Biographies   _____

Track Ad Return on Investment (ROI)

Objective: To invest in those marketing activities that generate the greatest return on invested funds.

Medium	Cost	Calls Received	Cost/Call	No. Act. New Clients	Cost/New Client
Formula:	A	B	A/B=C	D	A/D=E
Newspaper					
Classified Ads					
Yellow Pages					
Billboards					
Cable TV					
Magazine					
Flyers					
Posters					
Coupons					
Direct Mail					
Brochures					
Business Cards					
Seminars					
Demonstrations					
Sponsored Events					
Sign					
Radio					
Trade Shows					
Specialties					
Cold Calling					
Door Hangers					
T-shirts					
Coupon Books					
Transit Ads					
Press Releases					
Word-of-Mouth					
Totals:					

Internet Article Writing Template

1. Article Title
Maximum 100 characters (including spaces) - about 12 words.
Write it to catch the attention of readers and publishers. Start with your primary search engine keyword phrase. In printed media titles starting "How to…" or "10 top tips for…" are very popular, but they are not very helpful for search engines. The article title will go into the title of a web page.

2. Abstract
Maximum 500 characters - about 90 words but 50 or 60 is better.
Make it enticing to hook the publisher and make them want to read the full article. The abstract is primarily targeted at the publisher and will be displayed just below the title on the search pages in the directory, but is secondary to the title in getting attention. Some publishers may also use it.

3. Description – Meta Tag
Maximum 200 characters but preferably 150 – two lines of text.
This should be a shorter version of the abstract, which must contain your primary keywords. The Mega Tag is needed if you publish on your own website.

4. Keywords – Meta Tag
Maximum 100 characters - about 12 words comma separated
Start with your primary keyword of phrase then add the other relevant keywords that are used in the article.

5. Article Text
Length depends on your topic, market and writing style. Research suggests about 500 to 800 words, but some publishers want more of an in-depth analysis. Research your specific market and be flexible, with a prepared mix of lengths, including long and short versions of the same article. Write the basic article with no formatting. If you are using word, disable all the auto-formatting like smart quotes, automatic hypertext links and paragraph spacing because they will all cause problems later.

Include the 'Primary Keyword Phrase' into the first sentence. Include the liberal usage of keywords throughout the article, but don't overdo it. The article still has to be a good read. Remember that even though you are writing for several audiences, content must still be king. Do not promote your own products and services or your article will not be published. Also, do not include self serving links to your web site or affiliate sites in the body of the article, but rather save them for the 'Resource or Byline Box'. If you have links to resources show them as text, as many sites do not allow live html links in the body of the article.

Introduction
1. Brief outline of what will be covered in the article.
2. The motivating factor behind why this particular topic was selected and why you

233

    are qualified to address the subject.
3.   A brief statement on your credentials, experience and exposure.
4.   What you have achieved from your experience to convince readers that you know the subject very well.

Core Subject Matter
1.   Define the problem or address the subject areas that will define the gap between the uninformed and the knowledgeable.
2.   Provide the benefits the reader will realize from reading the article.
3.   Start with simple and general background knowledge, and gradually intensify the technicality of the subject matter.
4.   State the expected challenges to be faced in tackling the problem.
5.   Discuss the pros and cons of your proposed solution to create the link between the norm and the desired state.

Expand Upon Subject Matter
1.   Add technical information to convince readers of the merits of your solution.
2.   State a range of requirements needed to implement your solution and their options.
3.   Compare players in the market and promote good practice.
4.   Place emphasis on desired actions, taking a chronological approach to each stage.
5.   Attempt to indirectly answer any questions you think your readers may have.
6.   Give supporting points to gain confidence in the approach you recommend.
7.   Suggest other options based on price and availability.

Conclusion
1.   Summarize problem solution recommendations.
2.   Refer readers to other helpful resources.

6.   Copyright

Copyright, date, name, country. Few directories ask for this but it makes sense to put it at the bottom of the article or in the field requested.

7.   Resource Box

Maximum 500 characters, "including spaces and html code."
This is your opportunity to promote yourself but limit content to 1 or 2 self serving links. Refer to the links in the "Third Person." The directory publisher has to function with this link on their site or ezine so make it acceptable to them. Offer an incentive or reward for people to visit your web site, but make sure that live links show the web address not just keywords. If the publisher doesn't use live links, you still want to present your website address for later referral.

How to Get Started Marketing on Twitter

1. **Import Your Contacts**
   Import contacts from Gmail, Hotmail and your own address book.

2. **Make Sure that Your Profile is Complete**
   Fill in all the fields (both required and optional) and include your website URL. Personalize your Twitter page to match your company's branding.

3. **Understand the Dynamics of Twitter**
   Use Twitter as a social tool, not a classifieds site and follow these tips:
   - Don't spam others about your specials.
   - Follow other users.
   - Don't promote your company directly.
   - Tweet about an informative blog posting.

4. **Build Your Followers Base**
   - Put a link to "Follow Me on Twitter" everywhere (your email signature, forums, website, and business cards)
   - Every time you post on your blog, invite people to follow you on Twitter

5. **Balance Your Followers/Following Ratio**
   - Strike a balance between people you follow and people that follow you.
   - Grow slowly by adding 30 friends at a time, and then wait for them to follow you back.

6. **Make it Worthwhile to Follow You**
   - Tweet only interesting stuff.

7. **Learn from the Best**
   - Find users with several hundred followers and learn their best practices.

8. **Twitter Uses**
   - Use twitter to extend the reach of an existing blogging strategy and to deepen or further ties. Ex: Carnival Cruise Lines.
   - Use to announce sales and deals. Ex: Amazon.
   - Increase the ability for frequent updates to blogs or web sites or news.
   - Build consensus or a community of supporters.
   - Build buzz for a new blog.
   - Update breaking news at conferences or events.

Classified Ad Worksheet

Ad Budget: _____

Ad Objective: ___ Go to Website   ___ Request More Info ___ Mail a Check
              ___ Introduce a new product/service   ___ Announce a Sale
              ___ Increase awareness of product
              ___ Other _____

Target Market: _____

Target Market:
Demographics:
    - Age   _____
    - Gender   _____
    - Income   _____
    - Education _____
    - Location   _____

Reading Interests:
    - Daily Newspapers   _____
    - Weekly Magazines   _____
    - Magazines   _____
    - Trade Journals   _____

Product. Knowledge Level _____

Purchase Motivators   _____

Best Category Heading   _____

Select Type of Message
    - Strong Offer with Best Value for Money   _____
    - Point of Difference from Competitors   _____
    - Listing the Benefits   _____

Product Price: $_____

Ad Cost: $_____

Number of Responses: _____
Cost/Response: _____
Number of Sales: _____
Cost/Sales: _____

School Age Child Profile Form

Child's Name: _____
Child's Nickname _____

Name of School: _____
Address: _____ Phone: _____
School hours: _____
How will your child get to and from school: _____
Is a transportation company involved? (taxi, bus service) ☐ Yes   ☐ No
If yes, name of company: _____ Phone: _____

Family
Names of brothers & sisters   Birthdate
_____   _____
_____   _____

Names of others living in the home   Relationship to child
_____   _____
_____   _____

What language is spoken in your home:_____
Does your child have pets? ☐ Yes   ☐ No   Type: _____

Food
Describe your child's appetite: _____
What foods does your child dislike? _____
What foods does your child like? _____
Does your child have any food sensitivities? ☐ Yes   ☐ No
If yes, please identify: _____
What time does your child eat: Breakfast ____Lunch ____Supper ____
Will your child be taking a lunch to school? ☐ Yes   ☐ No
If no, when will child arrive at the child care & what time will they need to be back at their school? _____

Self-Care
Does your child need help dressing? Yes/No   Describe: _____
Does your child need help with toileting? Yes/No   Describe: _____
Sleep
Describe your child's sleep routine:_____
Social/Emotional Development
How does your child show feelings?
Affection:_____ Fear:_____
Frustration:_____ Anger:_____ Excitement:_____
Does your child make new friends easily?_____
What activities does your child enjoy? _____
What activities does your child dislike? _____

Is your child involved in any extracurricular activities? ☐ Yes ☐ No
If yes, list:_____
How do you handle discipline in your home? _____
What characteristics in your child's development would you like:
Encouraged?_____
Discouraged?_____

Please provide any other information relating to your child that would be helpful in understanding and caring for your child:
_____
_____

_____   _____
Parent/Guardian signature   Date

Toddler Profile Form

Child's Name: _____
Child's Nickname _____

Family
Names of brothers & sisters   Birthdate
_____   _____
_____   _____

Names of others living in the home   Relationship to child
_____   _____
_____   _____

What language is spoken in your home: _____
Does your child have pets? Yes/No   Type: _____

Food
Describe your child's appetite: _____
What foods does your child dislike? _____
What foods does your child like? _____
Does your child feed him/herself? ☐ Yes ☐ No
Does your child have any food sensitivities? Yes/No Describe: _____
What time does your child eat: Breakfast ____ Lunch ____ Supper ____

Self-Care
Is your child in diapers? ☐ Yes ☐ No   Comment: _____
Has training begun?   ☐ Yes ☐ No Comment: _____
Is your child trained?   ☐ Yes ☐ No Comment: _____
Does child need help? Yes/No   Comment: _____
Does your child need help dressing? Yes/No   Describe _____

Sleep
Describe your child's sleep routine (include naps & lengths of naps):
_____

Social/Emotional Development
Does your child separate easily from you? Yes/No
Please comment: _____
Is your child afraid of anything? Yes/No
Please comment: _____
Does your child have a favorite toy, blanket or soother? Yes/No
Please identify: _____
Does your child spend time with other children? Yes/No
Please comment: _____
How does your child show feelings?
Affection: _____   Fear: _____
Frustration: _____   Anger: _____

Excitement:_____
What activities does your child enjoy?
_____

What activities does your child dislike?
_____

How do you handle discipline in your home? _____
_____

What characteristics in your child's development would you like:
Encouraged?_____
Discouraged?_____

Please provide any other information relating to your child that would be helpful in understanding and caring for your child: _____
_____
_____

_____   _____
Parent/Guardian signature   Date

Infant Profile Form

Child's Name: _____ Child's Date of Birth: _____
____Pre-Mature Birth ____Full-Term   Child's Birth Weight: _____

Child's General Mood: _____Happy ____Fussy, ____Colicky, ____ Other_____
Has child stayed with anyone else besides parents? _____ If so who?_____

Is child Bottle or breast-fed? _____If using both, when do you use bottle vs. breast?
_____
How do you give bottle, room temp, warmed, cold? _____
If you warm the bottle, what procedure do you use to warm bottle? _____
Does the child hold his or her own bottle? _____
Is child on formula or milk? ____What kind of milk or formula do you use? _____
Is child on baby cereal? _____ List the kinds you use: _____
Is child on strained or other baby foods? _____
List the varieties you use fruits veggies etc: _____
Food likes: _____ Food Dislikes:_____
List amounts of food, types of food and times your child usually eats below:
Breakfast _____
Lunch _____
Snack _____
Will your child have a bottle or breast fed before arriving?_____
Will your child need breakfast? _____
Does your child use a pacifier? _____ When? _____
Does your child need a special comfort item to sleep? ___. What is it?_____
Does your child sleep through the night? _____ IF not how often do they
wake and what do you do when they wake – feed, rock change etc ? _____
_____
When does your child wake in the morning? _____
When does your child nap morning? _____ Afternoon? _____

Please list any other important information or special instructions on the care of your child below:
_____
_____
_____
_____
_____
_____
_____

Signature _____ Relationship to Child _____ Date_____

Phone Interview Log/Wait List

Date:_____

Name:_____ Phone Number:_____
Fax:_____ E-mail:_____
Referred By:_____

Start Date Needed:_____ Hours of care Needed:_____
Days: ☐Mon. ☐Tues. ☐Wed. ☐Thurs. ☐Fri. ☐Sat. ☐Sun.

Government Subsidy (assistance)? ☐Yes ☐No ☐Possible
Child(ren)'s Names & Ages:
1-
2-
3-
Interview Scheduled? ☐Yes ☐No   Date_____ Time_____
Materials: Mailed, Faxed, or E-mailed? ☐yes ☐no   Date_____

This Family is #___ on the waiting list.   Date for follow up call:_____

Notes:_____
_____

Phone Interview Log/Wait List

Date:_____

Name:_____ Phone Number:_____
Fax:_____ E-mail:_____
Referred By:_____

Start Date Needed:_____ Hours of care Needed:_____
Days: ☐Mon. ☐Tues. ☐Wed. ☐Thurs. ☐Fri. ☐Sat. ☐Sun.

Government Subsidy (assistance)? ☐Yes ☐No ☐Possible
Child(ren)'s Names & Ages:
1-
2-
3-
Interview Scheduled? ☐Yes ☐No   Date_____ Time_____
Materials: Mailed, Faxed, or E-mailed? ☐yes ☐no   Date_____

This Family is #___ on the waiting list.   Date for follow up call:_____

Notes:_____
_____

Family Child Care Registration Form

Date of Enrollment:_____

Name of Child:_____ Birthdate: __/__/__ Sex: M__ F__

Health #:_____ ID#:_____
Child's Doctor:_____ Phone:_____

Full name of Mother:_____

Full name of Father:_____

Mother's Address:_____
Home Phone:_____Work Phone:_____Cel Phone:_____
Place of work:_____ Hours:_____

Father's Address:_____
Home Phone:_____Work Phone:_____Cel Phone:_____
Place of work:_____ Hours:_____

Person(s) to contact incase of emergency/Authorized to pick up child:
1. Name:_____ 2. Name:_____
   Relationship to child:_____   Relationship to child:_____
   Home Phone:_____   Home Phone:_____
   Work Phone:_____   Work Phone:_____

Other Person(s) Authorized to pick up child:
Name:_____ Phone:_____
Name:_____ Phone:_____
Name:_____ Phone:_____

Names of other children in family:
Name:_____ Birthdate: __/__/__
Name:_____ Birthdate: __/__/__
Name:_____ Birthdate: __/__/__

Has child had previous experience away from home? Yes ( ) No ( ) If yes explain:
_____
_____

Are your Child's immunizations up to date? Yes ( ) No ( )
If no please explain:_____
_____

Note: attach a copy of immunization record

Child's Health History

Does child have any known health problems? Yes ( ) No ( ) (If yes attach documentation)

Check (v) any of the following illnesses the child has had:

☐Asthma	☐Earaches	☐Mumps	☐Whooping Cough	☐Bronchitis
☐Eczema	☐Pneumonia	☐Polio	☐Chicken Pox	☐Frequent Colds
☐Croup	☐Convulsions	☐Measles	☐Influenza	☐Rheumatic Fever
☐Diphtheria	☐Tonsillitis	☐Tonsillitis	☐Other:_____	

Please list any injuries child has had:_____
_____

Does you child have any know allergies? Yes ( ) No ( ) If yes, what are they and what are your child's reactions:_____
_____

Does your child take any medication on a regular basis? Yes ( ) No ( ) If yes please list the name of the medication(s) and the medical condition for which it is taken:
_____
_____

Do you have any concerns about your child's development? Yes ( ) No ( ) If yes please comment: _____
_____

Please comment on any other medical information/ or special need the child care provider should be aware of: _____
_____
_____
_____

I authorize the child care provider/staff to obtain the following services for this child if necessary: Public Health Nurse, Physician and or Ambulance in the event of an emergency. (ambulance fees and/or health care costs are the responsibility of the parent/guardian)

_____   _____
(Date)   (Signature of parent/guardian)

_____   _____
(Signature of child care provider)   (signature of parent/guardian)

Classified Ad Worksheet

Ad Budget: _____

Ad Objective: ___ Go to Website ___ Request More Info ___ Mail a Check
                ___ Introduce a new product/service ___ Announce a Sale
                ___ Increase awareness of product
                ___ Other _____

Target Market: _____

Target Market:
Demographics:
- Age _____
- Gender _____
- Income _____
- Education _____
- Location _____

Reading Interests:
- Daily Newspapers _____
- Weekly Magazines _____
- Magazines _____
- Trade Journals _____

Product. Knowledge Level _____

Purchase Motivators _____

Best Category Heading _____

Select Type of Message
- Strong Offer with Best Value for Money _____
- Point of Difference from Competitors _____
- Listing the Benefits _____

Product Price: $_____

Ad Cost: $_____

Number of Responses: _____
Cost/Response: _____
Number of Sales: _____
Cost/Sales: _____

Marketing Plan   Month: _____

Planned Accomplishments for month:
_____
_____

Describe target audience:
_____
_____

Success Measures:
Number of New Prospects   _____
Number of New Contacts to Referral Network
Sales Revenues of _____ by _____
Other measure: _____

Referral Network Action Plan:
We will attend the following events:
    Event   Date   Objective
_____
_____

We will contact the following people in my network:
    Name   Date   Reason
_____
_____

We will meet the following people in person:
    Name   Date   Reason
_____
_____

We will keep in touch with the following people by sending them information, including articles and newspaper clippings:
    Name   Date   Information Type
_____
_____

Past Client Action Plan:
We will contact the following past clients:
Method Options: In-person, Mail, email, phone.
    Name   Date   Reason   Method
_____
_____

Prospecting Action Plan:
Distribution Methods: Publications, Website, Organizations, Email, etc.

Method   Date   Subject   Distribution
                                                Method
Article   _____
Speech   _____
Newsletter   _____
Press Release   _____

Other Activities:
    Activity Type   Date   Target
_____
_____

Sample Flyer Template

Company Name
Address
City, State, Zip code
Website
Main Phone:
Email Address

Service Area:

What We Do:

Products:

Services:

Specialties:

Associations:

Awards / Certifications:

Open Hours

Special Offer:

Additional Info:

Coupon:

$_____ Off Any _____ Service

Name: _____
Address: _____
Phone: _____
Problem: _____
Expiration Date: _____
Offer valid for 90 days from _____ (date) . Limit one (1) coupon per contract. Cannot be combined with any other offer. Not redeemable on minimum service charge. Coupon must be presented at time of visit.